THE BEST FILM YOU'VE NEVER SEEN

Robert K. Elder

35 Directors Champion the Forgotten or Critically Savaged Movies They Love

CHICAGO REVIEW PRESS

A Cappella Book

For more interviews, movie posters, and photos, visit *The Best Film You've Never Seen* on the web at www.bestfilmneverseen.com.

Library of Congress Cataloging-in-Publication Data
Elder, Robert K.
  The best film you've never seen : 35 directors champion the forgotten or critically savaged movies they love / Robert K. Elder.
      p. cm.
  Includes filmographies and index.
  ISBN 978-1-56976-838-9
  1. Motion pictures. 2. Motion picture producers and directors—Interviews. I. Title.

  PN1995.E5583 2013
  791.4302'330922—dc23

                                   2013002783

Cover design: John Yates at Stealworks
Cover photos: (top to bottom) *Who'll Stop the Rain?* © 1978 Metro-Goldwyn-Mayer
      Studios, Inc., all rights reserved / MGM Media Licensing; *The Swimmer* © Colum-
      bia Pictures, all rights reserved; *Killer Klowns from Outer Space* © 1988 Orion
      Pictures Corporation, all rights reserved / MGM Media Licensing; *Eureka* © 1984
      Sunley Productions Limited, all rights reserved / MGM Media Licensing
Interior design: Visible Logic, Inc.

© 2013 by Robert K. Elder
All rights reserved
Published by Chicago Review Press, Incorporated
814 North Franklin Street
Chicago, Illinois 60610
ISBN 978-1-56976-838-9
Printed in the United States of America
5 4 3 2 1

For my dad, Rick, who is willing to rent any movie with an enigmatic poster. Among the cinematic rubble we found *Miller's Crossing*, *The Highlander*, Ralph Bakshi's *Wizards*, and, ahem, *The Best of the Best*. An education of classics, B-movies, and Z-movies—but some were haunting, some massively inappropriate for kids, and all gave me exposure to movies I would have never otherwise seen. I'm forever grateful.

Contents

Introduction

The Best Film You've Never Seen is an attempt to rewrite film history disguised as a search for unsung classics. In this book, thirty-five directors champion their favorite overlooked or critically savaged gems. Director Bill Condon (*Dreamgirls, Twilight: Breaking Dawn*) calls these "orphan movies," though I prefer "outcast classics."

If you're a movie buff, odds are you've seen at least one of these films. And that's by design. I didn't want a book that was inaccessible, about films you couldn't see or had to find on the gray market. I wanted to give you a way in to a festival of guilty pleasures, almost-masterpieces, and undeniable classics in need of revival.

On this list are unsung noir films (*The Chase, Murder by Contract*), famous flops (*Can't Stop the Music, Joe Versus the Volcano*), art films (*L'ange, WR: Mysteries of the Organism*), theatrical adaptations (*The Iceman Cometh, The Homecoming*), B-movies (*Killer Klowns from Outer Space, The Honeymoon Killers*), and even a couple of Oscar winners (*Breaking Away, A Man for All Seasons*).

I'll let each filmmaker defend why he or she chose the film they did—because I often play devil's advocate in our conversations. But whatever category these movies fit into, they all have one thing in common: their cinematic defenders want them to be loved, admired, swooned over. These films, they argue, deserve a larger audience and to have their place in movie history reconsidered. Some were well loved but are now faded or forgotten. Others ran afoul of critics or were just buried after a dismal opening run. Still others never even got proper distribution.

A few of these titles qualify as bona fide obscurata (*Le joli mai, ivansxtc, L'ange*), but now you can find most of them on DVD or via streaming from Netflix or Amazon—something that wasn't true when I started working on this book eight years ago. The more the merrier. I hope these conversations open these movies up to a wider audience, however you're able to find them.

Some of the things I loved most about these interviews were the tangents, the diversions, and the conversational side trips. Often, the interviewees provided me with as much insight into their own approach to moviemaking as into the film they discussed.

Spoiler alert: This book is full of spoilers. The directors and I talk about these films in detail, often dissecting the artistic choices made by the filmmakers, reaction from critics, and even alternate endings. So if you're one of those movie lovers who can't bear to know intimate details of a film's production or plot, watch the films first and read the chapters afterward.

The filmmakers in this book are the perfect hosts, often setting the tone, managing expectations, and giving advice about how you should watch each movie. (John Dahl, for example, suggests that you fast-forward through the first twenty minutes or so of his selection.) They're often brutally honest about a film's shortcomings or reasons why it was lost in the first place. Some steadfastly claim that the audience, not the filmmaker, was at fault for not seeing a movie's obvious brilliance. Time, they say, will correct the record. If they can speed up the process by championing it in a forum like this, all the better.

The companion project to this book is *The Film That Changed My Life*, interviews with filmmakers about the movies that made them want to direct or made them think differently about filmmaking. Each volume shares the same mission statement: to promote the love and discovery of film.

1

Austin Chick
After Dark, My Sweet

Austin Chick is attracted to charged, emotional interactions between characters. His films often explore the ways people either are or aren't able to work together and communicate. Chick's selection, James Foley's *After Dark, My Sweet*, has similar themes of alienation and that staple question of noirs: whom can you trust?

After Dark, My Sweet is an adaptation of Jim Thompson's pitch-black novel of the same name, and part of Chick's fascination with the film is with its bleak atmosphere. But asked to describe why he chose to defend this movie, Chick used two words: "Jason Patric."

"It's Jason Patric's best performance by far," Chick says. "He's always exceeding your expectations of who that character is . . . and then you realize that he's actually much smarter and more complicated than you initially give him credit for being."

Austin Chick, selected filmography:
XX/XY (2002)
August (2008)
Girls Against Boys (2012)

After Dark, My Sweet
1990
Directed by James Foley
Starring Jason Patric, Rocky Giordani, Rachel Ward, Bruce Dern, and others

How would you describe *After Dark, My Sweet* to someone who's never seen it?

CHICK: It's a thriller based on a Jim Thompson book about a vagrant ex-boxer who stumbles into town and meets a mysterious widow, who draws him into a kidnapping plot with others. They try to use him as the fall guy, and complications ensue.

I definitely first saw it on video, probably in film school. I remember being totally surprised by it. I felt that the inner monologue was kind of used as a crutch, but one of the things that's so interesting about the film is that the main character, Kevin "Kid" Collins (Jason Patric), is constantly reinventing himself. He's always exceeding your expectations of who that character is, and a big part of it is his inner monologue. You think he's one thing, and then you realize that he's actually much smarter and more complicated than you initially give him credit for being.

He is hyperaware of how things may play out and others' motivations—but not his own.

CHICK: It's Jason Patric's best performance by far. I was so impressed with him in that movie that I went and saw *Geronimo: An American Legend* in theaters. I was so into Jason Patric after seeing that, and *Geronimo* is a fucking terrible movie.

I had seen *Rush*, and everyone talked about how great he was in that movie, and I didn't really buy it. Then I must have seen *After Dark, My Sweet*, and I was like, "Holy shit, this guy is phenomenal."

Previously, he had been cast as the teen idol. He was in *Solarbabies*, but *The Lost Boys* was his big break.

CHICK: I had seen *The Lost Boys*. It was one of those movies, when I was a little kid, that was kind of big, and everyone was into that movie. It wasn't really my kind of film.

What are the dangers of relying on voiceover?

CHICK: Very often, it's a cheap way to deal with exposition or a cheap way to try to get an audience into a character's head. Generally speaking, it's not looked at as a very cinematic device. I have written scripts with voiceover, and I always feel like it's a cop-out. I've never made a movie with voiceover.

To use it when there's sort of an unreliable narrator or unreliable protagonists, like this movie does, the voiceover is giving you something other than exposition and other than talking you through what you're seeing.

So why does this film deserve recognition?
CHICK: For one thing, Jason Patric is phenomenal in the movie. It's beautifully shot—and I haven't seen all of James Foley's stuff—but to me it feels like a perfectly crafted, albeit small, piece of cinema. There's an overall sense of visual design to the film that you don't really see in the other James Foley films. *At Close Range* is a really interesting film, but it feels kind of dated.

But *After Dark, My Sweet*—from beginning to end—every frame and every camera move is clearly thought out and brilliantly, beautifully executed. It had a really clear, straightforward sense of visual design throughout the entire film.

How does this stack up against other Jim Thompson adaptations?
CHICK: *The Grifters* is an amazing film. I love that movie. The similarities between this and *The Grifters* have a lot to do with the complex relationships between the characters, the distribution of power, the dark take on what greed does to people and what paranoia can do to a relationship. The thing that's amazing about *The Grifters* is really the writing and the performances.

Perhaps *After Dark, My Sweet* is overlooked because it stands in the shadow of *The Grifters*.
CHICK: Yeah. I also feel like there are certain things about *After Dark, My Sweet* that are demanding of the audience, because a number of plot points are pretty subtle and hard to keep track of. *The Grifters* is much more straightforward. Psychologically, what's going on between the characters is easier to follow—as are the twists and turns and double-crossings. It's as interesting and complex, but it's a little bit more palatable for an audience.

Palatable for two reasons: *After Dark, My Sweet* **has a peculiar struc-ture, because Kid Collins initially walks away and the script goes off track for nearly twenty minutes—did it feel that way to you?**

CHICK: Yeah, and in some ways it suffers from being stuck in that house for so much of the movie. But the shifting power among those three characters—between Jason Patric, Rachel Ward, and Bruce Dern—is fascinating. The moment when Jason Patric takes the wrong kid in order to mess with Bruce Dern's character and the whole use of that *Vertigo* shot is a really great turning point in that film.

Rachel Ward said in an interview around the time of the film, "Thomp-son does not ask you to love his characters." Do you think that's true, and then how do you keep an audience interested?

CHICK: Maybe it's not the average viewer's response to the movie, but I think that Kid Collins is a very sympathetic character. Ultimately, he sacrifices himself. I don't know if you'd really call him a victim, but you definitely get the feeling he's been taken advantage of and stepped on throughout his life.

One of the things that makes *After Dark* **stand out in the Thompson canon is the presence of sexual attraction between the main characters, which was meant to make the story more palatable to audiences. In fact, the love scene is the only time when the characters seem to really connect. First, is my reading of that correct?**

CHICK: That fade in/fade out lovemaking stuff dates the movie a little. You're asking about whether or not the sexual attraction works in terms of making the film feel more commercial. It's on track to doing that, but then it derails too quickly to really satisfy that urge.

That first moment where he follows her into the bathroom and they start kissing seems like it should be the fulfillment of a desire that's been building through the whole movie, but . . . [*trails off*].

After that sex scene, it seems like it should be bringing them together, but then they cut it right off. If I remember, it's a hard cut. We come back, and those two characters, rather than being closer, they're at each other's throats. You come to realize that she's trying to do something by hiding the boy. In theory, she's trying to do something so they can get away and have a life together, but Jason Patric, being somewhat paranoid, immediately mistrusts her, and everything gets that much more complicated between the two of them.

My reading was just the opposite: It's the first time she feels close with Kid Collins, so he's no longer sacrificial. So she hides the boy to sabotage their relationship and narrow her options.

Chick: I assumed that she was hiding the kid because she was hoping that they were going to be able to run away together. That's definitely the way I read him, although he's kind of a dick to her even before he finds out the boy is gone. He wakes up feeling like he's going to get fucked. He wakes up mistrusting her, right? From the moment that he wakes up and she walks into the room, he's an asshole.

It's interesting that you chose this film, because this scene we're talking about contains echoes of your film *XX/XY*. Mark Ruffalo's character is looking for a sexual connection with two women, which ends up driving them apart and sowing mistrust with the one woman he could have a life with.

Chick: It didn't really occur to me. But to a certain degree, I can see the connection. Very often in films people getting together is too easy. Things aren't easy, and sex very often can complicate things and do the exact opposite of bringing people together emotionally.

It's been observed that sex scenes can stop a movie dead. Having had to direct them yourself, how do you approach sex scenes?

Chick: They're never easy to shoot. I've shot four of them. The first time I ever had to shoot a sex scene was the three-way sex scene in *XX/XY*, and we tried to rehearse just the blocking of it, because there were nudity issues with some of the actors. You end up getting into the situation where you say, "You don't have to show this; you have to show this." Everything has to be approved and signed off on before you get into production.

I thought that rehearsing just the choreography of it—who's going to move where, where the camera's going to be, how the camera's going to move—was something that would make it easier. Big mistake. That day ended in tears.

There are two different philosophies about shooting sex scenes from a production standpoint. Either you put it early in the schedule, with the hope that the actors will all be professional and do their jobs and do the sex scene, or you put it late in the schedule, with the hopes that the actors will be more comfortable with each other. But you also run the risk of the actors having grown to hate each other, in which case it becomes, you know, exponentially more difficult.

All the sex scenes that I've shot are about the discomfort of being intimate, but that one [from *XX/XY*] especially. It's about this character who's decided to do something she's not totally comfortable with, and over the course of the scene, she becomes really uncomfortable with it. So the fact that the actors were not really comfortable with it—you can see them giggling a little bit—that sense of discomfort worked for that scene.

The next sex scene that we shot was just between Mark Ruffalo and Maya Stange, and that one I was able to choreograph a little bit more. It was part of the overall visual design of that movie that the camera wanders around a little bit. We shot a lot of close-ups and landscapes of places. The third sex scene in that movie is probably the one that might draw the clearest parallel to the sex scene in *After Dark, My Sweet*. You feel the tension for a while, and then it explodes in this sexual impulse that then backfires.

What did you learn from *After Dark, My Sweet* as a director?
CHICK: There is some very simple technical stuff in that film that really made me rethink certain things. There's a moment where he runs away in the middle of the night. He packs up his shit, and he jumps out a window. You think you're going to hear the sound of him drop, but then we cut to the shot of the road. The camera pulls back to reveal that we're in the bed of the truck, and Jason Patric comes into view in the foreground. That moment made me think about sound differently—about playing against expectations and interrupting what might be the natural rhythm.

To what effect? What does that accomplish?
CHICK: That moment affects me on a visceral level somehow. It feels like a hiccup. If there's anything that I took from *After Dark, My Sweet* and used in *XX/XY*, it's the moment where Coles (Mark Ruffalo) and Sam (Maya Stange)

are on the phone and she's apologizing for having cheated on him, and she inhales. She's crying, and she inhales deeply. We hold it for a beat, we think she's going to exhale, and then we cut away. Withholding something small affects the rhythm—it keeps the tension there. It's subconscious almost.

A big part of my interest in the film has to do with the visual design. The use of Steadicam is brilliant, and the score is great. The light and the score create this very specific sense, this poetic sense of longing and loneliness. A big part of what's interesting to me about the film is the sense of atmosphere.

2

The Brothers Quay
L'ange

Flickering light, expressive figures caught in an ominous landscape—a description that could apply to both works of Stephen and Timothy Quay and the film they champion, Patrick Bokanowski's experimental *L'ange* (*The Angel*).

Their own enigmatic work with puppets and stop-motion animation make the Quays—who speak in one voice in this interview—perhaps the perfect ambassadors for Bokanowski's exploration of this ghostly ascent up a mysterious staircase, which defies narrative conventions. In the following interview, the twin brothers give rare insight into not only their friend Bokanowski's world but their own creative process as well.

"One should be prepared to be astonished and transported by this utterly unique film which has no reference points," say the Quays. "It's a beautiful comet rarely seen in a lifetime."

> **The Brothers Quay, selected filmography:**
> *Street of Crocodiles* (1986)
> *The Comb* (1990)
> *Are We Still Married?* (1992)
> *Duet* (2000)
> *The Piano Tuner of Earthquakes* (2005)
> *Through the Weeping Glass: On the Consolations of Life Everlasting* (2011)
>
> *L'ange*
> 1982
> Directed by Patrick Bokanowski

Starring Maurice Baquet, Jean-Marie Bon, Martine Couture, and Jacques Faure

How would you describe *L'ange* to someone who has never seen it?
QUAYS: *L'ange* is an absolutely startling and visionary film that could pass as one of the most disquieting and mystifying fables in cinema. You are singularly plunged into a febrile, poetic universe, and there are no handrails.

The film is a mere seventy minutes long yet took some five years to make and uses a most remarkable and virtuosic technique. You could possibly surmise that all the action takes place trapped in the late nineteenth century, around a mysterious and anonymous staircase, seen only in half-light, with rooms shooting off to the side, where dubious actions and occupations seem to be taking place. There is, little by little, a slow ascent into a final immolation of light. Apparently, it played nonstop in a cinema in Tokyo for over ten years.

When did you see the film?
QUAYS: We saw it in Paris probably around 1984, 1985. We'd read about it in a French animation magazine, and then a mutual friend—Olivier Gillon [maker of *Inukshuk*], an animator—told us it was playing in a program at Beaubourg.

How would you best prepare an audience for the experience?
QUAYS: One should be prepared to be astonished and transported by this utterly unique film which has no reference points. It's a beautiful comet rarely seen in a lifetime.

***L'ange* was often programmed with your film *Rehearsals for Extinct Anatomies* in U.S. showings. Other than similar release dates, do you perceive any thematic or aesthetic reason for the pairing?**
QUAYS: Programmers were obviously trying to make up a ninety-minute program. We'd been living in England a long time by then, and we knew nothing of this pairing. It's easy to see why they would have paired them, but *Rehearsals* is very feeble against *L'ange*. They should have simply programmed one of Patrick's earlier films, *La Femme qui se poudre* or *Déjeuner du matin*.

What are the influences you see Bokanowski drawing from in *L'ange*? Do you share some of these influences?

QUAYS: Clearly, he quotes from the history of paintings via old engravings, even an old Wilhelm Busch cartoon—also, the history of early photography, such as Étienne-Jules Marey, for example. And yes, we *do* share many of these influences. Maybe we even have some of the same books in our libraries. We love the late nineteenth- and early twentieth-century photography, especially Marey's work, which we're sure Patrick knows, certainly much better than us.

If your films are an attempt to "make a world that is seen through a dirty pane of glass," as you've said before, how would you describe *L'ange* in contrast?

QUAYS: It's as though the entire film were seen through one extraordinarily cut glass eye made by E. T. A. Hoffmann's Doctor Coppelia in his story "The Sandman." Or a kind of magnificent flayed retina.

I've noticed that Bokanowski treats human figures much like puppets, mirroring your own affection for humanoid puppets. *L'ange* often obscures the humanity of its figures with white, blank-looking masks.

QUAYS: What Bokanowski has charted most beautifully in this film is the use of the mask, which has nothing specifically to do with puppets and is quite unique unto itself. The mask most beautifully inflicts on us an instant otherness. You perceive these characters at once as extreme attenuated states, almost consumed by some great inner angst that threatens them.

What elements in particular made you both admirers of the work?

QUAYS: That utter and complete suspension of belief and narrative, where a trembling other life rushed to the fore, where music and image maintained an eerie and complete symbiosis in sustaining the power of the fiction on-screen.

What do you make of his use of symbolic repetitive motion? Many of the figures seem to be stuck in a loop.

QUAYS: It analyzes the beauty of a movement, even the most banal—especially the most banal—in precisely the way that Marey's photographs, as opposed to

Eadweard Muybridge's, equally analyzed a sense of motion not as separate little frames, but as one indissoluble continuum, an ever-unfolding flux and reflux almost leading one to the notion of a "loop." Music and dance have always done this, but it does seem to be the very special privilege of music. In this film, music and image are absolutely inseparable.

It occurred to me while watching the film that *L'ange* might be best suited to an installation, an art gallery showing, rather than the cinema hall.
QUAYS: *L'ange* should really be seen in a large cinema, as big as possible, and not on a ropy little monitor in a gallery. It simply diminishes its power.

Some of the critics of this film label it "tedious." The *Washington Post* wrote, "After the first of the sequences, a profound numbness sweeps over you at the thought that the same banalities will have to be examined from every conceivable perspective." Is this criticism justified, or did critics misunderstand it in some fundamental way?
QUAYS: Clearly, this film, and most experimental film, tends to separate the men from the boys. It's always a little distressing to know that something genuinely escapes us, when we ourselves are incapable of comprehending and understanding a piece of art, whether it be a film, a piece of music, a sculpture, or a novel. History shows us repeatedly that critics make abysmal judgments sometimes.

This film is mostly medium or full shots with only one or two close-ups. Often, images are obscured by flickering lights. How does this style serve Bokanowski's content?
QUAYS: The film makes great use of the tableau shot, which isn't an easy thing to do and something we often think of as being theatrical in the pejorative sense. But on the contrary, it works very well and locks you powerfully into a highly composed scene. Close-ups are rare, but when they do occur, they're all the more powerful and revealing.

Let's talk about the soundtrack, which reminds me very much of the musical choices in your own films. It ranges from terse, moody violin compositions to more avant-garde sounds, such as babies crying

and bubbles popping. *L'ange* uses sound almost exclusively to build and release tension.

QUAYS: *L'ange* presents an immaculate symbiosis between music and image, image and music. One is constantly feeding and perpetuating the other and even suspending it. We, along with a lot of other animators, have used music as the bloodstream for our puppet films. In fact, we've always had the music first before we've even filmed a single frame. Clearly, music is often, for us, the secret scenario and the great provocateur.

This soundtrack was composed by Bokanowski's wife, Michele. What are the advantages and dangers of working with family?

QUAYS: There need be no dangers, only advantages. They have worked together on many films, as we have, and the results are wonderful. We have no idea how they work. Does Patrick put together a rough cut of a scene and then Michele perpetrates her magic by proposing this or that? Is it a process of give and take? It's certainly the way we work; slowly building up the blocks.

Can you elaborate on this process?

QUAYS: For us, the process of making a film is always a laboratory setting. In other words, we might write out the idea for a proposal—to Channel Four or the BBC, for instance—on a single page, outlining the broadest of terms, a very specific direction that we're intending to embark upon. If the project does eventually get approval, then we almost invariably chuck this original proposal out, not out of any cavalierness, but simply because we know that as we start building the decors and the puppets, the script begins to grow and evolve very organically. It becomes a very hands-on process, and one where the hands often speak and know more than the brain, which then follows.

We're also very alert to the accidents or the famous but entirely normal chance encounter which can often set the work off in a totally different direction. We build on each other's initial, separate trajectories and then, over the proverbial glass of wine, we begin to collage and elaborate and find our way into the film's fiction. Like this, day after day, we microscopically build our film.

Then, at the filming stage, yet another adventure begins, both with the lighting and the animation. Each day, the film rushes come back in the morning, and you set them against the music, presuming that the animation is decent and doesn't need to be reshot. We're also simultaneously editing the film, so it builds very organically, very naturally and as slowly as the animation itself. Often we start our films partway into the story, as we're unsure of the beginning until we absolutely know the ending. We like the idea that a film might start metaphorically with a wrist, and then we discover the arm leading to the main torso, which leads to two short legs and maybe even a tail. Maybe, in the end, there's no real head or only a shadow of one, but sometimes that, too, can be very interesting, because it forces you to imagine the features. And even if the film limps, that, too, can be natural.

Both your films and *L'ange* reflect an interest in the fragmentary, in fetishism and the edges of madness. What is it about animation and stop-motion that lend themselves to these themes?
QUAYS: It's a really good question, but we don't know how to answer it. Live-action people have also approached these subjects.

Yes, but animation, even better than live-action films, seems best equipped to deal with such themes. Why do you think that is?
QUAYS: Possibly because these themes require a much more formal and stylized technique than the one that traditional live-action is really capable of, in order to transport you into these new, more unknown frontiers . . . this no-man's-land.

Bokanowski seems to draw attention to the fact that we're watching a film. For example, he uses test screens and the film breaks, much like Ingmar Bergman does in *Persona*. Why, do you think?
QUAYS: Bokanowski makes you very aware of atmosphere and light, in its palpable sense of densities and thicknesses, and all this being done by a camera's lens. He most likely would have ground the lens himself, which goes back to our metaphorical "glass eye" of Hoffmann's. He seems to bring in the images at a slower-revolving speed, which allows us to explore them almost as though they were under a magnifying glass.

The BBC said that your film *In Absentia* failed the test for people who are sensitive to stroboscopic light, and *L'ange* is saturated with the same technique. What's the allure of using it, as filmmakers?

QUAYS: With *In Absentia*, we were animating in our studio with real sunlight, shooting on black-and-white stock. It was during spring, and we'd start filming very, very early in the morning—5 A.M., when the light first started to appear.

So once the f-stop in our camera was set, we didn't change it. We began the shot in serious, technical underexposure. As the sun rose and began to travel slowly around to the different windows where we had mirrors variously placed to angle the sun's beams back onto the set, it got brighter and brighter and slowly began to overexpose the film stock, which is very beautiful and powerful—the way light can chew up and completely engulf something.

Sometimes, we also had amazing flickering effects, which were entirely due to clouds passing in front of the sun, but everything on that film was captured organically and genuinely on 35mm film.

How did your perception of *L'ange* change with subsequent viewings?

QUAYS: Alas, we've only seen it projected once in our lifetime, and the remaining times, we've watched it unsatisfactorily on lowly video. Naturally, you see more and feel more, and it's always a rediscovery and re-amazement, but it's frustrating not to see it on film.

Why hasn't it found a wider audience?

QUAYS: It's very well known in Europe, but it's inexplicable that it's not out on DVD yet. But Bokanowski is probably with smaller distribution companies who simply can't afford it.

Did you ever meet the Bokanowskis?

QUAYS: We've met them on several occasions and even saw their studio, which was, at that time, a vast empty space, but we saw some of the masks that were used on *L'ange*. We saw his *banc-titre*, or rostrum camera, used all the time in the shooting of all classical cell animation.

Bokanowski would shoot a scene in a normal way, as raw material. Later, he would refilm this original material under the rostrum camera, modifying and re-elaborating the chosen scene by making it longer, repeating it, or going in closer on it. It's in this sense that he's, as it were, animating his material. It was clearly a laboratory of wonderful experimentation.

How did *L'ange* influence your work? Are there any references or homages to it in your movies?
QUAYS: This film always pushes on you at every level: music, use of light, sound, movement, decor. Yes, we made our small and humble homage to *L'ange* in *Rehearsals*. It would obviously be the scene in *L'ange* where the woman wears the black-and-white striped cloth which matches the decor, as though one and all were representing an old engraving.

We'd found, by accident, a cloth like this in a street market, and as we were already into preparations to do *Rehearsals*, we unconsciously dressed the puppets in this striped cloth, realizing only a little later what we were in fact referencing. But by then we'd already done the decors, which made use of a very similar engraving technique.

How do you interpret the title?
QUAYS: Perhaps the angel is the figure who haunts the stairwell viewing man's past times and makes his slow upward ascent into the light. Maybe he is light.

3

Guillermo del Toro
Arcane Sorcerer

Guillermo del Toro's Catholic grandmother preformed an exorcism on him not once but twice—hoping to guard his soul from the monster movies and fantasy stories he loved. It's perhaps fitting then, that Del Toro's choice for this book is Italian director Pupi Avati's *Arcane Sorcerer*. This sixteenth-century story follows a disgraced young monk sent to look after an older monk whose soul may be in danger due to his knowledge of the occult.

But Del Toro had a tough time finding a copy of the film in the United States—until he found a DVD online. "It was a pretty bad-quality copy, but it had subtitles. And even in that absolutely ratty form, it completely compelled me," he remembers. "It was incredibly powerful to see."

Guillermo del Toro, selected filmography:
Cronos (1993)
Mimic (1997)
The Devil's Backbone (2001)
Hellboy (2004)
Pan's Labyrinth (2006)
Hellboy II: The Golden Army (2008)
Pacific Rim (2013)

Arcane Sorcerer
1996
Directed by Pupi Avati
Starring Carlo Cecchi, Stefano Dionisi, and Arnaldo Ninchi

How would you describe the film to someone who's never seen it?

DEL TORO: It's an incredibly well-researched, pastoral, spiritual horror movie. The rhythm and style of it are hard to describe. It's the *Barry Lyndon* of horror films.

Can you tell me about when you saw the film?

DEL TORO: I was at a showing of *Mimic*, and somebody said, "Your movies remind me of this movie, *Arcane Sorcerer*." So I found a copy on the Internet. It was a pretty bad-quality copy, but it had subtitles. And even in that absolutely ratty form, it completely compelled me. It was incredibly powerful to see.

And it became incredibly important for me in doing *Devil's Backbone*, for example. Just this idea that you can be pastoral in the landscape and imbue the movie with great horror, nevertheless. I love how Avati fuses the sounds of nature with the soundtrack—the cicadas and the crickets and the birds—until they become a source of mystery like they would've been at that time. The sounds of nature become the force of elemental creatures.

I'm a collector of old grimoires and old witchcraft texts and old occult literature. I have books from the seventeenth, eighteenth, and nineteenth century. I have a very nice library, and it's incredible how close the movie comes to feeling like a true undocumented account of how this story would've happened in the time. It has an incredibly deep knowledge of the occult. Avati has an uncanny ear for the tone of this type of story, and it's amazing!

And the story captures one aspect that is very rare in film or, for that matter, in modern literature, which is: prior to the seventeenth century and into the eighteenth century, the clergymen were incredibly knowledgeable and involved with the occult. They knew a lot about it. In fact, the best treatise on vampirism—or one of the best in literature—is written by a religious man, by Antoine Augustin Calmet, a Benedictine monk. And I think that it's truly amazing how the movie captures how these clergymen were toeing the line between the holy and the unholy.

People who know your work and know Avati's work might be surprised that you would choose this film. His other works, like *The*

Mazurka of the Baron, the Saint and the Early Fig Tree, **have that Fellini-like, fairy-tale influence that I think is reflected in some of your work. This film, on the other hand, seems to be almost a traditional gothic horror tale.**

DEL TORO: It's not as traditional as you would think. The stakes the movie posits are beautifully intangible—they are spiritual stakes. What is at stake is the soul of the person. He's not going to be destroyed physically; he's not going to be chewed. He may be murdered in a ritual, but the main fear you have is for the soul of this guy, and that is very close to the stuff I like. I have seen Avati's previous horror efforts, which were *Zeder* and *The House with Laughing Windows*, and I liked them both. I especially liked *Zeder*.

You've presented this film a few times in L.A. and Toronto. How does it play to contemporary audiences?

DEL TORO: It seemed to play very well. I frankly was so enraptured seeing a brand-new print of it. And this was Mr. Avati's print. So I thought it went well, but I didn't ask much [*laughs*].

I'm doing my best to bring this film to the world. Avati is a curious filmmaker, and because his political leanings are to the right, he's not a filmmaker that people analyze very deeply. I disagree with his political views, but I simply adore his filmmaking when it's hot, and this movie is irrefutably great.

On the more philosophical side, this is a film about knowledge and specifically forbidden knowledge. For you, is there such thing as forbidden knowledge?

DEL TORO: Well, I don't think so. I think knowledge, as long as it comes with a spiritual component, is always great. What I don't like is knowledge that is purely, purely intellectual, because that distances us from nature. I love the idea that knowledge can make us closer to the world, as opposed to making us feel superior to the world.

How do you think this film plays to people who were raised Catholic versus people who are outside the religion?

DEL TORO: I think it definitely echoes more strongly if you are a Catholic. Because first of all, you understand more the morbid side of the Church and the morbid side of Catholic ritual, even. It really is easier to understand. It is a very strong movie purely from a cinematic point of view. One of the people I spoke to after the screening was Edgar Wright, who, in fact, is the one who coined the phrase "This is the *Barry Lyndon* of horror movies."

He was completely blown away by it. I think if you know anything about the craft of cinema from a filmmaker's point of view, you understand how incredibly carefully crafted this movie is. A delightful confection. It's superb. The art direction is superb. The cinematography, staging, acting, design, pacing, music, sound design are superb.

In one of your introductions to the film, you wrote, "It is the director's eye for detail and pacing that makes us susceptible to the tenuous wonders at hand." Can you tell me about the scenes or images that stick with you long after this film has ended?
DEL TORO: Well, the pervasive atmosphere, certainly. I love the scene where a priest talks to what we think is a woman behind the portrait of the owl, which is, by the way, a highly significant bird in the occult. I love the scene where he sees the corpse that was buried, and his eyes are opened. That's very, very shocking. I mean, there are so many. I love the scene where he sees the apparition go through the library, and it's a magical, absolutely magical scene, and one with very limited resources.

Your grandmother, who raised you, performed two exorcisms on you because of your love of fantasy and monsters. Did that experience, being the subject of an exorcism, fuel your curiosity for fantasy?
DEL TORO: Well, it didn't hamper it [*laughs*]. It was already fueled. Quite frankly, I've been an addict of horror and fantasy since my earliest memories.

Sure, but there's a difference between watching *The Exorcist* and being the subject of an exorcism.
DEL TORO: Well, she was not a pro. She was an enthusiastic amateur. I think it definitely didn't take [*laughs*].

This film is also about a young priest who is seeking a mentor. Who filled that role in your life, and what did you learn from them?

DEL TORO: Several of my teachers were very influential in shaping my taste in cinema. My screenwriting teacher in Mexico, my first cinema teacher in Mexico—they were instrumental. And they demanded a lot of sacrifice and fidelity to the craft that made me very disciplined, and I still carry it with me to this day.

You were also a protégé of Dick Smith, a makeup effects artist who worked on everything from *The Godfather* and *The Exorcist* to *Taxi Driver*.
DEL TORO: Without Dick Smith, I couldn't have done any of the things I've done. Literally none. God knows what my life would be! He was incredibly generous with his knowledge, not only with me but with everyone and anyone that wanted to learn makeup effects. Before Dick Smith, what would be *Arcane Sorcerer*? Makeup effects were a secret occult knowledge that was only allowed to be handled by a selected few. And Dick Smith came in and literally burst open the doors of that. He freely started to share it with people, to allow people to learn from him. He divulged the treatment, the techniques, and all of that. So, he is truly that: the maestro, the mentor—the most important mentor in my life, probably.

What did you learn from him?
DEL TORO: The one thing he emphasized over any others was preparation. He used to say, "Prepare for the best, because that way you can deal with the unexpected." He was not advocating to be inflexible, he was advocating to be prepared, and I still do it to this day. I'm as thorough and as well prepared as I can be in my filmmaking, and that came from the discipline of having to work as a makeup effects artist many, many, many times in my life.

You've often mentioned this film in the same breath as Paul Verhoeven's *Flesh + Blood*. Did these two films share a link? They seem to hold a similar place in your heart.
DEL TORO: I think they do. Because Verhoeven also captures the period in an incredible way by capturing the rhythms of that period. And he has an incredible sort of fantasy horror scene in that movie, where characters lie under the gallows and they talk about the mandrake root. And it perfectly

captures the belief in the power of the occult and the supernatural as part of everyday life in that era.

Rarely anyone does that, because it's hard to capture the fact that those beliefs were completely matter-of-fact. They were not argued with. When you think about our transition from the Middle Ages, and you think about the Age of Reason coming to be, we were still living in a world that was full of magic, dark and light.

And bringing that full circle back to Avati, one critic wrote that Avati's films are often about the hidden or the obscure, especially his horror films. So why do we, as viewers, find that line so compelling, that tantalizing suspense until the moment we see what we fear?

DEL TORO: It's the same reason that we love hide-and-seek and love chases. One is the thrill of not knowing, and one is the thrill of knowing and experiencing. I think they are both fundamental columns of human narrative: to tease with a mystery or to pursue with action, so to speak.

But why, then, is horror so appealing? It's been said that, as humans, we're the only mammal that loves to scare the shit out of ourselves. Why is that uniquely human?

DEL TORO: We're the only mammals that arouse each other with tales or amuse each other with tales. The human act of storytelling is what sets us apart in the animal kingdom. There is no narrative drive, per se, in any other animal. The way, for example, bees communicate knowledge is through very, very precise geographic location, quantitative measures, where the flowers are, how much pollen can be extracted. But we adorn all these things with narrative. It's fantastic. That's what we do. And I think that that can be said about horror. Horror is one of the fundamental drives of storytelling. Comedy is another one, adventure is another one, and so on and so forth. You can end up identifying the genres through the millennia of narrative.

But why do we love to whack ourselves over the head with our own mortality?

DEL TORO: I think horror is fundamental because as socialized mammals, we don't get to experience the fight-or-flight and territorial battles in the way that other mammals do. We have socialized our existence, our geography, the limits of our geography and space, and social rules to a point where we cannot engage into a territorial fight that easily, and so forth. So we do it through movies and through narrative. Thinking and organizing life in a narrative that includes the beginning and the end—and what lies beyond—requires a storytelling process.

To bring this back to the *Arcane Sorcerer* and the afterlife, why is that spiritual theme more powerful?

DEL TORO: Well, the deepest horror is the one that deals with the worst kind of things. When you're dealing with somebody that may die or be maimed, you can always have the possibility of survival. There's always that part of you that says, "Well, if I lose an arm, I would always have the other one" [*laughs*]. "Well, if the monster tears up my leg, I can always have a prosthetic one made or something." But when you're dealing with the soul, there is no solution to that. There are no prosthetics for the soul.

4

Phil Lord
The Beaver Trilogy

Beauty can be found in variation, which is one of the things that draws director Phil Lord to Trent Harris's *The Beaver Trilogy*. One-third documentary, two-thirds docudrama, the film follows Groovin' Gary, an awkward young man with big dreams, who is then portrayed by Sean Penn and Crispin Glover in repeated and expanded variations of the same story.

"To me, it speaks to the way that you can do an infinite number of variations on a theme, and they can all be different, they can all be legitimate, and they can all be interesting in their own way," Lord says. "To me, it felt like it was a film-school education in eighty-three minutes."

Phil Lord, selected filmography, with codirector Chris Miller:
Cloudy with a Chance of Meatballs (2009)
21 Jump Street (2012)

The Beaver Trilogy
2000
Directed by Trent Harris
Starring Groovin' Gary, Sean Penn, Crispin Glover, Ken Butler, Elizabeth Daily, and others

How would you describe *The Beaver Trilogy* to someone who's never seen it?
LORD: I wanted to think of a really clever way to introduce it. When I've shown the movie to people—and I have the most beat-up copy, like a bootleg of a bootleg of a bootleg—I just tell them, "There's a movie; it's called *The*

Beaver Trilogy. You have to trust me. I don't want you to know anything; just sit down, commit eighty minutes to it, and prepare to be amazed." I showed the movie to Pam Brady, who wrote the *South Park* movie and *Team America*, and with that introduction, she was blown away.

The brief synopsis is, [in the initial documentary segment] there's a guy who's testing out a camera in a TV station in Salt Lake City, and he finds this kid in a parking lot who claims to be, like, the Rich Little of his hometown. One thing leads to another, and the cameraman follows the kid back to Beaver, Utah. The kid puts on this elaborate talent show that culminates in him doing a really embarrassing Olivia Newton-John impression. It's this incredibly funny thing and also really heartbreaking that this kid so badly wants to get into show business. Then, over the course of the next few years, the cameraman remade [the documentary footage] twice in a fictionalized way, once with Sean Penn and once with Crispin Glover.

How did you stumble upon it?
LORD: I had a roommate, a childhood friend of mine, who was a filmmaker and crashed with me. We don't know how it came up in conversation, but he was like, "You've never seen *The Beaver Trilogy*? Oh my God!" So he went to his friend's house that night, got it, brought it back, sat me down, and made me watch it. To me, it felt like it was a film-school education in eighty-three minutes. You see this moment that's a completely true, real moment and then watch it be interpreted in so many different ways by different actors and in different styles. It's a great treatise in storytelling and the different ways you can tell a story just with subtle changes.

What scene from this film sticks with you?
LORD: There are some things that are just incredibly memorable. For me, I think Gary in the parking lot saying "I'm kind of the Beaver Rich Little" was the moment that hooked me, because it's so antiquated in one way. It shows how hopeless he is. It's weird. He's hopeful and hopeless at the same time—that's what's incredible. Trent Harris just stumbles upon this kid who has no talent but is so compelling that he went and made eighty minutes' worth of material about him. So he's like a star, but he's not a star. I loved that character and wanted to see anything that he did.

The subject of the film, Richard LeVon Griffiths, a.k.a. Groovin' Gary, died in 2009. What sort of a legacy is this for him?

LORD: They screened this movie at Sundance. He shows up, and it was, like, the first time that he had publicly talked about the film and really enjoyed a moment of stardom. I think that might be in a *This American Life* piece.

It's funny—that movie reminds me of *Grizzly Man* a little bit, because there's kind of a wise, lunatic character in it who has big dreams. He's a great big dreamer. He has this dream to become famous and make an impact and share art with the world. And it seems like he's never, ever going to get there.

So by putting him in this film, Trent Harris basically makes his dream come true in the craziest, most oblique, twisted sort of way. It would be presumptuous to assume that he took some satisfaction, like, "Oh wow, I always had this dream, and look at that, before the end of my life it really came true." But the impact that it leaves me with is that naiveté, the hopefulness, the interest in sharing his creativity with everybody—it speaks to anybody who makes anything, and there's something really pure about that.

Let's talk a little bit about the performances of the Groovin' Gary character by both Sean Penn in 1981 and Crispin Glover in 1985.

LORD: Sean Penn does sort of an impression of Gary in the second one. And it's kind of a half-mocking but half-studied personification of the character. By copying something and repeating it, you're sort of honoring it and emphasizing it, and that's what his performance does for me. It's by doing as faithful an impression as he can. Sometimes he's really just mocking and parodying, because it's a much younger Sean Penn. You can tell that he thinks the guy is hilarious, but there's definitely an edge to it where he really understands the humanity of Gary. Just by reproducing it faithfully, it draws your attention to certain things. I think it draws your attention to his humanity.

And Crispin Glover?

LORD: The Crispin Glover version is really a little bit more of an original characterization. He takes it in his own direction, whereas Sean Penn, I think, was just trying to be faithful to the source material. Crispin's role explores more of the inner emotional turmoil of the character. You see the character at home; you see the character out on the town. There's this scene with Elizabeth Daily in a diner, and it's just a lot more fleshed out; there's a lot more backstory. And he's so known for being weird; that's another difference in the performance.

As you were watching this film, what was your reaction to it?
LORD: My jaw was dropping! And it drops a different level each time, because the original Gary is, like, this crazy person, and because I've seen a million crazy people on reality television shows, he fits into that field. They found a weirdo, and they're just kind of exposing his weirdness. I was presented the film without knowing that Sean Penn or Crispin Glover were in it, so it took me a good minute into the Sean Penn version to realize that it was Sean Penn, because he's *so* young, it's black and white, and I have the dinkiest, shittiest copy in the whole world.

Have you ever met anybody connected with the film?
LORD: No, never in my life. But I just missed the chance to go to Crispin Glover's house for some screening for a movie, and I regret that day. I regret that day.

One of the themes of the *This American Life* piece is that the filmmaker is repeating something—the sense of reality, the sense of grasping for fame—to get it right. But then it becomes like a snake eating its own tail. As a filmmaker, have you ever fallen prey to that? Did it appeal to the George Lucas in you?
LORD: I see what you're saying. So in other words, the act of remaking something to try and get it *just so*. Not at all, no, because each of those things is perfect in its own way. That's part of what's so great about the movie. Why go back and shoot this again? There's something he's saying inadvertently about the act of looking. There's something you're saying about the act of looking when you go back, repeat something, and try to re-create it; it changes your entire perception of everything. I certainly don't think that he succeeded in making it more perfect each time. I have to say that the original short, the original documentary, is the most perfect thing.

What you get by watching the other two pieces is that you're kind of a witness to other people's conversation about the original piece, their interpretation of it, and what they imagine transpired behind the scenes. A lot of my experience of watching the Gary character is trying to understand what went on in the original documentary. Each time it's expanded upon in the next two pieces, I think, "Oh, wow. I wonder if that's an invented detail. Is that something that they witnessed but didn't get on film?" To me, it speaks to the way that you can do an infinite number of variations on a theme, and they can all be different, they can all be legitimate, and they can all be interesting in their own way.

Has the film influenced your work in any way, directly or indirectly? Are there any references or homages to it?
LORD: I'm certainly not the only filmmaker who insistently writes awkward characters who want something that they are incapable of getting—the person whose ambition exceeds their ability is a really endearing character and is repeated again and again—but it's certainly something that I've been interested in. In terms of method, in an animated feature, you remake the movie three or four times, and it's really easy to get bummed out that the way you did it before didn't get green-lit, didn't get paid, and you're making a totally different version of that movie.

In our case, we made one version of *Cloudy with a Chance of Meatballs* which we loved, and at a certain point we had to start over and make a different version of the movie, which we also loved. As you go through enough of these experiences, you have to embrace the infinite iterations that the movie can go through. You have to say, "Well, yeah, there's a great version of that, too," and that's just another way of exploring this topic. Are we ever guilty of remaking something so many times, in an effort to achieve perfection, that it just kind of becomes weird?

I think the lesson here is you eventually get to Crispin Glover.
LORD: Exactly! You get a super-weird Crispin Glover version, which I love! That's the thing about this movie. The first time I watched it, I loved Gary, but the Crispin Glover version is by far my favorite performance. The second time around, I really appreciated Sean Penn's performance for his honest attempt to re-create it.

I mean, I've definitely rewritten a scene so many times that it became a bastardized version of itself. I don't think that's the case with *The Beaver Trilogy*, though. Each one of those things is its own. The thing about the Crispin Glover version is it's so much more expressionistic, and it has those flights of fancy where he's standing on a mountaintop and it gets really graphic. Those shots of him on the mountaintop in a wig, silhouetted against the moon, singing, couldn't be further from the aesthetic of that original documentary, and yet, it's expressing the same aspiration, the same longing. I'd say probably an equal amount of power, just different.

5

Neil LaBute
Blume in Love

In many ways, Paul Mazursky's *Blume in Love* could be called a precursor to the films that Neil LaBute has gone on to make, namely *Your Friends & Neighbors* and *In the Company of Men*—stories of infidelity, male desire, and moral uncertainty.

In *Blume in Love*, George Segal plays the title character, an unfaithful husband who finds out he's in love with his wife—only after they've divorced. But for LaBute, it's Mazursky's approach to his characters that draws him to the film.

"The telling aspects are his insights as a writer and his ability to elicit good performances from people, and that's what I admire about him," LaBute says. "It's all about what an interesting journey that character made."

Neil LaBute, selected filmography:
In the Company of Men (1997)
Tumble (2000)
Possession (2002)
The Wicker Man (2006)
Lakeview Terrace (2008)
Death at a Funeral (2010)

Blume in Love
1973
Directed by Paul Mazursky
Starring George Segal, Susan Anspach, and Kris Kristofferson

How would you describe *Blume in Love* to someone who's never seen it?
LaBute: It's the simple story of a man who realizes late in a marriage—inconveniently, after he's divorced—that he's in love with his wife and the increasingly desperate measures that he goes through to try to win her back.

When did you see the film?
LaBute: I first saw the film years ago on television, and I think the first time I saw it, I only saw part of it. That's one of the more intriguing ways to see a film—to stumble upon it, know not very much about it, have to dig through the *TV Guide*, and then try to see it again. We've lost a certain kind of searching and a certain kind of yearning for that aspect of film watching.

On the first go-round, there was something there that spoke to me in the way of the directors in the '70s. They all had a—compared to our present-day community of directors—more obvious link to the European directors of that time, and Mazursky even more so than a lot of his contemporaries. He, to me, has great similarities to someone like Eric Rohmer, whom I'm very fond of.

What scene hooked you—was the one that made you go back to watch the entire film?
LaBute: I was both intrigued and frustrated by what was happening. There's this fractured telling of the story—several trips to Venice, and the rest takes place in Venice, California. So I think there was attraction to it by the frustration of it—like, "What's happening here? What's the story?"

It never fails to amaze me when I watch a film like this and at the end, there's the Warner Bros. logo. I go, "This was a studio movie? Warner Bros. made this?" Warner Bros. made *A Clockwork Orange*. Not that it was all Warner Bros., but you know what I mean? These films that we admire from American cinema in the '70s—they were studio films. Not all of them, but a lot of them. And so you think, "God, what were the studio notes for something like this?"

Today working with a studio, they wouldn't even entertain a story like this. And then on top of that, you add this splintered narrative, you know, you're just begging for an audience to go, "I don't get this. Why don't you just put some subtitles on this and film it in black and white and kill everyone?

Why don't you just slowly put some gas into the theater? I mean, you're try-ing to eliminate us, why don't you just do it?"

Obviously, if you're not hooked by George Segal's character, by Blume, then it would be very easy to be repelled by the characters. This is something that I have dealt with in the handful of movies that I've made and the even smaller handful that have come directly from my own head. The question of, "Are these characters worth watching?" That's what people are asking when they say, "Um, who was I supposed to like in this? I didn't really like any-body." I always find that kind of a funny thing; I always think to myself, and sometimes I'll even say it, "Well, I don't really care if you like anyone. You're not supposed to date them; you're just supposed to watch them. You're sup-posed to be interested in them because they're fellow human beings, as long as their story is compelling and they're interesting." My personal mandate is that they're interesting.

I think Blume is immensely interesting as a person. He's incredibly human, and I think Segal makes him more than just interesting. Even though on first viewing it was difficult to follow the narrative, my interests were shaped by the way Mazursky made each scene painfully human.

One of the confusing aspects for me in the film is that Blume and his wife seem just fundamentally incompatible. Would you agree?

LaBute: Yeah, Blume cuts kind of a pathetic figure. For as hip as he feels himself to be, there's something pitiable about him in his little Republican tie and suit jacket. In the end, he's wandering around Venice in his beard, having his coffee and ruminating about love. But by extension, that makes him kind of adorable to me—how utterly small and human he was.

Mazursky is one of the more humane filmmakers in that way. He doesn't judge a scene or characters. He'll come up with the most interesting take on a conventional scene. Case in point, when Nina Blume's boyfriend, Elmo (Kris Kristofferson), comes back from going to see *Gone with the Wind* for the eleventh time and finds out that she (Susan Anspach) has been essen-tially raped by Blume, now her ex-husband.

Elmo doesn't just go berserk, he just asks if that's true. And Blume sort of says, "Yes." And Elmo smacks him in the face. But Blume holds on to Elmo, and Elmo bursts into tears.

It's a cumulative effect, the entire scene—Blume coming over and getting drunk and saying, "You wouldn't let me be here if you didn't really care about me," which leads to this rape. At that moment, before they both climax, you can see that she's remembering something or feeling something in the moment of the actual physical contact, and you long to know what would have happened, what the conversation would have been had Elmo not come home. What would it have been?

In Mazursky's autobiography, he writes that Susan Anspach and George Segal hated one another. Do you think that informs the performances?
LaBute: You can really look at it as a blessing. You can say, "A whole lot of this movie, at least one of them is not supposed to like this person." So usually you can easily believe those scenes.

Those were probably great days when Susan Anspach could arrive at work and go, "Oh good, this is not a day where I have to kiss him and pretend I like him—this is a day where I can tell him what an ass he is. Or tell him to get the hell out of my house," or whatever it was.

There were people like Elia Kazan, and he was a guy who would constantly—if he saw friction and it was healthy for his story—foster it. He wouldn't try to go, "Hey guys, we're all in this together; you're just actors. We gotta try and find a way to really communicate, and I know you're supposed to not like each other on-screen, but we've gotta make it."

What's your philosophy? How do you deal with that dynamic, or have you had to deal with that dynamic?
LaBute: I, luckily, haven't had to deal too much with that dynamic. I'm often creating an atmosphere that's fraught with tension, but I think there's no reason that the process can't be enjoyable. I love the work, so I'm always hoping every day is going to be great.

Actors, what they basically need is to just feel a great sense of trust, because you're asking them to make themselves look foolish. For me, it's more trust than pitting people against one another.

What are difficulties in having an unlikable protagonist at the core of your movie, as this film does?

LaBute: Again, it's arguable; it's subjective, because I don't dislike Blume. The very fact that he's on that journey is inviting, to me, and interesting. But yes, conventionally so, perhaps people found him less than likable, and I certainly have been told that a number of my characters have been that way. The difficulty is getting an audience to connect, to want to take that journey with them, to not just tune out.

You can see where Mazursky asks you to be a grown-up; he's challenging you to accept it on its own merits rather than conventional ones. That's the way the story should go, unlike the gentrified and palatable fairy tales that we take kids to now.

We take Grimm's fairy tales, and we make them something that a kid can look at, rather than the real thing. We've got into a place where we think people can accept basically anything as long as it ends right—as long as the bad person gets what they deserve and the good person comes out on top. They can take their evil in small, sanitized doses, but we're less comfortable with things that end badly—the hero dies on the quest; evil does not get punished.

This movie, for me, sadly, ends in a less than satisfying way. That's one of the things about the movie that I'm not thrilled by. The fact that not only does she take him back, that she does find herself, that his efforts have kind of won her over again—but that she shows up back in Venice. There's this classic scenario of two people coming together and wandering off into the proverbial sunset.

I picked this movie anyway as an underappreciated film in an underappreciated filmmaker's career. He meant a lot to me in the way that he dealt with people and his constant interest in relationships and the mechanics of the heart, rather than things on grander scales. He was in a really interesting decade and didn't seem to completely fit on either side of it but made some good films. So I think the work is indicative of someone who I admire for his tenacity in keeping after what it was that interested him.

Why do you think he hasn't received more attention?
LaBute: He's not an outspoken kind of character. I don't think Mazursky sings his own praises too loudly. I interviewed Mazursky for *A Decade Under the Influence*, that Ted Demme and Richard LaGravenese documentary on IFC. I sat down with Mazursky and talked about his films. Even then, he

was very gracious and happy with the work he'd done and spoke eloquently about the period but was not a grandstanding character.

I admire that his hands aren't all over the movie. *Blume in Love* is distinctly his own film, but he doesn't say "Look at me" all the time. The telling aspects are his insights as a writer and his ability to elicit good performances from people, and that's what I admire about him. It's all about what an interesting journey that character made.

I don't know enough about him to say whether he was an outsider or there wasn't enough box office, but there was always, in any given year that his films came out, a film that touched the zeitgeist, in a very zeitgeist decade, more firmly than his did.

In his own way, he is a pulse on that other side—the quieter side, that desperate side—of people struggling to understand what it was they wanted and how to get what they wanted. And that's Blume's frantic story: now that I know what I really want, how do I get it back?

He built these things on his own fantasies or longings or questions but realized that they were not solitary questions or pursuits; other people probably would be interested in watching somebody who was like them, who was profoundly human, making mistakes and constantly having to backtrack in their lives. He's pushing forward, saying, "Look, I'm trying to better myself, to figure this out, to make it right," and I don't think you can fault Blume or Mazursky on that fundamental level of someone who is reaching out.

After you met Mazursky and spent time with him for *A Decade Under the Influence*, did that inform his work at all for you?
LaBute: Well it always does, knowing you're able to ask specific questions about things. And just from a purely fan-based thing, it was nice [*laughs*]. You go, "Hey, there's the dude; he's right there." He's talking about *Bob & Carol & Ted & Alice*; he's not just this picture you see every so often in a magazine or something. He's there. You can ask him whatever you want. It enriches the experience, because you feel like you've looked the guy in the face.

So did you ask him anything at all about *Blume in Love*?
LaBute: No, I asked if he'd seen *Friends & Neighbors*, and he noticed that I'd actually ripped off one of his scenes where George Segal goes and sits on the

toilet and makes a phone call while his girlfriend's in the other room. That was my little homage to Mazursky in *Friends & Neighbors*. He said he had noticed, and I don't know if he was just being kind.

Are there other tangible ways this film has influenced your work?
LaBute: The theme of bed-hopping and lines like "All I know is I came three times in one night and I'm still depressed" [*laughs*]. There's a granddaddy there. I think *Blume in Love* has a greater heart than *Your Friends & Neighbors* does.

Your Friends & Neighbors can be a chilly experience for an audience [*laughs*]. It's not a movie that you just cozy up with someone and go, "I feel a lot of love for you; I just wanna share this with you." That's a surefire way to end a relationship or put one into question.

I think there's a great catharsis to it in the same way that people can watch soap operas and they can sit down and go, "Well, in retrospect, my life's not nearly as bad as I thought it was when I hold it up in relief to this." You can watch *Your Friends & Neighbors* in much the same way and kinda go, "Huh. I thought we were kinda having a bad go with it, but comparatively, I feel pretty good about us" [*laughs*]. It's meant to evoke the classic terror and pity that Greek tragedy was supposed to.

You and Mazursky are both interested in the same things: what makes the male animal tick, attraction, and adultery. What makes these themes so attractive that you can keep coming back to them?
LaBute: There's a constant probing of morality, of asking what I think of as those big questions: What is good and bad? What is sin? What is right and wrong? What makes us make those choices?

I think he seems to ask some of those things, so I find them interesting. I tend to be someone who looks for them in my characters as well. But I use them as a kind of gauge, as a Geiger counter of what it is to live, how to live—why this is wrong just because people say it's wrong and why it is right just because everybody's doing it.

I'm interested in those things. They're not purely spiritual; a lot of them are just secular and temporal—they're sort of both. I find an affinity in his approach to the common man yearning to know some of the bigger questions. That's why I think I'm drawn to his work.

6

John Waters
Boom!

John Waters loves *Boom!* so much that when he gushed to star Elizabeth Taylor about the movie, she thought he was making fun of her.

"It's the other side of camp," Waters says. "It's beautiful, atrocious, and it's perfect. It's a perfect movie, really, and I never tire of it."

John Waters, selected filmography:
Pink Flamingos (1972)
Female Trouble (1974)
Desperate Living (1977)
Polyester (1981)
Hairspray (1988)
Cry-Baby (1990)
Serial Mom (1994)
Pecker (1998)
Cecil B. DeMented (2000)
A Dirty Shame (2004)

Boom!
1968
Directed by Joseph Losey
Starring Elizabeth Taylor, Richard Burton, Noel Coward, and Joanna Shimkus

How would you describe *Boom!* to your friends?
WATERS: *Boom!* is actually the film based on Tennessee Williams's play *The Milk Train Doesn't Stop Here Anymore*. It's about Sissy Goforth, the richest

woman in the world, and the Angel of Death, a suitor who has a habit of making house calls on women right before they die.

It was a ludicrously wonderful play. When it was in Baltimore, I did not see it, and I hold my parents directly responsible for this [*laughs*]. I was only eight years old. It starred Tab Hunter and Tallulah Bankhead. Tab told me later when he starred in *Polyester* that there were so many gay people in the audience, every time Bankhead said a line, everyone started screaming. You couldn't even hear one thing. Then it opened on Broadway and closed five performances later.

The movie title was, at the last minute, changed. Universal panicked. It was called *The Milk Train Doesn't Stop Here Anymore*. You can even see Richard Burton say those lines, but they took it out. There's no sound when he says it in the movie. They ridiculously retitled it *Boom!* In America, it was with an exclamation point. Not on the credits but on the ad campaign. You wonder about the marketing meetings deciding on that exclamation point.

It was directed by Joseph Losey at a really good point in his career. He later said that it was the only movie to ever lose money with Richard Burton and Elizabeth Taylor. It was a giant bomb when it came out. It got terrible reviews and vanished in a week.

I saw it, and I think I was the only fan of this movie. It was very rarely shown, but I had a tape of it off television. I would show it when I had dates, a lot of times my first date, and if you didn't like it, I knew it wasn't going to work out. It is a great failed art film. We don't have failed art films too much anymore. I've said this before, but it's beyond bad. It's the other side of camp. It's beautiful, atrocious, and it's perfect. It's a perfect movie, really, and I never tire of it.

When was the first time you saw it?
WATERS: I don't remember the theater I saw it in; it could have been in New York or, if it was the summer, in Provincetown. But I remember loving it, and I remember going back and taking Divine to see it. No one really realizes this, but it was a huge influence on *Pink Flamingos*. There were parts of *Pink Flamingos* that were cut out, but in the script, Divine was in this trailer, hiding out, writing her memoirs—very much like Sissy Goforth, Elizabeth

Taylor's character. That really, really led to it, I think. The excesses of the ego, of being so famous that you retire to write about yourself and live in peace with your richness and filthiness, as Divine did.

I took Divine to see it, and Divine was a huge Elizabeth Taylor fan. He loved her. He even smoked Salem cigarettes because she did. In this movie, Elizabeth Taylor is really over-the-top.

There was only one print of it in the country, and I toured with festivals showing it: John Waters presents *Boom!* I've done it all over the world. Then the video came out, and they didn't even send me one. It's a bad video, too; it's a pan and scan, not a letterbox.

In a lot of these interviews that I do about overlooked or abused films, people boldly defend their choice as a good movie. But you, right up front, say that it's a failed—
WATERS: No, it's a great movie! It's not a good movie, but it's a great movie. It's a failed art film. That is possible.

On what level does it succeed in what it tries to do?
WATERS: You can never be sure if they are in on the joke. In Losey's biography, I read that they started every morning with Bloody Marys, so they were drunk when they made this movie. I love the fact that the part of the Witch of Capri was played by Noel Coward. In the play, it was always played by a woman. They asked Katharine Hepburn to do it, and they said she was insulted to have been asked. I love that!

Let's not forget, it's from Tennessee Williams, who I think is a brilliant, brilliant writer. There are moments of beautiful dialogue in it.

Also, it is directed in a very minimalist kind of way. It's almost like watching a play. I wished I lived in that house, in that villa. I think it was the best house I ever saw in my life; I want to live in that house. I was so obsessed with it. The flag she flies, I had made recently and put it in my art show in New York. Sometimes you love a movie so much that you can go into it and take a piece of furniture, something that is on the screen for a second, have it made, and you are *Boom!*

To me, the costumes are so amazing. They are credited to Tiziani of Rome. Well, Karl Lagerfeld, who I only met once, said, "I designed them. I worked for him, and I worked on the movie." So really, Karl Lagerfeld, as a kid, was working on *Boom!*

There are scenes in it—when she has a lunch of sea monster with Noel Coward and wears this most ludicrous kabuki outfit and does dialogue about memory. Or every time a wave crashes, Richard Burton says something like, "Boom! The shock of each moment of still being alive." It just makes me crazy.

It's, in a way, really, really good. But at the same time, it's so terrible. I'm confused all the time; I don't know which it is. I love to be confused, artistically. I love to be in on the joke, and I'm not sure if there is one.

Well, you may be the only person in on the joke.
WATERS: I think maybe I am—and Tennessee Williams, because he said it was the best [adaptation of any of his plays]. I believe it was a comedy, in a weird, weird way. And it is a comedy when you watch it now. I know from showing it to audiences; they are stupefied by it.

I'm a big Joseph Losey fan. In *Cecil B. Demented*, I had a thing where all the characters had their favorite directors tattooed on their arms. I would have Joseph Losey, which I think would be the only chic tattoo you could have. JOSEPH LOSEY on my arm, like a film lunatic.

There's that motif of Richard Burton saying "Boom!" He says it five times. To me, the hallmark of a bad movie is when they say the title of the film in the dialogue.
WATERS: Oh, I love it when they do that, especially in *What's the Matter with Helen?*, *Who's Afraid of Virginia Woolf?*, or *What Ever Happened to Baby Jane?* I always try to say the title in my movies, because it's so hokey. No one ever says "pink flamingos," though. But I love it when they use it in dialogue. Well, they never say, "Well, it's been a long day's journey into night." I don't know if they ever said, "Well, suddenly last summer," but I say that a lot in the summer. But Tennessee Williams had the best titles. Always. Every movie had such *great* titles, and *Boom!* isn't his.

It was called *Starburst* for a time.
WATERS: It was?

And then *Goforth* before *Boom!*

WATERS: And the only other person who told me they liked it was Martin Scorsese. He said he really liked it, too. He said, "Come over, we'll get a print." I was just so flattered . . . I'd never have the nerve to call him up and say, "Hey, Marty, remember that night you said get a print and come over?" He can get any print.

With Scorsese and Taylor, what kinds of conversations did you have with them?

WATERS: Well, he respected it. He likes Joseph Losey and liked it for the same reason I did: it is an incredible oddity from a time we don't ever see. But there are moments of greatness in it.

I was once in Elizabeth Taylor's house. I didn't know her, but she had a staff that knew me. It was a Fourth of July cookout, and it was the day after Princess Diana died. And she didn't cancel, I guess because she had all the food and stuff, but there were like helicopters overhead trying to get tabloid pictures. Elizabeth Taylor doesn't care—she'll have the party anyway! So I just covered my bald spot, because, you know, the pictures are being taken from above. Everyone just pretended they weren't there. And it was this amazing party. It was like Johnny Depp, Tab Hunter . . . Jennifer Jones was there. I mean you just couldn't believe it. But it was hot dogs and stuff.

I finally met her and told her how much I loved the movie, and she got *mad* at first. She thought I was making fun of her. She thought I came into her house to insult her. "That was a *terrible* movie," she says. I was in her house.

I said, "It's a great movie." And then she realized that I meant it. I talked to her for a long time about it; she didn't say much about it. She just was stupefied that somebody liked the movie.

When I left, I kissed her on the cheek and said, "Boom! The sound of knowing every moment you're alive." Of course, we'd had plenty of drinks by then.

How did she react?

WATERS: She was very sweet at the end. It was real nice. She realized I really did like it. I don't know if she ever read that I take this movie around to all these film festivals, but when I do, it's always packed. It's a bigger audience than the movie had when it came out, believe me.

People do see it. There was this huge article in the *New York Times Magazine* about how suddenly the fashion world, how Anna Wintour and everyone had to see this movie. I was almost a little pissed off by it. It mentioned that I had the poster in my house, so it gave me enough credit. They were all Johnny-come-latelies, and I don't know quite how all that started.

On the video box, it says something like "It's a camp classic!" But I'm guessing it didn't start out that way.
WATERS: I would never put it that way. They still don't know how to sell it. They should sell it as a classic. It is a classic. But basically, it should be sold with the Tennessee Williams quote, that it's the best movie ever made from one of his plays. That's the one they ought to use. But some of the quotes I found, some of their reviews are really hilarious. They are so mean about it.

Rex Reed wrote that during this period Taylor was "a hideous parody of herself—a fat, sloppy, yelling, screeching banshee."
WATERS: But nobody played it better. And, I mean, how about my favorite line: "Hot sun, cool breeze, white horse on the sea, and a big shot of vitamin B in me!"

Newsweek said it's a "pointless, pompous nightmare." Another put it, "An ordeal in tedium." *Life* magazine: "That title could not be more apt; it is precisely the sound of a bomb exploding."
WATERS: But they are so wrong.

I want to come back to the camp question. At what point does a movie become camp?
WATERS: Well, the best camp isn't in on the joke. *Showgirls* was great camp. I mean, *The Other Side of Midnight, Mahogany*—ones that didn't mean to be campy. *Beyond the Valley of the Dolls* was great camp but was totally in on the joke. A lot of them these days are in on the joke. But *Boom!*, you never know. You can watch that movie a hundred times and never know if Losey meant it to be camp. *Camp* isn't the right word. *Camp* means "so bad it's good." This is not "so bad it's good." This is so bad it's art. This is so bad it's

confusing. Or this is so great it's confusing. You don't ever know the tone of it. It is, to this day, mysterious to me.

Taylor's performance is camp in a way, only because it's a Tennessee Williams character. I mean, he wrote parts that drag queens have taken to their hearts. Rupert Everett played *Boom!* a couple years ago onstage in London and got some very respectful reviews.

The play itself actually failed twice on Broadway. In his memoirs, Tennessee Williams wrote that it was "really only successful, scriptwise, as the movie *BOOM*. . . . Despite its miscasting, I feel that *BOOM* was an artistic success and that eventually it will be received with acclaim." But it's funny. The quote on the box, it says "Tennessee Williams' favorite film." Do we know he said that, or is that the studio quoting you?
WATERS: Well, maybe I just started a lie. I don't know. Because you're right, I have the same quote.

That makes me believe that when they released the video, they were listening to you.
WATERS: They didn't even send me a video. I don't think they spent that much time researching it. I don't know. You might be right. I think that's the quote. But he did say it would be eventually received with acclaim. I'd like to think the first time I showed it at a festival was the beginning of that.

Tell me about the range of reactions you've gotten from showing it at festivals.
WATERS: Mostly, people love it. Some walk out. And I've had people say, "I'm sorry, I don't get why you like that movie." But mostly, people say, "Oh, I've never heard of that!" or "Can you believe that part!"

They like it. Certainly, they laugh. Not *at* it so much, but just like this artifact of "How can this movie be?" "What is this?"—because most people have never really heard of it at all, even people who know all about Elizabeth Taylor. But the fashion world loves it. I mean, it is a very gay movie. In a weird way, Burton is like a hustler who travels around. Certainly Sissy Goforth is a drag-queen role—Tennessee Williams had to be in on that. Like Edward Albee, I believe all his plays are written for women, not for men.

When Taylor was playing that role, she had a doctor write a fictional medical analysis of her character that concluded she was probably dying of leukemia, which would have given her those manic episodes.

WATERS: That one coughing scene is so hysterical. The audience goes crazy during that because she just *keeps* coughing. You actually think she's going to puke. She has the croup, it seems like, to me.

There was one biographer who suggested that she played this role with Vivien Leigh in mind, who died of tuberculosis.

WATERS: But as if Tennessee Williams wrote Vivien Leigh. That's a very, very different kind of gothic character. I can see that. But the woman who wrote *Gone with the Wind* was certainly not a favorite of mine like Tennessee Williams was.

I bought everything Tennessee Williams ever did up to the end of his life. I buy every book about him, every letter. Everything. As a kid—he saved my life. I read him when I was fifteen. I thought, "Oh God, I knew all that was a lie. You don't have to do all that other shit."

What specifically did you know was a lie?

WATERS: All of it. What they taught me in school, that everything was conformity and everything I had to do. He showed me that there was an alternate world. And I read *One Arm and Other Stories*. I don't know which one I read first, but I used to steal them from the library, because they wouldn't give them to kids. All the movies they made, even *The Seven Descents of Myrtle*, I saw every one of them. They all had good points in them, but *Boom!* was bewildering. It did matter that Elizabeth Taylor was too young for her role and Richard Burton was too old for his. It was miscast, but that miscasting— thirty, forty years later—gives it part of its greatness. Like fine wine, it takes a while for the true flavor of a mistake to come out to beautiful.

In the movie, Burton and Taylor don't get to a scene together until forty-eight minutes into the film. But in the play, they meet on page seven.

WATERS: It's all foreplay. The fact that all that stuff in the beginning, putting on those ludicrous white sunglass, how she's throwing things off the balcony and she's so hateful to the help is very, very funny today. It was certainly never thought of as a comedy when it first came out, which was a great marketing mistake. It certainly had comic lines in it, and excess. It's really talky for a movie.

Yes. There's a bit in one of Taylor's biographies about how she took direction from Losey on one particular line. It's when she's describing the demise of her husbands, and it's very, very rapid dialogue. The direction from Losey was, "Elizabeth, this is very funny stuff and you're not playing it funny." Her response was, "A woman who has lived such a life, I do not find funny." Is it different watching this film now? That perhaps she is thought of, in some light, like this character?
WATERS: No, I think she was the opposite. I don't think she acted imperious at all toward the end of her life. I mean, she was a charity worker basically, raising money for AIDS. There are other stars that do. But Taylor took her legend and, in a way, was comfortable and very kind of down-home about it. At the end of her life, she was still a big movie star and was incredibly gracious about it. I don't think she was like Sissy Goforth at all.

Losey seemed to get along with Taylor, because he directed her next movie, *Secret Ceremony*.
WATERS: Another bad one, but that didn't have the delightfulness of *Boom!* I don't think there's anything, except maybe *The Driver's Seat* [a.k.a. *Identikit*], where Taylor has to go out and find someone to have sex with her and kill her through the whole movie. Andy Warhol's in it. It's astonishing also, but not quite with the same excitement of *Boom!*

Is there a particular scene in *Boom!* that made you a fan?
WATERS: In the very beginning, when she puts those white sunglasses on. I have those white sunglasses, and I've only worn them twice, because I don't have the nerve. Not the exact ones, but I have almost the exact ones.

And when she throws the X-ray machine off the terrace: "Monkey off balcony!" which is a great line. Just those white sunglasses and that white outfit when she walks out on that porch with that view. That was it, to me. That's how I can always tell if an audience is going to go for it or not. They howl and applaud, usually. When I first saw it, there were probably four people in the audience that sat there in stunned silence. Slept maybe, I don't know.

It brought out my militancy, wanting others to experience it; this high, almost. It's like a drug if you see *Boom!* It's a weird drug that some like, most don't like, and a few are great enthusiasts for it. All that changed when I got the nerve to actually find a print of it and show it. They always applaud when I come out to introduce it, but I say, "But will you applaud me in a hundred minutes?"

What's the best way to view *Boom!*?
WATERS: It really helps to have an audience with it, and one that is willing. The fact that I'm presenting it usually puts it in the right tone. The people that come are ready to like it, unless they accidentally, at a film festival, buy a package ticket. Then, trouble.

I think you should be prepared to see a movie that is like no other movie. That redefines what is good or bad, really, in motion pictures. There is no easy answer to that. There are places in *Boom!* that are so astonishingly bad that they had to have been directed by Losey, unless it was an accident made in film heaven/hell that really seemed to work.

7

Richard Curtis
Breaking Away

Richard Curtis saw *Breaking Away* before his career at the BBC, where he wrote the hit comedy *The Black Adder*. It'd be ten more years before Curtis transitioned to features, but *Breaking Away* stuck with him.

"My initial inspiration was to write small, personal movies, and my first movie, *The Tall Guy*, shows that," Curtis says. "I remember thinking that *Breaking Away* was perfect when I saw it, and it's also brilliant about friendship."

He adds: "It's a bunch of friends being funny together, which is what I've always tried to do with my films."

Richard Curtis, selected filmography, as director:
Love Actually (2003)
Pirate Radio (2009)
About Time (2013)

Selected filmography, as writer:
The Tall Guy (1989)
Four Weddings and a Funeral (1994)
Notting Hill (1999)
Bridget Jones's Diary (2001)
War Horse (2011)

Breaking Away
1979
Directed by Peter Yates
Starring Dennis Christopher, Dennis Quaid, Daniel Stern, and Jackie Earle Haley

How would you describe *Breaking Away* to someone who has never seen it?

CURTIS: I would describe it as the perfect small, autobiographical comedy, friendship movie. *Breaking Away* is a beautifully written film. It's about a young guy (Dennis Christopher) who's obsessed with Italy and everything Italian. He speaks Italian at home, even though he comes from some small town in Indiana, and he spends his entire life trying to race bicycles so he can be like the Italians. One plot is the guy who's obsessed, and that's a very funny plot, because he annoys his family enormously. The other plot is about him and his friends hanging out.

It has this brilliant social dynamic, because he and his friends are what they call "cutters"; they're the sons of the men who cut the stone that made the town and, particularly, the university. Yet they can't go to the university that their dads built. So they're the working-class kids, hanging around and endlessly clashing with the university kids who treat them badly. It's Dennis Quaid's first movie. Very, very funny performance, great performance, angry performance.

It's a classic movie because it ends with a heroic bicycle race, and it's the university against the cutters. It has a great twist, and it's really exciting. It's very intimately and informally made, so when you get to the great big race at the end, it's not all pumped up and mighty music; there are endless shots of people in the crowd feeding apples to their children and laying out on chairs. It's a brilliant film.

When was your first experience with it? What did you learn from it?

CURTIS: I must have read a good review of it when I was in my early twenties, and I would have gone to see it at the cinema.

I remember loving it. I remember thinking that it was full of real low-key jokes. In my own films, I think I'm trying to reproduce what conversation is like between my friends and me at ten-thirty at night, slightly drunk, laughing at the world in general. It's a bunch of friends being funny together, which is what I've always tried to do with my films.

When people say, "It must be tiresome writing jokes all the time" or "How do you think of all the jokes?" I always say I'm only trying to be as good as you and your friends are every Saturday night. This is a movie like that, where every character has a particular voice. The relationship with their parents is funny. I just remember it being very romantic, very funny and meaningful.

How did *Breaking Away* impact your career?
CURTIS: My initial inspiration was to write small, personal movies, and my first movie, *The Tall Guy*, shows that. I remember thinking that *Breaking Away* was perfect when I saw it, and it's also brilliant about friendship.

Strangely, *Pirate Radio* and my other movies are possibly more about friendship than they are about love, even though they have the opposite reputation. There's much more screen time in *Four Weddings* about the friends and how Hugh Grant gets along with the band. I've always been interested in that. I was interested in that when I wrote sitcoms. I wrote groups of non-friend friends in tight spaces, and this *Pirate Radio* is about friendship, big characters crashing against each other and everyone trying to find their own way.

Tell me about your favorite scene.
CURTIS: There's a great line when they're all just hanging around, and one of their brothers, who has become a policeman, says, "How you doin', guys?"

And one of them says, "Well, we're a little disturbed by the developments in the Middle East, but . . ."

Then, there's a fantastic moment when he actually gets to race against the Italian cycling team, and the Italian team turns out to be cheats. That's such a heartbreaking moment.

There are so many. There's a great moment when Jackie Earle Haley punches the clock when they keep teasing him about how boring his job is and how he's compromised. He literally smashes the clock and leaves his work. It's full of delights.

One of the things that inspired me about *Breaking Away* was the idea that something small and personal could go on and win a best-screenplay Oscar. Steve Tesich won an Academy Award for it, and I thought that was really exciting. I think the biggest inspiration for my movies was Woody Allen, who made masterpiece after masterpiece when I was a young man. I also loved that his movies were so low-key, so intimate, so personal.

How has your relationship with the film changed?

CURTIS: The last time I saw it was when I showed it to my kids. They weren't crazy about *Breaking Away*, because of the fact that it has this slightly '70s kind of casualness, informality, and lack of manipulation about the rhythm with which it's shot, which I love in films.

I talked to them about genre and this issue of whether people who write comedy get forced into that genre more than they should. That's what I thought was really interesting about *Funny People*. Judd Apatow wanted to make a movie about a generally funny attitude to life. It dealt with a lot of subjects. It existed in a comic universe without him saying, "I have to deliver something which has these traditional comedy beats, start with a problem, make it even bigger, and resolve it."

I think that my kids are used to movies being quite manipulative with their understanding and knowing their shape. A movie like this, which can deal with all sorts of subjects, didn't fit into that sense of format, and I was trying to tell them that was a good thing, rather than a bad thing.

Your own film, *Love Actually*, seems to follow that advice.

CURTIS: *Love Actually* was a strange experience. I don't think anyone has ever written a compilation genre movie, where you took a romantic comedy, wrote ten plots, and put them all together.

I remember the wonderful day when we got the whole cast together in their normal clothes and they all read it. It all seemed to fit like clockwork, but when they put together the finished film, it didn't work at all. Editing it was like a game of three-dimensional chess, because you could literally put any scene, from any story, anywhere in the film. I had to remake a different film than the one that I'd written.

What was that like?

CURTIS: Very tough, because I suddenly realized that you had to interest the audience. The original movie was like a shuffled deck; it was one scene from each story in a row, then a second scene from each story. In the end, you couldn't do that; you had to have three scenes from one story to tell the audience you were actually going to get somewhere. I had to resolve one story halfway through the movie to give the feeling that it wasn't just an endless middle. It was a very, very complicated edit.

Did it teach you anything, other than that you never want to make a movie like that again?
CURTIS: I was thinking, if I ever did another movie in that style, I might just write the twelve stories, not even bother to interlink them, shoot them, and then interlink them in the edit.

In a way, *Love Actually* was the opposite of *Breaking Away*. The next film I write may be more like *Breaking Away*, because it was a genre movie, even though I got interested in stories that were less generic, sadder and odder in turn. In some ways, I think *Breaking Away* is quite a European movie, being about family and class. And what's strange is that the director is English, isn't that right? That is one of those peculiar things where an Englishman goes over to direct something like *American Beauty* or *Midnight Cowboy* and makes a quintessential American film.

What do British directors understand about Americans that we don't understand about ourselves?
CURTIS: I think it's that whole thing of people from another culture coming in and actually having an undisturbed view, in the same way Ang Lee came over to England and made *Sense and Sensibility*.

One of the great joys of my moviemaking is being at the test screenings of my films in America, because there's no difference in the reaction in the UK, except the Americans are slightly louder.

I'm a great believer that, in fact, we're all the same, and when people say, "What's the British sense of humor? What's the American sense of humor?"—actually, there's more in common between a surreal American movie and a surreal British one than between a surreal American movie and a college movie in America. So the truth of the matter is, we're all much more similar than we think.

8

Jonathan Levine
Can't Stop the Music

Can't Stop the Music—the Village People musical—has found an enthusiastic defender in Jonathan Levine. "I love this movie because it's incredibly, wildly entertaining," Levine says. "*Raiders of the Lost Ark* cannot hold a candle to this movie as far as entertainment."

The 1980 musical signaled the death knell for disco—and knows it. Characters proclaim the Village People "the sound of the '80s" without irony, but with a hint of desperation. It also won the first inaugural Razzie for Worst Picture. All of this, Levine says, just makes *Can't Stop the Music* a more compelling cultural artifact.

"The film is very much a celebration of the culture that spawned these guys," Levine says. "The '70s now, with the benefit of hindsight, were fucking awesome."

Jonathan Levine, selected filmography:
All the Boys Love Mandy Lane (2006)
The Wackness (2008)
50/50 (2011)
Warm Bodies (2013)

Can't Stop the Music
1980
Directed by Nancy Walker
Starring Steve Guttenberg, Valerie Perrine, Bruce Jenner, Alex Briley, David Hodo, Glenn Hughes, Randy Jones, Felipe Rose, and Ray Simpson

How would you describe *Can't Stop the Music* to someone who's never seen it?

LEVINE: It's a musical movie with the Village People, a triumphant tale of this ramshackle band that includes an Indian and a leather guy and a construction worker and a cop. It's like *A Hard Day's Night*, but if you replace talented musicians with the Village People and a coherent narrative with this movie.

How did you first see it?

LEVINE: I have a vague memory of seeing it as a kid. When I recently went back and looked at my old records, it was like I had the soundtrack to *Can't Stop the Music* and the soundtrack to *Rhinestone Cowboy*.

I have vague memories of it as a very young kid, but then I have specific memories of looking through the liner notes of the record and opening the record up. So these images from the record are etched in my head. I really was into *Grease* and *Saturday Night Fever* and movies like that.

I would say within the last five years, I've rewatched it, and since then I've shown it to a lot of people. It's a really good movie to show to people at a party if you want to have a few laughs. It's just so fantastic.

Did you see it in the theater or on television?

LEVINE: Maybe I saw it on TV, because I don't think my parents would have taken me to see it in a movie theater. Plus, it doesn't seem like a family-friendly film.

So let's talk about the elephant in the room: this is a very straightened-up version of a very iconic gay band. When might it have occurred to you that these men were not interested in the women they were dancing with?

LEVINE: This is the first I've heard of that. These are gay people? [*Laughs.*]

But the Village People being gay did not occur to me until I was in my twenties. But to me, George Michael was the most sexually potent heterosexual guy. And it didn't occur to me until much later that "I Want Your Sex" was not directed at a woman at all. So I guess my gaydar is not very good. Now I watch *Can't Stop the Music* and think it's an important step in the mainstream culture embracing homosexuality—whether they knew it or not.

Seeing the movie in a modern context, how is the subtext hidden?
LEVINE: One of the more amusing things about the movie is the ways in which the filmmakers just dodge these guys' sexuality. These guys are clearly gay, and the women are swooning over them as well.

The kind of disconnects between the reality of the movie and the reality of these guys' lives becomes a very entertaining subtext for the movie. But I would imagine that off set, in their day-to-day lives, they're not hiding their sexuality. I think disco was very embracing of all sexual preferences.

What's your favorite scene?
LEVINE: Just when you think the movie could not get more entertaining, more nonsensical or crazy, they trump it. It's not so much scenes but evocative images, like Bruce Jenner in a midriff-baring T-shirt. The milkshake musical number is incredible. But to me, you can't beat Guttenberg roller-skating through New York. That's an incredible montage.

It's Steve Guttenberg's first role. He plays a DJ named Jack Morell, basically a stand-in for French producer Jacques Morali, who discovers and assembles the Village People. And it was directed by Nancy Walker. . . .
LEVINE: She's an actress! I definitely did a little research on her. She's an actress, and then she was a TV director.

She was a TV director for *The Mary Tyler Moore Show* and other shows. But I think many of our readers would remember her as the Bounty paper towel spokesman for twenty years.
LEVINE: Really?

The New Jersey waitress in the diner.
LEVINE: This is a true renaissance movie, Mr. Elder. But those opening three minutes—they'll just hook you no matter what. And some of the effects in the musical numbers I find to be very, very cool and very kind of forward-thinking.

The great thing about watching the movie . . . it's marked by incredible kinds of jumps in narrative logic and characters who just do things for no reason, and I think that's fantastic. I would love to intensely make a movie like that.

The only other point I want to add is that there was a person who worked on *The Wackness*—I cannot remember who it was, and she should probably remain nameless—but she told me that on the film, at the craft services table, there was a giant bowl of cocaine. I can neither confirm nor deny that. It is pure conjecture. But if you look at the movie, it makes a lot of sense.

The movie awkwardly straddles two decades and was first titled *Discoland: Where the Music Never Ends*. The title changed, of course. And you can see them trying to stake a claim in the new decade.

LEVINE: Someone says "The '70s are dead and gone. The '80s are going to be something wonderfully new and different." It's just strange, because everything about the movie just smacks of desperation.

It was probably green-lit in the wake of *Saturday Night Fever*, when disco was just this hugely popular thing. Then the disco backlash started pretty quickly, and so they were just fucked, basically. So they had to kind of keep proclaiming their relevance throughout the movie.

It was produced by Allan Carr, one of the producers behind *Grease*.

LEVINE: He also took a writer credit. An ill-advised writer credit, I would say, for Mr. Carr.

It's also notable that the Village People was an assembled band. Victor Willis, the original lead vocalist who you hear on "YMCA," left the band before *Can't Stop the Music* started filming. Did you even know it was a different guy?

LEVINE: I had absolutely no idea. No, but that's pretty funny [*laughs*].

Tell me about the Village People themselves. Does anybody stand out as a particularly good actor, or does anybody turn in a memorable performance?

LEVINE: The Indian guy (Felipe Rose) is pretty good. One of the more fascinating narrative constructs in the film is how the Village People get together. And it's basically done in one montage. Valerie Perrine (who plays a model named Samantha Simpson)—she just basically happens to have all these archetypes in her constellation. All these different archetypes, which I think is very lucky for her, and they're all incredible singers, which is also like a huge stroke of luck. It's sort of like this supergroup, like the Avengers.

The Avengers, I think, maybe steals a lot from *Can't Stop the Music* [*laughs*]. But the way the group is assembled—I don't think they spent a lot of time on that part of the script.

Actually, the filmmakers tried—in some cases—to stick close to their biographies. For example, Glenn Hughes, who plays the leather man, was literally discovered at a tollbooth. They tried to keep a little bit of semblance to reality in there.
LEVINE: I don't think there's any reality that is as surreal as the reality of that film.

It has been said that it was a double feature of this film and *Xanadu* that inspired John Wilson to start the Razzies. In fact, *Can't Stop the Music* is famous for becoming the first winner of the Worst Picture Razzie. Does it deserve that history?
LEVINE: I don't know the criteria for the Razzies, really. For me, the worst movies are the ones that bore me to tears. But perhaps as the celebration of something whose quality level may be somewhat dubious, I can think of no better candidate than this film. If we're looking at the Razzies as a badge of honor, then *Can't Stop the Music* wears it proudly, and I'm proud to be a champion of it.

But what won the Razzie last year? Like, Adam Sandler's *Jack and Jill* or something like that? I'd much rather watch *Can't Stop the Music*. Other bad films can't even aspire to be as bad—as greatly bad—as this film.

How could this have been made a better film?
LEVINE: In the traditional sense? Because I personally think it's a perfect film. I think that a lot of the script's pretty lazy. A lot of the characters' motivations are very, very poorly drawn.

It's also worth noting that *Can't Stop the Music* has three main characters, none of whom are Village People.

LEVINE: That's part of the charm of the movie. It's so ill-conceived. The Village People can't act, right? So then they have to create protagonists for the narrative.

No disrespect to Bruce Jenner, great Olympian, but this is probably the worst thing he did since fathering a Kardashian. I mean, wait—is he a father of a Kardashian?

He just married into it. He's their stepfather.
LEVINE: Okay, well, *Can't Stop the Music* is the other bad decision he made in his life.

I would recast Bruce Jenner if I could.

I think a lot of the performances are a little big. Guttenberg, clearly, has since learned how to focus his energy. He's a little bit of a loose cannon in this movie. When I do get the opportunity to remake this film, you know—I don't want to give away too many of my secrets right now, because no one will go see the remake [*laughs*].

Why, ultimately, did you choose this movie?
LEVINE: I love this movie because it's incredibly, wildly entertaining. It's probably one of the funniest movies I've ever seen. On a pure level of entertainment, you can do no better than this film. *Raiders of the Lost Ark* cannot hold a candle to this movie as far as entertainment.

It has been influential, I think. There are two things about it I see in some of the stuff I do. One: it's a total portrait of a city, and it tries to present you with a picture of a time and a place, which I think I tried to do in *The Wackness*. Two: it's the marriage of music and image, which is something that I pride myself on in all my movies; no matter what, they're music-driven. Those seem to be the touch-points, the reasons that it has a place in my heart.

I do believe in things that you watch for fun. I went to film school, and I do not have a hugely vast knowledge of film, but I've seen a decent amount of movies. And no matter how I try to have the really great, classic films influence me, it's the ones I saw on TV when I was eight that have more of an impact on who I am and what I want to do as a filmmaker, for better or worse.

What conversations spark from showing this film?

LEVINE: Oh my God, it's amazing. People just stare at it with their jaws dropped. It's like, you can break it up into little chunks, so it's perfect for the YouTube generation. Every little three-minute chunk has a gem in it, so you don't necessarily have to watch the entire two-hour feature. But I do recommend that everyone does that, because that's the way that it was intended to be viewed. And on the big screen.

***Can't Stop the Music* marks not only the end of disco but the end of the '70s. It's at the beginning of the AIDS epidemic. Jacques Morali, who put together the Village People, actually died of complications from AIDS. Does this overshadow modern viewings of the film?**

LEVINE: If you watch it closely enough, there is a bit of melancholy hanging up over the movie. As we talked about, they are trying to proclaim their own relevance, and there's something kind of sad about that.

But the film is very much a celebration of the culture that spawned these guys. The '70s now, with the benefit of hindsight, were fucking awesome. The music was awesome, the movies—it was a defining decade for movies in the history of our country. So you can tell that it's coming at a crossroads in time, and everyone knows that, and there is that struggle to identify exactly what that is. If nothing else, it is a fascinating historical artifact, this movie.

It's also rated PG, which is interesting, because if you pay attention during the "YMCA" number, you can see Valerie Perrine topless and some fleeting, full-frontal male nudity.

LEVINE: Wait! It's PG?! Dude. Wow [*laughter*].

Well, in 1980, they didn't have many choices. It was PG or R.

LEVINE: If today you were to make the Village People movie and you showed one of their dicks, you'd probably get an R. I'm just guessing. I would love to make a PG movie with a lot of dicks in it. Perhaps now I can use that with the MPAA as precedence.

Wait, I'm going to go back and recut my movie *Warm Bodies* and just throw in a construction worker singing with his dick hanging out, just as an epilogue.

9

Guy Maddin
The Chase

"A pretty dark flower" is how Guy Maddin describes *The Chase*, a 1946 sur-realistic thriller starring Robert Cummings as the hero, Steve Cochran as the heavy, and the iconic Peter Lorre as a jealous thug.

Perhaps Maddin's love of the film is only increased by the fact that only murky copies seem to be available, adding to the dreamlike atmosphere of the film. Maddin traces movies such as *Memento* and *Blue Velvet* back to the twisted narrative of *The Chase*, as well as some coded "queer mischief" from gay mystery writer Cornell Woolrich.

"I know it's confusing to people, implausible," says Maddin. "But for me, it's confusing and implausible in just the right way."

Guy Maddin, selected filmography:
The Heart of the World (2000)
The Saddest Music in the World (2003)
My Winnipeg (2007)
Footsteps (2008)
Night Mayor (2009)
Keyhole (2011)

The Chase
1946
Directed by Arthur Ripley
Starring Robert Cummings, Michèle Morgan, Peter Lorre, and Steve Cochran

How would you describe *The Chase* to someone who's never seen it?

MADDIN: The movie opens up with sweet Robert Cummings, the hero of the movie. Somehow he just projects a warm apple pie just slid onto the windowsill. He's got a very pleasant voice and a pleasant, open face. But he's out of work, finds a wallet, and takes a dollar and a half out of it to have lunch. He then returns the wallet with the other bucks in it to its owner, who turns out to be a savage gangster (played by Steve Cochran).

Cummings accepts a job from this gangster, because he needs it, as his chauffeur. The gangster's a control freak and flips open, from the backseat, a separate set of accelerator and brake pedals and starts driving Robert Cummings from behind.

One of the extraordinary things about *The Chase* is that it uses no dialogue for the first two and a half minutes.

MADDIN: It's got one of the great openings in film noir; it's just so economical. It does seem like some sort of ancestor of *Blue Velvet* as well—that sweetness that's represented by Kyle MacLachlan in Robert Cummings and the lunacy of Steve Cochran as a Frank Booth–like character. There's something just so raw and primitive about the performances in both movies at times, and it's very effective. There's just something honest about it.

What film noir does best is show a delirious war veteran doing something wrong in the film's opening minutes. The graph of the movie's trajectory looks like a steep downward slope into the protagonist's open grave.

Who recommended the film to you?

MADDIN: It was my friend Dennis Jakob. He's in his late sixties now, dropout from the film industry. He edited the acid-dropping sequences in *The Trip*. He went to school with Jim Morrison and Francis Ford Coppola and really knows his stuff. He's a real cinema buff, and he sent me a copy of *The Chase*, or at least referred me to it, and I tracked it down somewhere. All copies of it are in horrible condition, and I kind of love that. It just opened up to me like a flower. I stuck my nose in a pretty dark flower.

Why did you choose this particular film to champion?

MADDIN: It's got something surrealist going in it. There's something mysterious and confusing emanating from all those shadows. This is maybe the
most delirious of all film noirs ever made, because it turns out that not one
but two of the major characters, both the protagonist and the antagonist,
have amnesia of some sort or are shell-shocked war veterans with severe
mental traumas that aren't made apparent until later.

There's some great queer mischief going on there. Homosexual domi-
nance, moments which just make a mockery of the production code. At
one point, the employer/employee relationship seems to have been con-
summated, and their other employee, Peter Lorre, is registering some
vague jealousy.

So Cummings promptly, with a logic that only can be found in film noirs
and in real life, falls in love with Cochran's wife, within about four minutes,
and decides to help her sneak away. Thus begins one of the chases the movie
refers to, a paranoid dream in which Cummings and Michèle Morgan flee
to a nightclub in Cuba. At this time, his guilt, perhaps over a theft, or just
guilt over wartime atrocities, forces him to kill this girl and get tangled up in
some plot in which he desperately tries to prove his innocence.

It gets more and more convoluted, more so for the literal-minded viewers out there that need tangible explanations for things. And just when it
gets so far-fetched with tangible explanations and it's getting dreamlike
again, he wakes up from his dream, restages the escape to Cuba with the
girl, this time successfully, and they live happily ever after. Except that, as
I've instructed all my slack-jawed students, the protagonist is probably not
such a hero, but probably doomed to kill his wife and kill countless other
people because he's totally fucked.

Robert Cummings's character is not exactly the most stable marry-
ing material. In the opening shot of the movie, he's popping what seem
like Rolaids, but they're clearly some serious meds. He might be the most
medded-up guy in film noir history. And *Memento* sure owes something
to this picture.

**This movie mystified even the *New York Times* critic. Why does it
appeal to you?**

MADDIN: This movie may well remain an orphan forever. It just might. I've shown this movie to so many people. I teach it every year in my class, and my students write just a one-page response to it every time.

I like the level of confusion. I think it's perfect. At times, when it starts getting convoluted with plot late in his dream, it starts getting perilously close to the explanations at the end of a *Murder, She Wrote* episode. Things really take off as a dream when it starts overlapping a little bit with working methods of *The Big Sleep*, the most famously convoluted noir ever.

I normally loathe whodunits, because they always get tangled up in an anticlimactic explanation involving psychologically bogus motives and things like that, but what drives *The Big Sleep* is that none of that stuff matters. And what really matters is that Humphrey Bogart is determined—no matter how often Lauren Bacall is implicated and almost proven guilty of something—he's determined to scrub her vagina clean so that he can love her. I find there's a madness in that. Maybe having seen *The Big Sleep* enabled me to enjoy the almost-as-intricate explanation in the late stages of that dream within the middle of *The Chase*.

This film has all the hallmarks of a film noir. It's got the dame, the murder—it's even got Peter Lorre. What does he add to the movie?
MADDIN: I just saw him in his very last film the other day, Jerry Lewis's *The Patsy*. He's clearly dying right in Technicolor, right before your eyes. Good God, those eyes. They just look like a pug getting ready to be put down. Peter Lorre's ever-morphing, unhealthy body and amazing voice are always welcome. He's one of my favorites.

How does Arthur Ripley, who later directed Robert Mitchum in *Thunder Road*, distinguish himself as a director?
MADDIN: He seems to understand the set pieces quite nicely, and code mischief is kind of fun, too. Novelist Cornell Woolrich wrote the books behind *Rear Window* and *Black Angel*, which is another fantastic *Memento*-like amnesia picture. There's just so much dark and coded queerness in sailor-suited Cornell's writing. He lived with his mother and kept a cruising sailor suit folded up neatly under the bed for night use. That really sort of drives the movie.

So much of noir is aimed at penetrating past the censors so quickly that they won't even notice what hit them—such as Steve Cochran's jail domination and the murky situation he has with Peter Lorre. The two of them just lie around postcoitally all the time. For guys that are real go-getters and really successful, they just seem to lie around with languor, listen to music to agitate themselves. Who knows who Robert Cummings is falling in love with? It might be Steve Cochran. He might be running away from his guilt for betraying Cochran. That might be the real chase.

It's a movie that very smartly and correctly identifies the fact that we can't identify what it is we're really running away from or chasing after. Robert Cummings could be successfully chasing Michèle Morgan, or vice-versa. It's a real odd look at how mating rituals work in the human marshland. It seems to acknowledge that there are a lot of dark, fuzzy corners for all of us. And all of this is enhanced by my Sinister Cinema copy of it, which is even fuzzier and murkier, and by the knowledge that a better copy of *The Chase* doesn't even exist anywhere.

Usually film noir is about the unredeemable characters on a quick trajectory to damnation. But this one embraces both this path and the romantic notion that people are redeemable. Do you think there is some sort of message to the audience?
MADDIN: Robert Cummings doesn't end up in the grave after it's implied that he's going to. It does seem to be a realistic warning that America in 1946 has got an army of civilians that are in rough shape that need some help.

Can we believe the ending?
MADDIN: No, it seems dreamlike, especially the fact that he's even in the very same horse-drawn hack and shot from exactly the same camera angle. There's something loopy about that, and perhaps you're watching another dream, or a memory of the dream, or a wish-fulfillment fantasy. I know it's confusing to people, implausible. But for me, it's confusing and implausible in just the right way.

Have you found people who share your love of this film?

MADDIN: Well, other than Dennis Jakob and my upstairs neighbor, Steve Snyder, who's a film professor, I haven't encountered anyone who loves this movie properly. And all I can say is, clean off your glasses for a closer look at this incredibly murky picture.

An alarming number of viewers, even at the fine arts university where I most recently taught, are incredibly literal-minded when it comes to cinema. We even have trouble with flashbacks, let alone movies this delirious. You hear people complain that Steve Cochran just wasn't that likable. Of course not—he just slapped a manicurist! I don't think people know how to process coded scenes anymore, and they need their women to be strong and hoof men in the balls. Too many people watch movies with a propagandistic eye now. They want movies to be about the way life should be, not the way it is.

10

Danny Boyle
Eureka

Danny Boyle describes Nicolas Roeg as a director "who makes truly inter-national films and wants to make films for a huge audience. They're highly idiosyncratic films. You can spot a Nic Roeg film within a heartbeat." The same could be said of Boyle's kinetic sense of self-reinvention, and it's easy to spot a kinship between their bodies of work.

Boyle chose *Eureka* in part because of its obscurity in the Roeg canon. "That is a wrong, a severe injustice in the cinematic world," Boyle says. "It's an extremely wild pleasure."

Danny Boyle, selected filmography:
Shallow Grave (1994)
Trainspotting (1996)
A Life Less Ordinary (1997)
The Beach (2000)
28 Days Later (2002)
Millions (2004)
Sunshine (2007)
Slumdog Millionaire (2008)
127 Hours (2010)
Trance (2013)

Eureka
1983
Directed by Nicolas Roeg
Starring Gene Hackman, Theresa Russell, Rutger Hauer, Mickey Rourke, and Joe Pesci

How would you describe *Eureka* to someone who's never seen it?

BOYLE: It's about Jack McCann (Gene Hackman), who discovers gold in the Yukon, immeasurable gold, and becomes the richest man in the world. It's about how dissatisfying his life is.

Why did you choose this film, and Nicolas Roeg in particular?

BOYLE: Nic Roeg is probably my favorite director. I love saying that because he's a Brit as well, but he's a Brit who makes truly international films and wants to make films for a huge audience. They're highly idiosyncratic films. You can spot a Nic Roeg film within a heartbeat. There's something about them; you just know you're in the middle of one straight away. I've been a big fan of his. I've seen *Don't Look Now* and *The Man Who Fell to Earth* as a young man and again [more recently]. This, unlike *Apocalypse Now*, was a film whose baggage buried it.

I remember going to the theater on a Friday afternoon to watch it, and I was ready for it. I wanted to see it so much, and there was nobody in the cinema; it was just me. I was absolutely blown away by the film. I went back to see it the following Wednesday, and it had already been taken off. It had disappeared. It's one of the absolute shames, I think, of my experience of modern cinema.

The notes I've seen from the studio said it was too violent and too incomprehensible. Critic David Sterritt wrote, "Few filmmakers are more talented than Nicolas Roeg, and few are more infuriating."

BOYLE: One of the key things about a Nic Roeg experience is that he tries to disorientate you, and he wants you to be in a state where you're not ready for it. That's basically his technique. He will use any tool to create that disorientating effect. He doesn't use a zoom lens here like Robert Altman uses a zoom lens—he wants to seek out an actor, and the actor doesn't know it. It gives him that control, in a way. He often uses bad performances for minor characters like a zoom lens. He's trying to make you feel slightly off balance, really.

Can you talk about his approach—how is it informed by his experience as a cinematographer?

BOYLE: What I like about him with his use of the camera is that he's a jack-of-all-trades with it. He's not a purist with it. He'll often use handheld cameras in extraordinary circumstances where it's very inappropriate, like in Hackman's great speech. It ends with him saying, "Once I had it all, now I just have everything."

I think that camera is handheld in that scene in a very kind of inappropriate, awkward way. You wouldn't notice it was handheld, except that it's not perfect, and it should be. He's a kind of anticlassicist in a way. And he's prepared to cut. The way that he's prepared to cut is more interesting than his history as a cinematographer. His editing technique is his greatest tool, and there are so many examples of it in *Eureka*.

The film basically warns that if you reach ecstasy or your goals too soon in life, there's nothing left; you're dead after that.
BOYLE: It's a fairly commonplace idea that it's all in the pursuit and the chase and not the fulfillment, really. I think Philip Larkin has an amazing phrase he uses about it. He calls it "fulfillment's desolate attic." It's not unique to Roeg. In a funny kind of way, he's much more interested in seeing people who are in that state, what happens to their consciousness. That's Roeg's obsession, to find out what tricks are being played in our subconscious world.

The problem with the film is that this extraordinary creation of Roeg's, Jack McCann, he kills two-thirds into the film. It's almost like his absence kills the film.

The final third is a courtroom sequence.
BOYLE: Which is shot—ironically, once McCann is absent—in an entirely conventional manner. The freedom of the film to go anywhere and do anything accompanied McCann, and his life is lost. I find that extraordinary, watching that again, just to see how Roeg lost his touch as soon as McCann lost his life.

That's what Roeg's screenwriter Paul Mayersberg points to as being the central difference between English films and American films. American films have a point; they know where they're going. It's not necessarily predictable, but it's an arc you can follow. Whereas in

English films, it's about getting to the end, not necessarily even knowing where that will be. Is that a fair critique?

BOYLE: It's certainly true in terms of Roeg. The studio system says that you shoot in order to edit; basically the two are a unified process. For Roeg, as I understand it, they are very separate things. He shoots, and then he sees how he can edit it. Which is really interesting, because it is anti-product, and you can see why it drove Universal mad on something as huge as *Eureka*. If you bring that idiosyncratic approach to something as expensive as *Eureka*, there's going to be trouble.

There have been parallels drawn with, for example, Orson Welles and *Citizen Kane*. *Citizen Kane* is another film that is evoked all the time when talking about *Eureka*, that McCann is just a gold-prospecting Charles Foster Kane. But it's also been said that Roeg is also McCann. The *Guardian* wrote that Roeg resembles McCann, "a man with style who had it all and spent the rest of his life considering what to do with it."

BOYLE: Excellent. Sounds very true to me. That's very good. I mean, I don't like the *Citizen Kane* stuff in the film, I think it's unnecessary. I personally find that my love of the film really isn't based on its relationship to *Citizen Kane*. It seems a shame to me that it invokes it. It has enough of its own to stand alone. McCann's emotion is gold. It's gold in his veins. I think that whole sequence where he discovers it, the whole setup of that—the intercutting of the discovery and of nature and the orgasmic death pangs of his lover—it's just pure Roegian genius, really. His death and the orgy that Rutger Hauer takes the girls to—both sequences are Roegian, Roeg as his greatest.

McCann reaches ecstasy too early, and he'll never be able to reach that point again. How do you feel about this parallel that's made to filmmakers, that their early work never reaches the acclaim of their later films in a lot of cases?

BOYLE: The ten-year theory. There's probably no greater application of it than to Nic Roeg. I think it's literally a ten-year period between *Performance* and *Walkabout* and *Don't Look Now* and *The Man Who Fell to Earth* and *Bad Timing* and *Eureka*, an example of a golden period of a filmmaker. They're so individual and idiosyncratic, yet they're huge films. I think that's why you can spot a Nic Roeg film within three shots. You know you're in a Nic Roeg film.

But how do you feel knowing you, personally, are beyond that ten-year span?
BOYLE: Yeah, but there's not much you can do about it, is there? Other than retirement. I think there's probably a period where you work up an energy that isn't too self-conscious, and that's certainly the best way to make films. There probably does come a point in your career when you start to become too aware of what you're doing, too self-conscious about it, rather than going with the flow.

Is there a way that you've found to circumvent that?
BOYLE: Yeah, because certain stories can regenerate you or techniques can regenerate you, approaches to certain stories that you can stumble across can revitalize you.

Can you give me an example of something you've been revitalized by?
BOYLE: Well, for me, it was digital cameras. I came back from Thailand, where we'd made *The Beach*, and I made a couple of very small films for the BBC in Manchester for television on the digital cameras. Subsequently, I used that experience, then, to feed into *28 Days Later*. And that revitalized me. It made me feel kind of centered again. When something in a film asserts itself, you can feel it making itself.

You mentioned that within three shots you know you're in a Nic Roeg film. What are the hallmarks?
BOYLE: Free association. You feel when you're watching him, "Jesus Christ, he'll intercut anything, this guy!" But there is a scheme that is working on you emotionally. And it's hugely powerful.

His preoccupations certainly show up in *Eureka*. There's his obsession with being lost, the unknowability of truth, and sex. He became known for his very lyrical, naturalist sex scenes.

BOYLE: I always think the scene in *Don't Look Now* is the best sex scene ever. That's what I call free association, the way he cuts that sex scene in *Don't Look Now*.

How does he accomplish that? It's been said there's nothing less sexy than sex on film.
BOYLE: Directors tend to be quite rigid. When you watch a Roeg film, you realize he's got a very liquid mind. He's quite prepared to take anything on board. He doesn't have any rigid frameworks at all. He's prepared to tolerate, and he's interested in anything. And that, sometimes, can lead you up blind alleys. But it also can open up huge meadows of wonder. I don't have a free mind like that at all. God knows how he manages to keep that liquid sense when you've got the huge pressure of a forty-million-dollar film.

What was it like meeting him?
BOYLE: I've met him twice. I used to take my kids to swimming lessons at this pool in central London. Also at this pool, taking *his* kids to swimming lessons, was Tony Blair. There was another guy there as well, and it was Nic Roeg.

In fact, when we were leaving once—I never went up to him, because I'm very shy like that—in the car, driving home, I pulled up, and he was just about to cross the road. I literally wound down the window, and I said to him, "I fucking love your films, you know."

And he said, "Oh, thank you very much. Thank you." Then I drove off.

I told him that story when I did meet him properly. I got an award for *Trainspotting*, and he presented it to me. *Empire* magazine said, "We're gonna give you a prize. Who would be your ideal person to give you a prize?" I said, "Oh, it'd be Nic Roeg!" And so he did! He was absolutely chuffed to be invited, because he felt he'd fallen out of fashion totally, and so he was delighted to be invited back into the club.

Why do you think he has fallen out of fashion?
BOYLE: I don't know, actually. What amazed me just having a look back at *Eureka* is how modern it is. I think it just happens. In one minute, when you look back, you're suddenly no longer in the race.

When you go back and you look at the casting, it has Mickey Rourke, Joe Pesci, Rutger Hauer, Gene Hackman, and Roeg's wife, Theresa Russell. It's strange casting, because he had made his name as a cult director. He'd worked with Mick Jagger, David Bowie, and Art Garfunkel. What do you think of Roeg's casting?

BOYLE: I suppose the unusual part for the casting is Hackman, because he was an establishment star. The thing I've always admired about him is that he's got these highly ambitious ideas, and yet he knows he wants, in his blood, to get them to as many people as possible. He will use people who have a persona that will bring publicity to the film.

Is there a scene or sequence that riveted you that you still go back to?

BOYLE: The orgy scene. It's like some kind of voodoo scene or trance scene. I remember being on my own in this rather plush cinema, being absolutely breathless watching this scene. His presentation of sensuality is a full-on, unashamed experience, although the girls are ashamed by the end of it. I was blown away by that, I remember. And of course, McCann's death, the violence of his death.

I've been around movies many, many years and seen many violent deaths, but I actually looked away from the screen during McCann's murder. What was your reaction to it?

BOYLE: When I watched it again, you realize what's incredible about it is Hackman's performance in the fifteen minutes leading up to that. He knows he's going to die. In this incredible scene with Jane Lapotaire—he's fantastic in it—he suddenly calls her back to bed, and they make love. And he knows, because there's always that link in Roeg between death and sex, so they make love, and then she leaves in the car, and she's smiling, because for women in Roeg's films, sex always leads somewhere. For men, it never leads anywhere. It's a death, really.

The most acute moment of the murder scene is when he goes into the house and he says, "You can do better than that." He staggers into the house and kind of watches his killers as they come up the stairs, and he chucks something at them.

There's so much brutality in this scene. He's chased, beaten, and burned to death.

BOYLE: Yeah, and yet there's no sense of a fight. There's always a sense of Hackman letting it happen to him, because it's got to happen to him now. Yet, there's a defiance there, and he's almost unkillable. I'm sure that's why, unless they can literally burn his flesh off his bones, he won't die. He seems to stay alive there. We've seen him cheat death at the beginning of the film; you see him cheat death there.

Screenwriter Paul Mayersberg has said *Eureka* is basically about a man, why he died, and how he contributed to his own death.

BOYLE: As it often is in Roeg, there's a literal symbol, which is that he has substituted his blood with gold. He substitutes his lonely quest for the gold instead of emotion, contact, and the love of that woman at the beginning, who he clearly does love and pines for later.

Where he's made vulnerable, of course, is when his daughter (Theresa Russell) says, "I don't want your gold, I want flesh." The next moment, Rutger Hauer dresses her in McCann's gold. His emotional life has become stunted by that early fulfillment, and he's been left nowhere to go emotionally. Everybody wants it, and he found it, but he sacrifices his emotional life for that.

Tell me about why you ultimately champion this film.

BOYLE: It's partly people's ignorance of it. I don't mean ignorance in a pejorative way, I mean it in a way that the film is virtually unknown. That is a wrong, a severe injustice in the cinematic world. It's an extremely wild pleasure. For the kind of people who like the films I make, watch the first three-quarters of *Eureka*; there are wonderful things to discover in it.

11

Henry Jaglom
F for Fake

In *F for Fake*, Orson Welles portrays himself as a magician who can't be trusted. It's been called a pseudodocumentary, which is not entirely fair or accurate. Instead, it's best described as a cinematic sleight of hand, a documentary that becomes something else entirely.

Henry Jaglom, Welles's friend and sometime collaborator, calls it "the most autobiographical of [his] films"—and does not want to hear any criticism of it. None. Not a quote from a contemporary review, nothing. A masterpiece is a masterpiece, he argues, and the movie does not need him to champion it.

"Ultimately, it is about the creative act and the confession that all creative acts are fraudulent," Jaglom says. "I think it's one of the greatest films never seen."

Henry Jaglom, selected filmography:
A Safe Place (1971)
Someone to Love (1987)
Venice/Venice (1992)
Déjà Vu (1997)
Festival in Cannes (2001)
Going Shopping (2005)
Hollywood Dreams (2006)
Irene in Time (2009)
Queen of the Lot (2010)
Just 45 Minutes from Broadway (2012)
The M Word (2013)

F for Fake
1973
Directed by Orson Welles
Starring Orson Welles and Oja Kodar

How would you describe *F for Fake* to someone who has never seen it?
JAGLOM: It's a film about a painter, Elmyr de Hory, who paints copies of the great masters and passes them off as authentic—and about a writer, Clifford Irving, who is doing a book about this painter. Later in life, Irving wrote a book he claimed was the autobiography of Howard Hughes, which in fact was a fake, and he ended up in jail because of it. Ultimately, it is about the creative act and the confession that all creative acts are fraudulent. I think it's one of the greatest films never seen.

Is it just filmmakers who are liars that tell the truth, or is it that, at some level, all artists feel vaguely fraudulent?
JAGLOM: Well, you're making something up, you're telling a lie and you're trying to get the audience to believe it as if it were real.

You remember early in the movie Orson says, "During the next hour, everything you hear from us is really true!" And then he shows his girl-friend, his real-life lover of twenty-five years, Oja Kodar, having an affair with Picasso. And I was shocked! I didn't know she had an affair with him . . . so it's a tremendous kind of confession from a magician. Orson loved magic. Magic is fakery.

How did you first see it?
JAGLOM: Orson showed it to me, in his house, on the video. I just fell in love with it; I thought it was sensational. Orson considered it his greatest accomplishment, and I said, "Why?"

He said, "Because I found a way to beat the process. I made a film for no money."

And he thought that everybody was going to acclaim it, and he'd be set for the rest of his life. It never even got distribution. He was more dejected by that than by any of the other things that happened in the other films. He really thought that he created a whole new form. It is the film as the ultimate confessional as he shows us all of these boxes within boxes of people being fakes. It is a confession of a filmmaker who essentially—like all filmmakers, storytellers, and artists—is a fake. It is the most autobiographical of Orson's films, for me.

Can you talk about that new form, define it?

JAGLOM: It's boxes within boxes within boxes. Instead of having a beginning and an end, or going circularly within itself. There's no structure like it in any other film that I've seen. It is a film that's created in the editing, not in any shooting. It is a film about editing, which is what creative filmmaking is really about.

How is this film best viewed?

JAGLOM: With as many people as you possibly can, because you're doing so many people a favor, and they'll never see it otherwise. Everything worth anything has to be seen on the big screen, but this film, because of its nature—it's not about the visuals, so it doesn't matter. See it on video or DVD, but you should crowd the room with people for this one.

Aside from Welles himself being in the first three minutes of the film, how do you know *F for Fake* was his? What makes this a signature Welles film?

JAGLOM: I don't know, but I know . . . The first of my films that he saw, *Tracks*, he set out in the dark in the screening room. I'll never forget that. It was him and me and one other person in the screening room. And he said, "I know immediately that this has to be your film."

And later I said, "How do you know that? You haven't seen any of my other films?"

He said, "I bet you say the same thing on every film you ever make," meaning the themes.

And he considered that the sign of a filmmaker, as opposed to a movie director for hire. So he certainly was the exemplar of that. I don't know how to define what it is in his films, but you can't reduce it to camera angles or dialogue. It can be by nobody else.

Some of the first spoken dialogue is "Why not? I'm a charlatan." And we talked briefly about Welles casting himself as a magician—and you cast him as a magician in *Someone to Love*.

JAGLOM: He was a magician, and I like using people for the essence of what they are. That's what he was: he was a fraud. He was a magician who felt like he could no longer do his magic. He felt like he was a failed magician.

Did Orson have a full awareness of that, his public persona?

JAGLOM: I would kick Orson under the table at lunch when somebody would come over to the table and he would do this Orson Welles thing that would scare the shit out of them. And I would kick him. He called me his "Jewish conscience." He would say, "I don't need my Jewish conscience kicking me under the table."

And I would say, "Why do you do that? Why do you do that? You're so sweet and open and vulnerable. Why do you put on this intimidating ogre act?"

And his answer was, "Well, they don't want to see this," and he pointed to his nose. He said, "This little nose? There's nothing here, so I give them a nose" [a facade —ed.].

When he did *Someone to Love*, his final film, I finally got him to take off the mask. The reason he wanted to do it was because he had seen *Always*, and I play a person going through a divorce who is very stripped emotionally. He said, "You show yourself warts and all, and I'd like to do that just once on film."

And I said, "What about your little nose?"

And he said, "I would do it for you! I would do it for you!"

So I said, "Great, the next movie." And when he came to the set, he came with this huge, elaborate nose and a Russian accent. I said, "What are you doing? I want this to be you, Orson."

"You don't like this?" he said. "Look!" And he put on an Arabic accent. So he wanted to hide. He didn't think he was sufficient. That's why he put on this act that he finally got trapped behind. When you see *Someone to Love*, you see him as he really is, as if you had lunch with him. He was such a sweet and open and unintimidating man.

What specific lessons did you learn from *F for Fake*?

JAGLOM: It reinforces a great lesson Orson gave to me in my life. As I'm talking to you, it's over my editing machine. Every day, I come in here to edit my movie, and there it is: "The enemy of art is the absence of limitations."

He said it to me one day at lunch, and it's the most valuable thing anybody has ever said to me. It means simply that if you have no limitations, if you have all the money in the world, all the time, you can create a lot of things, but it's not about art. You can get special effects, you can get great production . . . but if you don't have it, if you're limited in money or time, you're forced to be creative, to find a creative solution and an artistic answer to a question. That's exemplified for me, more than anything, in the great work that is *F for Fake*.

It just reinforced, tremendously, that film is a magic place where you can do anything, and you should not be bound by any rules.

Editor's note: Lasse Hallström's The Hoax, *which stars Richard Gere as fabricator Clifford Irving, had not yet been released when Jaglom spoke to me about* F for Fake. *Irving appears as himself in* F for Fake, *and his story in* The Hoax *dovetails nicely into Welles's documentary segments. But before you see* The Hoax, *watch* F for Fake.

12

Richard Kelly
Fearless

For Richard Kelly, *Fearless* had a palpable effect on his career. "The impact it had on me definitely motivated me to follow through with going to film school," he says.

In this interview, Kelly speaks about the fear of being pigeonholed, making challenging films, and the example *Fearless* director Peter Weir sets for him to do just that. Weir—best known for movies such as *Dead Poets Society*, *The Truman Show*, and *Witness*—cast Jeff Bridges in the challenging role of a plane-crash survivor struggling to make sense of his life.

Kelly calls *Fearless* an "incredible emotional, metaphysical thriller" that is "brutally honest and emotional without ever being manipulative or cheap."

> **Richard Kelly, selected filmography:**
> *Donnie Darko* (2001)
> *Southland Tales* (2006)
> *The Box* (2009)
>
> *Fearless*
> 1993
> Directed by Peter Weir
> Starring Jeff Bridges, Isabella Rossellini, Rosie Perez, and John Turturro

How would you describe *Fearless* to someone who has never seen it?
KELLY: It's about Max Klein (Jeff Bridges), an architect from San Francisco, who walked away from a horrific plane crash with barely a scratch on his body and emerges from this accident completely unafraid of anything in

life. He's then unable to connect with his family, with his friends, or really with anyone other than this survivor (Rosie Perez) of the plane crash who's lost her child.

Director Peter Weir said, "I think I've always been tough on [*Fearless*], tougher on it than the public. For me, it's always been a thriller with a grace note." What's your take?

KELLY: I would definitely see his take on it as a thriller, in the sense that it opens with an incredibly suspenseful, gripping scene. It certainly operates as this incredible emotional, metaphysical thriller.

For me, it is this existential suspense film on whether or not he's going to choose to live or die after this accident. It's also a platonic love story between two strangers who experience the same horrific experience. There's such a clean precision to the cinematography in the film. There isn't a wasted shot. The lead character is an architect, and I think that design is very apparent in the film.

How did you first encounter it?

KELLY: I first saw the film about a month after I arrived in L.A. I was a freshman in college, and my parents came out to visit me for the first time, and we went to Universal CityWalk, and we just happened to decide to go see this film *Fearless*. I was always a fan of Peter Weir growing up, so it seemed like a good choice.

I remember walking out of the theater and being completely blown away. That was not at all what I was expecting. The impact it had on me definitely motivated me to follow through with going to film school.

***Fearless* was made eight years after *Witness* and three after *Green Card*. The reason Weir attached himself to this is, he asked for scripts that were in "raw shape." From your perspective, what about this film is so unusual that it might have been rejected by other directors?**

KELLY: There's never been a film made like it. There are no villains, and the hero is not exactly heroic. He is heroic in the sense that he saves several people, but he does not behave like a sympathetic character for ninety percent of the film—which, to me, is a very interesting character arc that I'd never seen before and one that wasn't encumbered by artificial obstacles. There was nothing contrived about the screenplay. It just unfolded in this day-to-day shock and recovery that one must endure after a horrific experience, like a plane crash. I found it to be brutally honest and emotional without ever being manipulative or cheap.

Weir did not want this film set in front of test audiences, because he said he believed "it would be at least 24 hours later until a viewer would wholly endorse the experience," that the film yields more on a second viewing. Is that true for you?
KELLY: Absolutely. Every time I see it, I get something new out of it. It is a very disturbing film, and it's probably the most honest depiction of grief that I've ever seen. The characters are never forced to be sympathetic for purposes of pleasing the audience. They behave reprehensibly in some cases, yet you never hate any of the characters. You don't judge any of these characters because, ultimately, Weir isn't judging them; he's painting them in an honest way.

On one level, it's this metaphysical thriller, and on another level, it's a love story. Not really that much happens in the film, other than people connecting in various scenes. A viewer walking into the theater expecting the twists and turns of a traditional story might be turned off or disappointed by it, but upon further viewing, you find that the film has so much going on. This is a subtle, understated film in terms of what it accomplishes: not only the most realistic plane crash ever depicted on film but also the most realistic depiction of the emotional toll that such an event could take on characters.

Tell me about sequences that stick with you.
KELLY: From the first horrific images, Max's dilemma forces you to identify with him. The film opens with some of the most brutal, horrific images that I've ever seen a film open with: no opening credits, and there's this smoke drifting through a cornfield, and you see a figure emerge through the corn. It's Jeff Bridges holding this infant, and there's this little boy, and you don't know who they are or what they're doing there.

As they emerge from the cornfield, you come upon this horrific plane crash and the wreckage and the charred bodies. There are Mexican farm workers kneeling down. There are firemen and rescue workers coming to the scene and a fleeting image of a wine bottle rolling across the gravel, a man in a silver, fire-retardant suit.

This sort of eerie, dreamlike opening is incredibly disturbing because you understand exactly what these characters are going through and from then on, that you have to surrender yourself to this film.

In a flashback sequence, Bridges and his partner choose not to make calls home from the doomed flight. If you knew you could die, whom would you call and what would you say?
KELLY: I honestly don't know if I would make a phone call, because I don't know what I would say. I think that, in a strange way, would be conceding defeat. It would be making the assumption that it's over. You don't want to believe that it's over; you want to believe that the plane is going to land.

Some say this is one of Bridges's definitive performances. What makes him so magnetic here?
KELLY: He is one of our most underrated actors, and I don't think anyone else could have done what Bridges did in this film. He's not always a sympathetic character, but he behaves the way real people act. His character doesn't play into the plot mechanics. He behaves in a very erratic, unpredictable manner that fits the design of the film.

He's a chameleon. It's impossible to compare any of Bridges's performances to one another, because he's probably one of the more versatile actors out there. He's this character actor trapped in the body of a leading man. It's actors like that who end up aging like fine wine. [After this interview, Jeff Bridges won a Best Actor Oscar for 2009's *Crazy Heart.* —ed.]

***Fearless* didn't do that well economically, and Weir said, "I find that films are elevated there [in the United States] purely in terms of box office," and if the film doesn't click, there's this sort of embarrassment.**
KELLY: I had that experience with *Donnie Darko* in the sense that the film didn't make money and it didn't turn a profit in its initial theatrical release. I definitely felt the negative impact of that. There is this obsession with the top five films at the box office. It's become this measure of success or failure.

Studios will fudge the numbers just to get that number one, the bragging rights and the marketing value of being number one.

In Europe and other parts of the world, they aren't as obsessed with being number one. There is more longevity to the way the films play at the box office. There, films are allowed to settle in and find their way, the way that they used to be here.

What impact do you think that has on fostering new artists?
KELLY: It prohibits studios from taking risks, because if a film doesn't perform on a weekend, it's often deemed a failure. I wasn't a viable filmmaker to the studios until about six to eight months after my film came out on DVD.

Time is the judge of any film. There are some films that have been nominated for best picture and made a hundred million dollars, and several years later, everyone looks at one another and says, "What the hell were we thinking? That's the biggest piece of shit! Why did we deny this other film?" It's just a matter of timing. Sometimes the moviegoing population can flock like sheep to *My Big Fat Greek Wedding* or something that happens to catch on like lightning in a bottle, and a film like *Fearless* can get left behind or ignored on that opening weekend, and it can't recover from something like that.

Some have called the middle of the film slow, to put it mildly. How did you experience it when you saw it?
KELLY: I was taken with the honesty of the characters. Some people just can't open their minds to a stream-of-consciousness kind of film. A lot of reviewers were programmed to digest the film in a certain way. They're so used to drinking Diet Coke that when they get the real thing, they can't swallow it because they aren't used to the taste.

Bridges's character behaves in a way that is very honest to that unnatural way of experiencing life. You see the other filmmakers who are obsessed with making your lead character sympathetic in every scene and actors who are afraid to ever appear unsympathetic. Sympathetic people aren't always that interesting.

Weir is one of these directors who says, "I make my films completely around music." I noticed that in your work, too.

KELLY: He's a big influence on me as a filmmaker, because I start with music, too. It's the first thing that comes into my head in any film that I begin to write or begin to direct. I design a film around a series of songs that I burn onto a CD. I give it to the crew. I give it to the people who read the script. I time it out for the script specifically.

In *Fearless*, Maurice Jarre's score is very minimalistic. He uses U2, some other classical pieces, and even the Gipsy Kings and the Henryk Gorecki classical piece Symphony No. 3. I think that our greatest filmmakers are the ones that can connect in ways that very few can, are the ones that understand the impact of music, those who can place music with images in such a way that they are interdependent and they elevate each other to places they couldn't exist on their own.

Do you have a favorite scene?
KELLY: I can't name a favorite scene, but I've certainly been taken by some of the bizarre and disturbing scenes of the film, like when he puts Rosie Perez in the back of his car with the toolbox and they drive it into a wall.

You're seeing two completely insane people, but at the same time, Weir makes you identify with them on such a deep level that their insanity makes complete sense in the context of what they're experiencing. It's a very brave scene that very few filmmakers can pull off. There are moments like that— they exist as these little metaphysical action sequences invested with great suspense, and I hadn't seen a filmmaker do that before.

Critic Ron Weiskind wrote, "Weir's filmography suggests a fascination with men who control others or who create such a scenario for themselves." Would you agree with that?
KELLY: Like any filmmaker, there are common themes, but he's never made the same film twice, and there are very few filmmakers you can say that about. I would not know how to categorize Weir, because he can do anything.

Weir said, "It's a terrifying thought that your first film was your best. But that's why we love young filmmakers. There's a certain recklessness. For whatever reasons, I felt that reckless feeling coming back again,

and I approached this film in that spirit." As someone who is at the relative beginning of his career, are you aware of this perception?

KELLY: Absolutely. Studios want to put every director in a category so they can pigeonhole that director, and they can pass him to whatever genre they need him to work in. Everything in the marketing and distribution process in America is geared towards putting things into categories to sell. That's something that you definitely have to fight against, to prove to people that you can't be categorized.

That can be a difficult thing, because some directors can get rich very quickly in one particular genre, and then no one will ever give them the chance to do something different. If you're aware of this imminent danger of categorization as a young filmmaker, you can do everything you can to dodge those preconceived notions about who you are. That's great advice to hear from someone, and it's definitely something I'll take into account as I choose each subsequent project.

You always need to remember to reinvent yourself, and it's a frightening thing to do. If you've found a niche that works, it can be a prison. Our greatest filmmakers throughout history have also been the greatest risk-takers.

Did you or have you ever met anyone connected to the film?

KELLY: I had lunch with Weir. He was a fan of *Donnie Darko*, and he wanted to meet me, and we were talking about maybe collaborating on a project. It was great to meet him in person and get to have these discussions over lunch in Beverly Hills.

We talked all about *Fearless*. He seemed pleasantly surprised that someone had this much affection for it, because I think when they mention his name and put his films in parentheses after his name, they always mention *Dead Poets Society* or *Witness* or *The Truman Show*. They only mention the box-office successes. I think I was the one doing most of the talking. He smiled and nodded his head most of the lunch.

13

Atom Egoyan
The Homecoming

To say that director Peter Hall's adaptation of *The Homecoming* enraptured Atom Egoyan might be an understatement. "It just *completely* transfixed me," Egoyan says. "It was a huge upheaval, and I couldn't watch it enough."

The movie, part of the American Film Theatre series, adapts Harold Pinter's play about a prodigal son's return to his family's London home with his wife for the first time, after the death of his mother. What follows is Pinter's brutal investigation of how families negotiate intimacy, loss, and the shift of familial power.

"I just lost myself completely in the really perverse and quite hilarious black humor of the piece," Egoyan says. "This veering between sentimentality and brutal hatred was just intoxicating to me."

Atom Egoyan, selected filmography:
Exotica (1994)
The Sweet Hereafter (1997)
Ararat (2002)
Where the Truth Lies (2005)
Adoration (2008)
Chloe (2009)
Devil's Knot (2013)

The Homecoming
1973
Directed by Peter Hall
Starring Ian Holm, Vivien Merchant, Terence Rigby, Michael Jayston, Paul Rogers, and Cyril Cusack

How would you describe *The Homecoming* to someone who has never seen it?

EGOYAN: The ultimate dysfunctional family movie. A lot of the play's power and motivation is mysterious, even to the people who are inside of it. But to me, it's all quite clear: It's about people—the brothers and the family—trying to assert their sense of identity after the catastrophic loss of the matriarch. And then suddenly, a new matriarch finds her way in through one of the brothers. They're all scrambling to calibrate their personalities in relationship to this new presence.

I just watched it again recently, and it confirmed what I really love about this film, which is that it completely reinvents a way of photographing people. Some of the compositions are jaw-dropping. And in terms of being able to demonstrate completely original ways of just placing people in a frame, the film is really striking.

Now, that being said, because of the peculiar tensions and energies that are being investigated, one's allowed to get away with some of those compositions, which would probably be too awkward in a traditional drama. But it's just really interesting to watch.

When did you first see the film?

EGOYAN: I saw the film in my early twenties, and at that point, I became quite obsessed with it. When I saw this movie, it just *completely* transfixed me. It was a huge upheaval, and I couldn't watch it enough. I've calmed down a little bit since then, but it did have a huge effect on me at that point.

It seemed to me there were issues I was dealing with in my own family, and I just lost myself completely in the really perverse and quite hilarious black humor of the piece. The territorial nature of how the characters position themselves in relationship to each other, the dark histories alluded to but never actually articulated, the way they punish each other continually. This veering between sentimentality and brutal hatred was just intoxicating to me.

What do audiences who don't know playwright Harold Pinter need to know about him going in?

EGOYAN: Pinter is fascinated by the inherent mystery of any meeting between two people. That could be people even in a family, but he's obsessed with how inherently mysterious that process is, that there's nothing casual about people meeting. There's a wealth of subtext and innuendo in the most casual conversation.

What about his style? His famed pauses?
EGOYAN: Given those issues I was talking about, silence is a very potent place. It's a place where all sorts of other issues are being negotiated. We're used to seeing drama where the character is usually articulate and quite lucid about their circumstance and knows where they have to get to in order to satisfy a whole set of expectations. In Pinter's drama, very often, the motivations are kept quite mysterious. That's something that's either really intriguing and seductive to people or really off-putting. His drama really divides people. But it has been a huge influence on me, a huge influence on my work.

Can you point to any one or two things you learned from Pinter?
EGOYAN: The reason I was so thrilled to be working with Ian Holm in *The Sweet Hereafter* was because of the work I saw him do as Lenny in *The Homecoming*.

And a lot of the moments he has in that film, where quite silently he's trying to assess a situation, trying to understand his position to the other people in the room—that's what I think Pinter's all about. That's why it's so exciting to work with a Pinter text, because you have to really be on your toes. You have to always try to understand your relationship to everyone around you in a way that's really kinetic at all times. Even though not verbally so, you're trying to assess and justify why you are in a certain place. It's a central issue that a lot of actors are trying to identify at all times.

There's this line in *Exotica*, the first line exactly, when the customs officer says as he's looking through the glass window, "You have to ask yourself what brought the person to this point." He's talking about trying to assess at what point someone should be suspicious. He's trying to teach someone else how to identify people who are suspicious. That notion of suspicion and how to arouse and sustain or try to abolish someone else's suspicion in you is a really exciting territory, dramatically.

Did you talk with Ian Holm about *The Homecoming*?

EGOYAN: Absolutely; he knew I was obsessed with it. As a matter of fact, one of the prized gifts he gave me was a signed copy of *The Homecoming*. One of my largest professional regrets was that I was invited to direct the revival of *The Homecoming* at the Lincoln Center a few years ago, but I couldn't, because I was too busy with *Ararat*.

It's one of the greatest plays of the last century, and this film version is really intriguing. Not only are the performances just so stupendous, but there's an incredible awkwardness to a lot of framing, which is actually really exciting to me. With every composition, it's almost as though they asked, "What would be an alternative way of presenting this?" So, very rarely does the camera use conventional setups.

The other thing is, because of the way they were working, they were able to pump a lot of extra light into the set. Technically, they were using longer lenses, stopping them down in such a way that they have a huge depth of field, the focus seems like they were using wide-angle lenses—a very interesting effect.

Most of Pinter's plays were a reaction against the realism of the 1950s. What are the difficulties in filming unreality or a surreal situation, as opposed to presenting it onstage?

EGOYAN: Since my background is in theater, I don't have that difficulty. I immediately understand that it's a play. Photographing it as innovatively as I described before makes it a very exciting film experience for me. I've never seen the film projected in a theater; I've only seen it on television.

What's interesting about the American Film Theatre series [which distributed *The Homecoming*] was that the films were originally only meant for theatrical presentation. The intention was to re-create the ephemeral nature of the theater experience: the work is only in a place for a certain amount of time, and then it disappears. But what happened, of course, is that the prints survived and were transferred to DVD. It was a really glorious experience for me to watch it on DVD—a really exciting piece of drama that has been successfully rendered visually because of the quality of the performances, the detail of the performances, but also the very original approach to the photography.

Cinematographer David Watkin, whom most of us know from films like *Out of Africa*, has done an exquisite job of making the tensions in the piece really palpable through the framings. As I said before, there are a number of sequences in this film that are just jaw-dropping. For example, when the two brothers encounter each other for the first time in the hallway, the series of cuts made there is just really brutal and quite shocking, because it is so unexpected. And, again, you can say that there's an awkwardness to that, but I think it all works for this particular movie.

What kind of filmgoer might enjoy *The Homecoming*?
EGOYAN: If you like the kind of oddball humor of movies like *Being John Malkovich* or a lot of the Charlie Kaufman material, you'll like this. Kaufman is clearly really inspired by Pinter. There's a sense of the absurd that comes off in these incredible contradictions.

The father, Max, talks about his late wife in these very sentimental terms; he'll talk about missing her and say, "Mind you, she wasn't such a bad woman. Even though it made me sick just to look at her rotten, stinking face, she wasn't such a bad bitch." A line like that, where you're just suddenly thrown from one place to the other, shows real bravura. The writing is just so audacious. You have to see it in the context of being very firmly rooted in absurdist theater. There's a direct lineage between that and the work of Monty Python, and from that to the work of Charlie Kaufman and Spike Jonze.

I wanted to talk a little bit more about Pinter's style: the pacing, the placement of what have been called his "juicy" words. With so many unnatural pauses, what effect does his style have on the action?
EGOYAN: To me, it's seductive, because I wonder what is going on. It draws me in because I'm intrigued. Now, other people might find that it closes them off.

I'm always drawn to things that I don't understand [*laughs*]. It might be a peculiar quirk of my character, but for me, the point is whether I trust the dramatic intention. In *The Homecoming*, Pinter deals with several issues. How do people negotiate loss? How do they negotiate loneliness? How do they negotiate intimacy? Those are all huge issues. They're given a very careful reading in the film, and the silences are full of those moments of attempted resolution.

Pinter called his early plays "a very strange brew." He couldn't talk about them, he couldn't watch them. I've talked to a lot of artists who can't watch their own work once it's finished. As a director, do you have any insight into that psychology? What is your relationship with your early films?

EGOYAN: It's true that after a period of being completely involved in something which consumes you, and often needs to consume you professionally for years—especially in film, where you have to check every print, and also the video transfer—there is the moment you let it go. It's a very deciding and quite definitive point.

The moment that happens, you just want to flee. It's almost a strange punishment, this repeated viewing that is a necessary part of the process. You have to endure it for having made the film in the first place.

It must be like going through rehearsals in theater. You just have to watch the performance again and again and again. But then there's the point at which you have a premiere, when you watch it with an audience for the first time. You may be intrigued to see how different audiences respond, but there's no question that you have to let go.

Is there also a disconnect from the material?

EGOYAN: Not for me. I certainly know who the person was who made those early films. And for all their flaws and all of the things that they didn't achieve, I still understand where they came from. I think that, maybe often, Pinter is trying to avoid his own interpretation of something, because he knows it will assume an orthodoxy, and he wants to keep the work open. He wants to let people have their own views and their own way of interpreting things.

Pinter has said, "I have no explanation for anything I do at all." Do you think Pinter's wish is to not dismantle the creative process? Or is genuine confusion a theme of his work that he doesn't want to put a dent in?

EGOYAN: Pinter's absolutely scrupulous with the detail of language and the reasons people say certain things, so it's inconceivable that he wouldn't be able to defend the internal logic of the decisions he has made as a writer. Whether or not he wants to talk about them publicly or make them known is another issue. But I think that he must have a very clear idea of what he's trying to do.

Pinter's early works were labeled "comedies of menace." Do you think that's a fitting description, or can you come up with a better one?

EGOYAN: Menace is just one part of the energy. They're dealing with the nature of anticipation—why and how we expect things to unfold and resolve themselves in a certain way, which speaks to our most secret wish/fantasies of how other human beings are supposed to act.

How has your perception of the film changed since your twenties?

EGOYAN: When I was in my early twenties, I couldn't define why it had a very peculiar attraction to me. I think now, it's clear that not only are the performances so completely committed, but there is also a really exciting mise-en-scène. The directorial and cinematographic approaches are really strident and quite audacious. I've never seen another film that does what this film does, in terms of the way it presents these figures.

Pauline Kael wrote of Pinter, "We are so aware of the absence of goodness and of the usual melodramatic conflict that we wait eagerly to see what he will provide in its place." What in *The Homecoming* does he provide in its place, and why is that so magnetic for you?

EGOYAN: Pinter provides extraordinary humor and cruelty. He provides an extraordinary pleasure in the unexpected and of an intoxicating glee with the construction of language.

Pinter's wife at the time, Vivien Merchant, plays the returning brother's wife in the movie. Do you think that as the movie plays out, this adds any layers of interpretation for you?

EGOYAN: It does, but I think in considering her as an actress, there's a rhythm to her voice, and Pinter seems to have clearly written the role for her. She never feels like she's actually pausing. She feels like she's in the moment of trying to get from one thought to the other. It's very visceral and tangible. She's an extraordinary actress.

But there's this interesting dynamic: when you bring a girl home, you want your family to *like* her, but it seems that Pinter brings this to its absurdist extreme. And for me, having that be his *wife* is telling. Does it add any dimension to the film for you?

EGOYAN: Sure it does. But I think you've just touched on something really interesting there. When we introduce people who are close to us, we *do* want them to be liked, because it's an affirmation of who we are.

What we see in this film, and in this play, is an incredible resentment directed towards the brother who's gone away, and the extraordinary ritualized humiliation of the brother through the reactions of the rest of the family to this matriarch, to this wife.

It's almost as if I don't want to acknowledge that she's the wife. There's this incredibly funny moment where he says, "She's my wife," but they don't seem to register that, or don't want to register it; they just want to sort of move on. It's a complete betrayal of everything you're led to expect from a family, or how a family should respond.

Pinter wrote that this is the most liberated woman who he has ever written, but liberation does not come without its price here. There are all sorts of feminist readings about exactly what she gains or how much decision she has in the end. Have you thought about those issues in *The Homecoming*?

EGOYAN: To me, the least satisfying part is the ending. Schematically, it works, but it's so beyond anything plausible—that she would end up working as a whore for her pimp brother-in-law and leave her family behind is a little bit of a stretch, in terms of the Syd Field approach to screenwriting, I'm sure [*laughs*].

Everything else in the play, to me, seems almost identifiable. As extreme as it is, it seems that I can understand everything *but* her final decision, which seems patently unacceptable. And yet, of course, that's a provocation. We're left with something completely absurd. I don't think there's anything remotely possible about it—though, of course, human beings are capable of anything.

14

Todd Solondz
The Honeymoon Killers

Todd Solondz has spent a career exploring the lives of outsiders, which makes *The Honeymoon Killers*—the story of two mismatched, misfit serial killers—a logical choice.

Not to say that Solondz isn't critical of the film. "Its flaws are all too apparent. It may come across, to the uninitiated, as something somewhat amateur," he says. "But if it is amateur, it is of the highest form of amateur."

Todd Solondz, selected filmography:
Welcome to the Dollhouse (1995)
Happiness (1998)
Storytelling (2001)
Palindromes (2004)
Life During Wartime (2009)
Dark Horse (2011)

The Honeymoon Killers
1969
Directed by Leonard Kastle
Starring Shirley Stoler, Tony Lo Bianco, Doris Roberts, Dortha Duckworth, and others

How would you describe *The Honeymoon Killers* to someone who's never seen it?
SOLONDZ: Well, it's a fictionalization of a true-life story of a couple who murdered women for their money. It's very lurid and sordid, and yet, by turns, it's campy and moving and funny as well.

How so?

SOLONDZ: Well, first of all, it doesn't seem the movie was paced with an audience in mind. Despite its obvious low budget, it does, at times, look quite stunning; at other times it looks terrible. And the acting is uneven, to put it mildly. Its flaws are all too apparent. It may come across, to the uninitiated, as something somewhat amateur. But if it is amateur, it is of the highest form of amateur. It is a film that requires a certain patience and generosity.

We've talked about its faults; let's talk about its graces. Why is it a great film?

SOLONDZ: Well, it's a remarkably intriguing work, because its faults are part of what makes it compelling at the same time. The actors, Shirley Stoler and Tony Lo Bianco, do some remarkable work, and yet at other times, you feel it is a kind of parody, or camp. It's navigating this fine line between sublime horror and, on the other hand, well, the incompetent.

Do you remember when you saw it or who with?

SOLONDZ: I saw it about twenty years ago or more at the Cinema Village in New York, which is now a very fine triplex art-house theater. At the time, when I saw it, it was a retrospective house with one screen, and it was a very sordid, very seedy theater—in fact, like the movie.

It was a theater where you would raise your feet so that you would not have to worry about any scampering mice. It was that kind of a setting, which was ideal for a movie as unsleek as this one: unslick and unsleek.

You would laugh at times, yet you could never feel superior to the material, because it would always take turns that would be terribly haunting and moving. The pathos was all too apparent and affecting and yet would continually be interrupted by these moments of camp and narrative incompetence.

Francois Truffaut called this his favorite American film. Can you tell me about what drew you to the film? Is there a sequence that is particularly powerful to you?

SOLONDZ: I don't know if it's any particular sequence. When the Latino guy, Tony Lo Bianco, is dancing to the cha-cha, you just see him below the waist as he's exciting the mother. It sort of reminds me of Charlotte Haze in *Lolita* or something.

It's the overall pull of it that you can't rub out—just when you want to brush it aside as something either amateurish or campy, it suddenly has this pull that you cannot help but be affected by.

Martin Scorsese was the first director of this film, but he was later replaced by the scriptwriter Leonard Kastle. Two of Scorsese's scenes survive the film. Do you see or sense his fingerprints on the film?
SOLONDZ: No. I would never have known that if I hadn't been told. I don't see it; maybe others do. I haven't seen him really make a movie like this.

Kastle is, by training, a composer. Do you see any evidence of this musical background in his directorial style?
SOLONDZ: I know that he likes Gustav Mahler, but I wouldn't know he was a musician from watching the movie. The choice of the music demands a certain kind of seriousness, a certain kind of gravitas—and at the same time it can upend things and lend the proceedings to unintentional camp. There's this constant back-and-forth between these moments where you feel the filmmaker has discovered something new and frightening and moving—alternating with the question "Why am I even watching this?"

Kastle said he envisioned it as the anti–*Bonnie and Clyde*. He said, in fact, he was revolted by that movie, because, "I didn't want to show beautiful shots of beautiful people in color." But it seems to me they're almost bookend films, because they're of the same era. Was *Bonnie and Clyde* a reference point for you when you saw this?
SOLONDZ: The movie is so deeply "anti," not just anti-Hollywood but anti–*Bonnie and Clyde*, and all the conventions that are set up are tweaked in ways that I'm not even sure the director is fully aware of how radical the film was.

One of the reasons it's effective is that many of its shortcomings were budgetary. Rather than being seen as a kind of handicap, I think they're exploited. The look of the film was something that would never have been attempted if there had been a real budget. You're sort of forced into certain kinds of creative decisions when you have so little money, and there were some very brilliant choices: the way it's lit, the way it looks. It looks, at times, like a documentary—you know that movie *Salesman*? *The Honeymoon Killers* has kind of a cinema verité look, which is very much of its time.

Bonnie and Clyde, of course, is very rebellious and antiauthoritarian and so forth; it is also a very glamorous film, and this is very much anything but. *The Honeymoon Killers* asks of its audience to care for these outcasts, these ostracized "losers," characters that couldn't be anything but marginalized in a movie like *Bonnie and Clyde*. Reference points will come up—John Waters will come up, you'll think of Divine. You'll think of *Badlands* also.

They're very much a kind of alternative to what John Cassavetes was doing at the same time. This was also, you could say, Warhol—or Waters—meeting Cassavetes. This was a film of its time, representative of the independent movement that existed back then.

It's interesting that you bring up John Waters, because he is one of the few directors who has had a woman of size—Ricki Lake in *Hairspray*—as the star of his movie, as *The Honeymoon Killers* does. In using an overweight actress in your movie *Palindromes*, did you learn anything from audience reaction to her?

SOLONDZ: It really requires a certain kind of openness to experience and opening yourself up to looking at people who are not glamorous. But of course, it's so extreme. People have certainly asked me, "Well, why do you make films about such ugly people?" But I always say, "Well, for me, they're not ugly." I understand the question and I think I understand what's meant by it, but I think it's more telling about the questioner than it is about the person making these movies.

I don't think there's any doubt of where Kastle's affections lie, where his sympathies lie. It's not with the victims, certainly, and that's what makes it a morally complicated film—one that I think for many people would be repellent, morally and aesthetically.

Martha Beck, the real-life murderess, told the press during her trial, "What am I being tried for? Murder or because I'm fat?"

SOLONDZ: What I find interesting is the director's unambiguous emotional attachment to this character. Not only is Martha Beck physically the antithesis of glamour, she is mean and ruthless and even—at certain points—evil. But there's this roiling passion underneath that brings a kind of dignity to what would otherwise be a cruel joke.

Kastle had a fight with the censors in France because they had cut out most of the murders and violence in the film. And he went to the censors and said, "You've made a moral movie immoral by not showing the horror, the banality of the evil." Do you buy that point of view?
SOLONDZ: Well, yes and no. I don't know about it being banal. It's pretty horrific and intense and drawn-out, dramatic—showing just how difficult murder can be, as Alfred Hitchcock had done famously in *Torn Curtain*. There's a whole scene where he tries to show how hard it is to kill someone.

One can argue that the film doesn't glamorize violence but shows it in all its sordidness and horrificness. And yet at the same time, whether or not he's aware of this, there certainly is a pulp fascination and thrill from this terrorizing. There's this murder scene where he spends a long time just focused on the eyes of the woman lying in bed. You hear all the sounds, you hear all the offscreen dialogue, and you know that the other shoe's going to drop, so to speak, and finally, it does, and the gun goes off. He certainly plays with the audience, teases.

It's hard to see this as truly a moralistic movie, though I think Kastle *does* see it this way. I see it and admire it, however, insofar as it lends unexpected dignity to these profoundly wretched lives.

Kastle actually argued with the censor and was able to have that footage restored. You seem to have circumnavigated censors altogether with the use of a red box over the MPAA-offending material in *Storytelling*.
SOLONDZ: Yeah, I did use red boxes. I put it in my contract that I could use red boxes and/or bleeps as need be in order to procure an R. But, look, the MPAA fulfills a function, and this is a whole other conversation.

If you complain to them, they'll say, "Look, we don't work for you, the director, we work for the parents of America." So they don't see themselves as censors; at least in this country they will never describe themselves as such, even if de facto censorship is often the result. In France things certainly have changed. I never had any problem with having to alter my films, as far as I'm aware, in any territory except the U.S.

In the most chilling murder scene, a woman is hit with a hammer and strangled with a tourniquet made by her own scarf. What does Kastle achieve by having one murder on-screen and almost all of the rest off-screen or portrayed in reaction shots?
SOLONDZ: Well, it's different ways of getting at the same thing. In a sense, the movie does function as entertainment. I mean, there's a kind of sick thrill that he's providing. And while he may want to make a kind of anti-violence statement, it certainly may not quite have that effect on many people in the audience.

It's creepy and sordid, certainly, but I'm not sure it's suspense per se that he's after. It's unlike Hitchcock, where there's a plot set in motion with different set pieces of suspense and a story, a well-oiled machine. You've got a structure there that's very cleverly put into motion.

Here, in *The Honeymoon Killers*, there's not much plot. They go after one lonely woman, and then they go after another, and then they go after another. It's much more character-driven, driven by the erotic fixation and frustration and desperation of this woman than it is by anything Hitchcockian.

I think there's no film that so clearly links sex and violence. After a swindle or even a murder, they have sex at least twice immediately after. What did you make of that link?
SOLONDZ: I think sex and violence is the classic combination. I don't think it's unique in that way. There's always been a link between the two; it just manifests itself in different ways.

The movie has a combination of elements. On the one hand, compassion. And on the other, a kind of contempt for these victims, for these women, who in some sense are typed. As much as they are lonely hearts, they are also in some sense representative of certain kinds of mainstream values—political, religious, and so forth.

And there's that great scene where a woman is singing "America" as Martha is going through her purse.

SOLONDZ: Right, right. I mean, it's all so over-the-top. It's so silly—and even annoying, listening to that singing, and yet then, of course, she goes in for the kill.

What's more radical is the morality of *The Honeymoon Killers* and the ways in which certain expectations—via the casting—are subverted, where one is forced to question where one's sympathies lie, where the nature of violence itself is being not in some sense "fun" but rather something that is a felt experience.

When you rented this again and watched it, did your perception of it change?

SOLONDZ: The first time I saw it, I was much more just wrapped up in the luridness of the story. I remember it having a big impact on me. I was affected by the story, of which I had really known very little. I like watching movies in a movie theater in a big, dark room, even if I'm the only one who shows up. It does affect things. And so when I rented the video twenty-odd years later and stuck it in my VCR, well, naturally it wasn't the same. In fact, it was a bit laborious.

I never rent for pleasure. I only do it for work or when someone like you asks me to rent something. When I started watching it, I said, "Oh my God, this is terrible." But then, eventually, it took hold. Patience is required. As I continued watching, I could appreciate it more intellectually and analytically than I did when I first saw it. Also, I wasn't a filmmaker when I first saw it.

It's been remade, you know. Arturo Ripstein did a remake in Mexico. And the movie really does not come close to what Leonard Kastle achieves, in spite of the fact that it's very well shot and very well played. There's nothing amateurish about it, and yet it doesn't have any of the power—that sticks with you, that sticks to the bone—that the original possesses and savors.

I think that certain people invest themselves in the character of the work in ways that other people, with all of their technical proficiency, can never achieve. When you are less experienced, you may think that all your so-called mistakes and flaws are a stain on your achievement.

But in fact some of those very flaws are what ultimately create what becomes inimitable and even, at times, ineffable. I'm not saying that it's good because of these flaws, but they do play a role in the strange power of the film.

Am I right in sensing a kinship in the way that you and Kastle treat your characters?
SOLONDZ: You know, it's funny you say this. I hadn't really thought about the film in ages, and I've done so many interviews for all my movies over the years and I've never brought up this movie. Not out of avoiding it; I just had forgotten about it. And when I watched it, I said, "Oh my gosh, there is so much of what he was trying to achieve that is really not so foreign to what I as a filmmaker aspire to as well."

Every filmmaker, every storyteller is trying to get at a certain kind of truth that—even if it doesn't maybe sit so well with what one is taught—has the force and courage of his convictions. Spending time with the outcast, the tormented, the reviled can be wearing, if not excruciating, but most felicitously, these characters also make for good stories and, in Kastle's lone movie, remind the more fortunate of us that we're not as different as we might like to believe ourselves to be.

15

Arthur Hiller
The Iceman Cometh

This is the second movie a director chose from the American Film Theatre series, fourteen film adaptations of plays released from 1973 to 1975. Atom Egoyan champions *The Homecoming* in chapter 13, and below, director Arthur Hiller spotlights John Frankenheimer's adaptation of Eugene O'Neill's *The Iceman Cometh*.

Hiller has a particular insight into the series, not only as a fan but also as a contributor. He shot *The Man in the Glass Booth*, an adaptation of a Robert Shaw play. But he chose to talk about *Iceman* because it stuck with him all these years. "It got a hold of me and kept me. It made me see not just with my eyes but with my gut," Hiller says. "It made us look at ourselves and realize the time and emotion we spend supporting and living the illusions we live by. Yet we need to have these dreams to live."

Arthur Hiller, selected filmography:

The Americanization of Emily (1964)

Promise Her Anything (1965)

Penelope (1966)

Popi (1969)

The Out-of-Towners (1970)

Love Story (1970)

The Hospital (1971)

Man of La Mancha (1972)

The Man in the Glass Booth (1975)

Silver Streak (1976)

The In-Laws (1979)

Author! Author! (1982)
The Lonely Guy (1984)
Outrageous Fortune (1987)
See No Evil, Hear No Evil (1989)
The Babe (1992)

The Iceman Cometh
1973
Directed by John Frankenheimer
Starring Lee Marvin, Fredric March, Robert Ryan, Juno
Dawson, and Jeff Bridges

How would you describe *The Iceman Cometh* film to someone who's never seen it?
HILLER: All these people who've really lost faith in themselves or their dreams and have nothing to live for and just sit there in a saloon. And Hickey (Lee Marvin)—who was one of them at one time—comes to visit and to save them. He's changed his whole life and comes to change them.

He wants them to give up their pipe dreams.
HILLER: And later we're surprised by what really brought him. I saw this film in 1973, because I was a subscriber to the American Film Theatre series. It was set up by producer Ely Landau to bring theater to the whole country. They were films made from interesting and provocative plays that didn't lend themselves to being translated into a commercial film by a studio. And what studio was going to make *Man in the Glass Booth*, or *The Homecoming*, or *Butley*, or *Rhinoceros*?

At the time you saw it, only John Frankenheimer's abbreviated version was screened. They showed it only at three hours. But what was your first impression of it?
HILLER: I thought it was a wonderful movie of a wonderful play; it was wonderfully acted and directed. But it's done in a very dramatic and, granted, sometimes even an overdramatic way. And yet I think it made you, the audience, feel and believe its emotional ups and downs.

It made us look at ourselves and realize the time and emotion we spend supporting and living the illusions we live by. Yet we need to have these dreams to live, and we see these guys when they've lost that.

Lee Marvin stars in a role that was made famous by Jason Robards, who was considered the quintessential O'Neill actor. But how do you think Lee's performance holds up?
HILLER: He was damn good. I thought they were all great. I wouldn't say all terrific, but almost. Robert Ryan was terrific; Fredric March was terrific. I think Lee Marvin maybe was the least terrific, but only because the others were so terrific. He was damn good, you know what I mean? He had more range, and I thought he handled that very well.

For Fredric March and Robert Ryan, these were their last roles. March plays a man who's dying, and Robert Ryan plays a character who has . . .
HILLER: Lost his faith in life.

Yes. Does that lend any weight to the film, do you think?
HILLER: It may well have. Although both of those guys were terrific actors, so it's hard to know whether they were acting that and saying to themselves, "This is ironic; I'm on my way out and I'm playing a character who's on his way out." They wouldn't have undertaken the roles if they didn't feel they could do something. But obviously, everything they know affects the performance when you're an actor.

It's a very, very heavy play, and uncut it's 239 minutes long. How do you think that stands up with modern audiences?
HILLER: Well, I feel it still would not reach the vast audience. And I think that's true of almost all the plays in that series. Who in their right mind sets up a series like that? Because they cared.

How did they sort of sell you on it? You directed *Man in the Glass Booth*; what was their approach to you?
HILLER: They asked if I'd like to do it, and they showed it to me.

It didn't take a lot of convincing?

HILLER: No, not at all. When we did press for the film, writers would ask why we did these films. And everybody said, "Because we want to bring theater to the rest of the country." And I said, "Because nobody else would let me do this movie." It just was a challenge and a worthwhile challenge, and that's why I worked at it that way. I rehearsed about twelve days with almost the whole cast.

Another question the press always asked was, particularly of the director and the star, "Why would you do this with so little money?" We made the movies for a million dollars [each], so obviously the director is working at scale and the lead actor is working at scale. You're working at a lot less than a tenth of your normal salary.

The story is set in a saloon below the boarding house in the summer of 1912, and it's during the same season as *Long Day's Journey into Night* was set. And in 1912, O'Neill attempted suicide in a boarding house just like Harry Hopes's bar. Do you think that's reflected in the play?

HILLER: Well, to some degree yes, because look how many have given up on life. The point of the play is getting back to life. Yes, you have to have dreams, but you have to face them with self-realization, and that's the way to fulfill your life.

A recurring theme in his work seems to be the universal horrible marriage. The alcoholic with the bad marriage, like all those guys in that bar were married to the same woman and had the same problems.

HILLER: [*Laughs.*] I hadn't thought of it that way, but I see what you're saying.

Is one tied to the other necessarily, or was this O'Neill just airing out his own issues?

HILLER: I think a lot of it sure comes from his own life. What do you draw from? You draw from your own feelings, and he just had a way of expressing them. That's true with most writers and actors. You still have to draw from something within you.

Especially *Long Day's Journey into Night*, that's why he wanted it produced after his death. There's a quote like, "It was written in tears and blood," and so he was definitely one of those playwrights who wrote close to the bone.

What are some of the inherent difficulties of translating a play into the medium of film?

HILLER: You have to think about it differently. But it always amazes me, like when I saw *Amadeus* onstage, I just loved it so much. I was just so bowled over by it as a theatrical event. I loved the directing, I loved the acting, I loved the play—just everything. I came out off the ground, thinking, "Boy, that's theater!" And I felt it so strongly that I couldn't go to the movie when it came out. I thought, "It's just never going to live up."

Finally, after a few months, I did see it, and I loved the movie. And the same writer, Peter Shaffer, wrote both. And I presume that he or Milos Forman realized they had to change it because onstage it was basically Salieri and God. And in the film it was mostly Mozart's story and they could be a lot more visual about it.

And we made changes in *Man in the Glass Booth*, but only because I felt that, onstage, it was intellectual game-playing. And I thought, that's not going to work as well on film; we need more emotion. And so we worked on it that way. And Robert Shaw was very upset with us. Eddie Anhalt wrote the screenplay. And Shaw was so upset with the way we were doing it, even though we were saying we were going to be really honest to him, that he wouldn't put his name on it. And he wouldn't even let us say it was based on his play.

Let's talk about Ely Landau. What was he like to work with?

HILLER: He was very determined and very caring about the theater. He was trying to bring theater to the whole country, not just to major cities. But [to see the American Film Theatre productions] you had to subscribe to the series. Usually, it was a Monday. That's the night with the least amount of business at the theater.

And you'd see an interesting and provocative play that didn't lend itself to being a commercial film. But at the time the intention was that the films would not be seen again. They were just meant to be seen that one time and that's it. And indeed, not many people have seen them.

What Landau and the American Film Theatre didn't realize was that they were preserving stage theater on the screen. And by releasing them on DVD, they're going to let a lot of theater jewels be seen or reseen by hopefully a bigger audience.

Frankenheimer said that this was his greatest ensemble feat. Reflecting on the film, what do you think your attraction to it was?
HILLER: It got to me emotionally. And it got a hold of me and kept me. It made me see not just with my eyes but with my gut, and that did it, it did it for me. Frankenheimer and I, we always said live television, if it was still around, we'd rather do that than film.

Really, why?
HILLER: It's unbelievably exciting, because no matter how prepared you were, no matter how organized you were when the clock hit the top, you had to pray, because anything could go wrong, and you couldn't stop it and do it again. It was there, that's it. But you got good rehearsal time and good actors and then camera rehearsal over and over again. You had to do it while you were doing it, figure out things. It was like opening night.

16

Michael Polish
Institute Benjamenta

Michael Polish almost didn't choose the Quay Brothers' *Institute Benjamenta* for this book, because of the parallels to his own life and work. Not because they share similar themes or styles—it was simply because he wanted to avoid pairing himself with another set of identical twin brother filmmakers. (Michael collaborates with his own twin brother, Mark.)

Yet the pull of *Institute Benjamenta* was too much. *Institute* was the first live-action feature by the Quays, Philadelphia natives who had only made esoteric, puppet-populated stop-motion animation in England. Polish says, "*Institute Benjamenta* really makes you take a step forth into their own realm and participate in a way that you are just not normally participating in movies."

Michael Polish, selected filmography:
Twin Falls Idaho (1999)
Northfork (2003)
The Astronaut Farmer (2006)
The Smell of Success (2009)
Stay Cool (2009)
For Lovers Only (2010)
Big Sur (2013)

Institute Benjamenta
1995
Directed by Stephen and Timothy Quay
Starring Mark Rylance, Alice Krige, Gottfried John, and Daniel Smith

How would you describe *Institute Benjamenta* to someone who's never seen it?

POLISH: It's hard to really give a plot, because it is all atmosphere and atmosphere-driven. I think if somebody says, "What's it about?" you'd say, "Look, it's an institute for servants and servitude, the whole movie's about servitude, and at the end of the day, we all end up servicing." But that doesn't do it justice.

Institute Benjamenta unveils itself after the opening. It sets you up for a riddle in pictures, because they're gonna put these pictures side by side, and you're gonna have to put them together in the puzzle. And you're gonna force yourself to find a narrative structure when there really isn't one. But it's amazing how as an audience member, or as somebody who writes stories, you just automatically try and do it. You're in their dream, and it's a dream that the brothers envisioned, and you have to participate or not participate.

What was interesting to me, though, is it's a school for almost a masochistic form of servitude—almost to the point of self-flagellation.

POLISH: Yeah, it's choreographed. It's choreographed in a way that it flows. It's almost a fetish, a fetishized quality.

When did you first see this film?

POLISH: I saw this film in '96. I think it opened for a week at the Nuart, but I just remember this was sort of its last run. And I remember I scratched my head and thought, "Yeah, the Brothers Quay, they did all those animation shorts that I saw in college." And I go, "This is their first live-action; I'm gonna go check it out."

I went to go see it on a Sunday, and it was a one o'clock showing. There were only a couple of showings, and there weren't very many people in it. The first image came up, and it looked like you were looking through gauze. It was so heavily layered, through filters, and I can just remember saying to myself, "Here we go. You're gonna stick on this, or it's gonna really freak you out."

But it was exciting, and that was what was neat about it—that no matter what I felt, it was exciting. It was exciting to see that for all the films that you've watched, this instantly tingled you. You had that feeling around when you watched it, like, "Wow, they put a lot of thought behind this." It was their overall appreciation.

The story was taken from Robert Walser, a Swiss writer. He wrote novels and poems and then committed himself to an asylum in 1929, refusing to write anymore, saying that he was "not here to write, but to be mad."

POLISH: From what I understand, his writing is very experimental, and that goes hand in hand with the Quay Brothers. They have taken that literature and inherently turned it into a visual, and it seems to go really well.

Let's talk a little bit about theme of repetition in the film.

POLISH: I went to the California Institute of the Arts, so I remembered "institute" as one of the connections. The school I went to was repetitious—the first year was very heavy repetition. You had to draw black lines, India-ink black lines with a ruler for six months before you could do color. And so it was this repetition of how you saw lines and the width of lines, and it was really rigorous—it was very Swiss, the way they taught how to look at paintings and art in general. So yeah, prepping your canvas in art school was just as important as painting on it.

So it was one of those same repetitions when I saw that. And I saw those guys [servants in training] setting those forks and doing the napkins, and I was like, "Wow, somebody got it."

Did your Cal Arts education and focus on preparation carry over into your filmmaking?

POLISH: Yeah, because I also learned, doing film, that you can never be overly prepared. What you're trying to do in filming is trying to delete all the accidents that might come in. What I try to do is prepare visually and have this film as set up as possible through storyboards and pictures, and control as much I can. That doesn't mean I won't change it or won't make some alteration when we're doing it. You're trying to eliminate all the possibilities so you know exactly what you're doing when you get there. If anything goes wrong, you have an answer for it.

What is your favorite scene?

POLISH: It's when the spider monkey answers the door. It's a very frail monkey that in some cultures is represented as very spiritual and very magical. You look at Indian culture, you look at others; they were painted so heavily, these monkeys, that it was nice to see that type of monkey answer the door—that he had his own door.

Would you agree that this is a difficult movie to understand?

POLISH: It's no doubt a difficult movie to ingest. I watched it again and I just thought, "It's still a difficult movie to get through." It doesn't get easier. It's incredible. You might get used to it, you might get used to the images, but for the first few times, it's gonna keep you off guard.

Reviews of this film say that it is exquisitely crafted but remote and emotionally barren. Critic Michael Wilmington wrote that the characters seem more puppet-like than the puppets in their earlier films. Is that a valid criticism?

POLISH: It's a valid criticism. They're coming from a world where they can tweak everything. It is live-action, but it's not that unlike what they were doing before. They are the master puppeteers, and to make a live-action movie, it's gonna be hard to remove that control that they've had.

The only thing they probably can't control is the heartbeat of the actor. Anytime you put live-action, or a live actor, in your movie, you're gonna witness something that you can't control—just their breath and how the camera picks up the intuitiveness of somebody's soul.

With them controlling everything, they end up making things colder. It's not going to be accessible, which is automatically gonna turn off 90 percent of the population.

But it's not without humor. . . .

POLISH: It has its humor, and what I find amazing is that they also have very provocative images, too, with that lady sweating. That it's sexy at the same time.

Yet their obsessions resurface as well, with their characters searching for pieces of themselves.

POLISH: There's this serious oppression that you feel with their work, and their love of Kafka and those writers of the Eastern Bloc comes through a lot. There's a sense of oppression and that idea of the one person against the world. But it's pushed way into the Brothers Grimm realm.

And what do you make of the signs shown in the background throughout the film? Those signs that say WORK MORE, WISH LESS. It plays against the modern fairy-tale perception, because so many people think that modern fairy tales are about simple wish fulfillment.
POLISH: Yeah. I think you're right with that analysis of the fairy tale, because you're the second person I've heard compare it to a fairy tale and the way they construct the fairy tale. And I think they're going back just to the way they started animation, growing up in a very Disney-oriented world. I think they've been trying to break through that.

They're reclaiming it, making it the way they would like to have tweaked the Disney movies.

What did *Institute* teach you?
POLISH: We all, as artists, love to get instant gratification, because that's what validates us. We get a sense of validation when our work is on display and it gets appreciated. When that doesn't happen, it does shut down a little bit of your progress. You can't be one hundred percent of an artist and say it doesn't matter. But you would love for the Brothers Quay to come out to a wider audience.

But the independent world is just as ruthless as Hollywood; independents eat their own. Independent filmmaking and this community—this ruthlessness is part of the game, but it's no different when you're working with a studio. At least the studios are up-front with what they want to do.

I'm sure you hear what I'm saying about the discovery of now and the discovery of later. They're two very powerful things, and they're each their own. It's just unfortunate sometimes that the person who suffers the most is the person who created it.

What are the hurdles with translation to the screen, of never having it turn out on film the way it does in your head?

POLISH: I feel that comment is directly about *Northfork*, because that movie is as close to the dream state that the *Institute* has. Trying to get *Northfork* made for eight years, even after doing two other movies before that, felt like I had a commitment to bringing that screenplay as close to what I visually imagined as possible—even if that meant stripping all the color out and filming it through gauze. It had to feel a particular way for everybody to believe that it was rural Montana and on that ride. The Quay Brothers reinforced that it's great that people are doing this work. You don't have to be totally arty to get something unique on the screen.

The film is directed by identical twin brothers. Did you intentionally choose this film because you are an identical twin?
POLISH: That's weird, isn't it? I almost didn't pick them because of that.

Why?
POLISH: Well, they direct, they do things together. Me and Mark, while we are identical twins, are very decisive in what we do. I direct. He produces and writes. I have my share of writing involved, but what makes us good is that we don't have a singular vision; we have two different interpretations of what we write. Me being the director, I get the overall say, which drives him nuts most of the time.

But the arch in *Northfork* is from my drawings, and that's the way I wanted to see it. It's acceptable because he wrote that scene, but I don't think it's the same arch that he thought that he saw.

Do you think that there's anything about the Quays' fraternal relationship that you understand?
POLISH: I think confidence behind the visuals that they both reinforce is probably the same support team that Mark and I have. What's nice about their relationship that parallels our relationship is that we reinforce each other's ideals without having to go to get each other's opinion. Our visions become very particular—become our own quicker—because we have a support team. I didn't know they were twins for the longest time. I just thought they were brothers. But they are so twins. They are so much more than what me and Mark are.

The Quays have said that it's best to abandon the idea of translating the action in a literal sense. Their justification: if somebody tells you about an extraordinary dream, you don't pick it apart later and say it had a lousy story; you accept it as a whole.

POLISH: Dreams have a symbolic nature. They come to you in symbols, because it's very hard to put a narrative structure to a dream. You might be linking pictures in a narrative way, but the way they are coming at you, you accept them. Maybe that's what they were leaning toward: you accept a dream, but you are not really controlling it. You are participating; that's all you're really doing.

Is that one of the reasons why this film is difficult at times?

POLISH: Yes. And I also find that connection with *Northfork*. You're more of a participant, and we are allowing you to think much more than you are usually allowed to think. It's allowing people to make up their own conclusions. But ours isn't as complicated or as complex, maybe, as what the Brothers Quay were doing. *Institute Benjamenta* really makes you take a step forth into their own realm and participate in a way that you are just not normally participating in movies.

The Quays have said, "We can't be responsible for the meaning of our work; the viewer has to determine that for themselves." As a filmmaker, what is the inherent danger in that philosophy?

POLISH: The danger is that as an audience, you feel that there's a reckless abandonment to your work in the way you are getting what you want, and you're not asking for approval. They're kind of extending themselves.

It's tough, because ultimately you are responsible for your work, even if you say you're not; you're putting it out there. You have rappers today saying go shoot this person, go shoot your girlfriend, but you have to be somewhat responsible for saying that. By saying they're not, they really are. They created it. There's meaning behind what they created. Ultimately I don't know what that means, but I'm going to put it out there anyway.

As an artist, it's hard not to say that you're not responsible. I could easily say I don't have responsibility for the meaning of *Northfork*, and yet it lives and it breathes and it's a reflection of who we are. Ultimately, you are not responsible for anything you put out there, but it's a reflection of you.

17

Joe Swanberg
ivansxtc

Sometimes a movie is about a central performance. Even if the other elements of a film don't support it, a single performance can be a mesmerizing force that gains your loyalty and admiration.

That's what happened to Joe Swanberg while watching Danny Huston in director Bernard Rose's *ivansxtc* (also known as *IVANSXTC*, *Ivan's XTC*, and *ivansxtc.*).

"It's rare to see something so alive on the screen, something that feels so unforced, where somebody's humanity is that big and that present," Swanberg says.

The film follows a drug-addled Hollywood superagent (Huston) through his last days, in a story based partly on Leo Tolstoy's *The Death of Ivan Ilyich* and partly on Rose's own agent.

"It was digging a hole in my brain until a couple of days later, I went and saw it again . . . but I couldn't help it. I couldn't stop thinking about it," Swanberg says.

Joe Swanberg, selected filmography:
Kissing on the Mouth (2005)
Hannah Takes the Stairs (2007)
Nights and Weekends (2008)
Alexander the Last (2009)
Silver Bullets (2011)
All the Light in the Sky (2013)

ivansxtc
2000

Directed by Bernard Rose
Starring Danny Huston, Peter Weller, James Merendino, Adam
Krentzman, and Tiffani Amber Theissen

How would you describe *ivansxtc* to someone who has never seen it?
SWANBERG: It is a moralistic parable about Ivan (Danny Huston), a scummy
Los Angeles agent, and his slow creep towards death. It's an update of Leo
Tolstoy's *The Death of Ivan Ilyich* but set in Hollywood.

When did you see the film?
SWANBERG: I was living in Los Angeles, the summer of 2002, and I was by
myself in an apartment that was unfurnished. I basically had an air mattress
on the floor, two frozen pizzas in the freezer, and my laptop. So I would try
and find two movies a night that I could go see so I would spend as little
time in that apartment as possible. And one of the places I was frequenting
is the Laemmle Fairfax, a really off-the-beaten-path movie theater that was
showing really weird stuff. And there was a movie called *ivansxtc*, and I
didn't know anything about it, and I took a chance on it.

What was your experience seeing it?
SWANBERG: Well, the first fifteen minutes of the movie nearly had me walking out. I felt it was really terrible acting and really weird photography, and
it was shot on video . . . everything about it was off-putting to me.

Then, about halfway in, I started getting into it. And by the end I was
totally blown away. Not so much by the movie but by Danny Huston's performance, which was the most living, breathing, vibrant thing I had seen
in a movie in a really long time. It still remains one of my favorite performances of all time.

I was completely caught off guard, especially because I was so uninterested
in the movie. When I got home, I had no idea what happened. I knew that
I had seen something that I really liked, but I couldn't quite put it together,
because there was a lot of stuff in there that I thought was really crummy.

It just stayed with me, and it was digging a hole in my brain until a couple of days later, I went and saw it again, which I rarely do in the theater.
But I couldn't help it. I couldn't stop thinking about it, and I was like, "Fuck,

man, the only way I'm going to figure this out is if I see it again." So I saw it again, and I didn't figure anything out. I was just more amazed by it, because I knew the structure more, and I've watched it several times since then.

This is a Bernard Rose film. He also directed *Candyman* and *Immortal Beloved* and then went underground after his adaptation of *Anna Karenina*, also a Tolstoy novel, was taken away from him and recut. *Ivansxtc* seems to be his response to that experience.
SWANBERG: *Ivansxtc* is so angry, and there's nothing commercial about it. It feels very much like a response—in a good way and in a bad way. It's like teenage angst, like somebody throwing a temper tantrum, which is fascinating to watch and also really repulsive at the same time. You're interested but embarrassed.

But that's an incredible quality, and movies don't usually get to have that, because movies are hard to make, and they're expensive, and you don't do it by yourself, you do it with other people. So usually you don't get to watch somebody throw a temper tantrum on-screen. And he somehow convinced a crew of people and a group of actors to come throw the temper tantrum with him.

I did see Bernard Rose speak in person at Roger Ebert's festival in Champaign, Illinois, and he was so upset when I saw him speak. He was talking about these dolls he had, these action figures he had made for *Candyman 2* and how he had helped visualize and create this character of Candyman. And they didn't give him any of the licensing money for these action figures, because they claimed that the character, that the action figures, were from *Candyman 2*, not from *Candyman* one. But it's the same character that he created.

He took it as a personal affront. So I knew that about him before going to see *ivansxtc*. And that was the filter through which I watched *ivansxtc*— knowing, damn, this guy's been beaten up by the system.

Ebert gave it four stars. *Variety*, however, said that it's "aesthetically messy and far from trenchant in that it has nothing new to say about [Hollywood]."
SWANBERG: I'm so uninterested in what the movie has to say about Hollywood, but that's the way I watch most movies. I'm always that guy who

missed the point or wasn't paying attention to the storyline because I'm so fascinated by characters.

But like these critics are saying: we get it already. Even people who appreciate Hollywood movies understand that Hollywood's shallow and lame. It's such an easy joke to make. But the thing about the movie that I love is the pain of what happened to Rose as an artist. So he can poke a million holes into Hollywood, but the pain of having his movie taken away from him is very much there. You feel it in that movie—that he's wounded.

Rose charges that Creative Artists Agency helped suppress the movie. He said it was because *ivansxtc* is based, in part, on a CAA agent named Jay Moloney. He was Rose's own agent, who also represented Steven Spielberg, Martin Scorsese, Bill Murray, Tim Burton, and Leonardo DiCaprio. He was fired from CAA for cocaine use and ultimately committed suicide.
SWANBERG: I can't remember if I ever read that. I know it now. I don't think you're losing anything by not knowing it.

That this is about, at least tangentially, a guy that he knew. But do you gain anything by knowing it?
SWANBERG: It's a pretty daring point to make, which is that Hollywood is a corrupt and evil place where they will love you and use you, and essentially, once you become a burden for them, they will fire you and turn their back while you sort of disappear off into the world and kill yourself. It's a very bold statement to make. And if you can base that statement on actual life, it gives validity to it. So I think that if you do know that, then you do gain something. But I don't feel like it's necessary information.

Tell me about just your own experience with Hollywood.
SWANBERG: I've been surprised in recent years by how receptive Hollywood has been to the Mumblecore films and filmmakers. As the studio system moves almost entirely toward remakes, reboots, sequels, and spin-offs, Hollywood actors especially seem receptive to this smaller, more personal work. I've been shocked and excited to discover how many well-known actors are fans of my films and would like to work with me.

Television is another factor in this. Television has lost its stigma over the last decade, to the point where it's now attracting well-respected directors and actors. But the television schedule is very rigorous, so many of these actors are looking for film work that satisfies them creatively, because they're making plenty of money from their TV gigs.

Many New Yorkers are also moving out to Los Angeles as the city becomes more interesting and New York becomes less interesting, so Hollywood's image is changing. It doesn't feel like the city in *ivansxtc* anymore. The agents I have met and worked with are very helpful and respect my films and my process. I don't know. It's surprising. I still live in Chicago, away from the industry, but I really like going to Los Angeles.

Peter Weller plays Don West, a high-powered, horribly spoiled actor. Have you ever had to deal with this kind of personality?
SWANBERG: Yeah, sure. Being the director, I get to see different sides than most other people get to see. But it's in an actor's best interest to be on their best behavior in front of me and to try and make a good impression. But if you ask my wife whether she's experienced people like that, I bet she would say yes, because they're less interested in sucking up to her and winning her approval. So it's something that she and I constantly talk about. We know the same people and oftentimes have completely different impressions of the same people. I have come across those people, but I just am not privy to their temper tantrums . . . yet.

What dialogue or scene, as you said most poetically, dug a hole in your brain?
SWANBERG: It starts from the very beginning. The opening credits in this movie are old-school, because Rose put them all up front. And the very first time I saw the movie, I felt like I accidently came in during the end credits or something like that. It's like this opera music, and it's a really long sequence over shots of Los Angeles.

Wagner's *Tristan and Isolde* is playing.
SWANBERG: Yes. And you're seeing billboards with actors and movies on them, and something feels very weird about it. So right away, the movie

had me on edge, because I couldn't quite figure out what was going on. Of course, I love it now. And I'm doing it with my own movies too, which is a direct influence. I'm putting most of my credits up front and just having it say THE END at the end, sort of the way old movies used to.

That's because of *ivansxtc*, definitely. There are several scenes that left a big impression on me—some for better, some for worse. The scene in the beginning where they're at the agency, and everybody's sort of sitting around the table talking . . . it's so bad and over-the-top.

Most of those people are real agents.
SWANBERG: Exactly. But it's, like, exactly that. It's that they're real agents. These things make the movie work on the third viewing—which is a really risky thing to do as a filmmaker and something I'm always struggling with.

Do you make a movie for the third viewing? Or do you make a movie where, if you're lucky, people will see your movie once? It seems like Bernard Rose said, "Fuck it. I'm going to make a movie for the third viewing, and the things that are going to seem off and weird will eventually make sense or feel more right." And I like that about it. Danny Huston's performance really grabs me. I forget which scene it is, but I feel like it's the first time we meet the guy. He's walking through the office and talking to some girl who's supposed to be doing coverage on scripts or something like that.

Any other scenes that stick with you?
SWANBERG: There's the scene where Peter Weller does cocaine off the vagina of Ivan's girlfriend. Very near the vagina. It's so crass that it must be based on a true story. It's one of those things that as soon as I saw it, it felt so disgusting and like such a violation that I couldn't stop thinking about it. As a human, how do you get to that point? It was so removed and still is so removed from the world I live in. Just the audacity to do something like that without even asking for permission.

Well, he does ask permission.
SWANBERG: But he doesn't, really. He tells her. It's so weird, because there's no elegance to any of it, to any of that movie. It's not an elegant movie. It's a very clunky, clumsy, crass movie, and it should be. It's the same with this

party scene. They are up in this penthouse, and there are strobe lights going off, and it's so lame. There's nothing cool about that party. And he shoots it in the most typical, like, '90s techno party. But you know that's what it's supposed to be like.

As an artist, he has to overcome his ability to make things beautiful and to make things elegant and revert back to a reptilian, crass brain. To me, that's brave filmmaking. To basically open yourself up to the worst kind of criticism, which is that you're untalented, and he's not untalented. But if you watch that movie, it looks like he is, and it feels like he is. It feels like he's bad at directing actors. It feels like he's bad at camera direction, a bad screenwriter. And all of these things, they're very scary things to do as a filmmaker, because he's not bad at those things, and you know he's not bad because of the central performance, which is totally subtle and incredible and alive. It's like that's where you see him truly at work, and all the rest of the stuff is just lame. But it makes Hollywood seem lame in just the right way.

But is it lame because it is so much of a screed and he can't help himself?
SWANBERG: That's part of it. He's blind to a lot of this stuff because of his anger. He must be. But also, something like that party scene, there's no better way to make something look like it's no fun than to make it be that kind of fun. Like nobody's enjoying themselves and half of them don't want to be there or feel obligated to be there. No one even remembers what it was like to have fun at a party, because it's become work to be there.

To come back to Tolstoy, this is really a film about someone coming to grips with the inevitability of death and the question of "Does God exist?" And if so, why is suffering allowed? I question, as a viewer, if a behind-the-scenes Hollywood film is the best place to search for that.
SWANBERG: I know. And that part of it doesn't really ring true in the movie either. The whole ending sequence with the nurse and the bright light and all that stuff just feels a little lame.

But that's direct from the Tolstoy. That's actually how *The Death of Ivan Ilyich* ends. Vladimir Nabokov said, "The Tolstoyian formula is: Ivan lived a bad life and since a bad life is nothing but the death of the soul,

then Ivan lived a living death; and since beyond death is God's giving light, then Ivan died into a new Life, Life with a capital L."

SWANBERG: Well, it's a nice thought. But it doesn't quite go along with even Bernard Rose's anger. For him, maybe it's nice to think it's about the forgiveness of the sins he feels have been perpetrated against him.

But with that kind of anger, you want to get the sense that these guys die and go to a fiery hell as punishment for not only living miserable lives themselves, but making the people around them miserable. But you don't get that sense. You get the sense that he's finally freed. If that's how Bernard Rose feels, then that's great. I have a feeling that he doesn't really feel that way and that it was his attempt to be more true to the source material than they let him be on *Anna Karenina*.

I want to make clear to somebody who's reading this that the movie itself is so important to me really only because of Danny Huston's performance. If there's a crime about things being overlooked, it's that people don't talk about him in this movie. And I think he's incredible. *Ivansxtc* is his movie, and I was really disappointed at the end of the year that not only was I the only person I know that had seen it, but that larger institutions and bodies were not giving this guy his due. It's rare to see something so alive on the screen, something that feels so unforced, where somebody's humanity is that big and that present. And to give that sort of performance while you're playing a coked-out asshole is just really amazing to me.

It does more to prove Bernard Rose's point than anything, which is this guy should be a great, warm, healing human being and have the ability, the humanity, to do that. But instead he's a miserable, sniveling creep who's wasted this big humanity.

TOP: Jason Patric and Rachel Ward as an ex-boxer and his troubled love interest in the noir thriller *After Dark, My Sweet* (1990). © LIONSGATE ENTERTAINMENT

LEFT: Lovelorn Stephen Blume (George Segal) in *Blume in Love* (1973). © WARNER BROS.

TOP: From left to right: Elizabeth Taylor, Richard Burton, and Noel Coward in *Boom!* (1968).
© UNIVERSAL PICTURES

BOTTOM: Orson Welles's muse and girlfriend Oja Kodar plays herself in *F for Fake* (1973).
© JANUS FILMS

LEFT: Cyril Cusack (left) as Sam and Ian Holm as Lenny in the 1973 adaptation of Harold Pinter's play *The Homecoming*. © KINO INTERNATIONAL

BOTTOM: Ray Fernandez (Tony Lo Bianco) and Martha Beck (Shirley Stoler), the title couple in *The Honeymoon Killers* (1969). © EURO-LONDON FILMS

TOP: Fredric March (left) as Harry Hope and Lee Marvin as Hickey in *The Iceman Cometh* (1973).
© KINO INTERNATIONAL

BOTTOM: Joe Banks (Tom Hanks) and Patricia (Meg Ryan) wait for an audience with the Waponi chief in *Joe Versus the Volcano* (1990). © WARNER BROS.

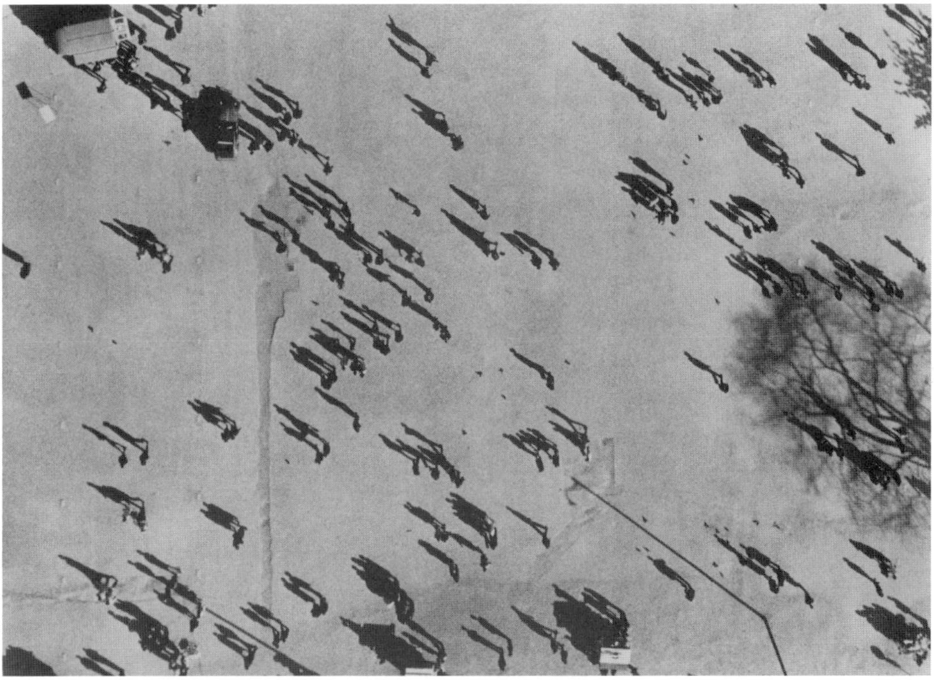

TOP: A Parisian aerial scene from *Le joli mai* (1963).
© SOFRACIMA

LEFT: Hit man Jef Costello (Alain Delon) takes aim in *Le samouraï* (1967). © FILMEL

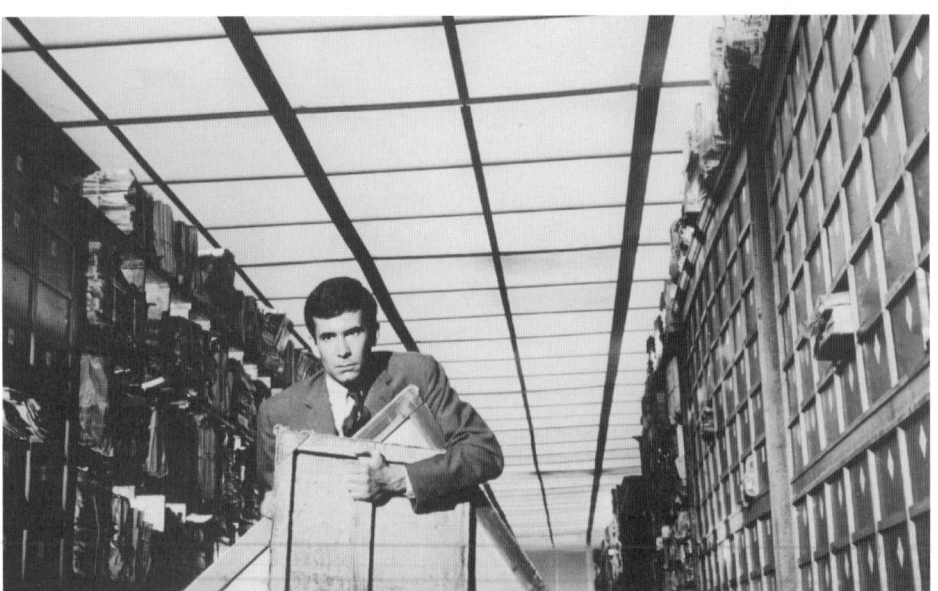

TOP: Frank Sinatra plays a troubled writer opposite Shirley MacLaine, who earned an Oscar nomination for her supporting role in *Some Came Running* (1958). © WARNER BROS.

BOTTOM: Josef K. (Anthony Perkins) in Orson Welles's *The Trial* (1962). © CANTHARUS PRODUCTIONS

LEFT: Gaston Monescu (Herbert Marshall) shares a tender embrace with lover and fellow thief Lily (Miriam Hopkins) in *Trouble in Paradise* (1932).
© UNIVERSAL PICTURES

BOTTOM: The ethereal Lady Wakasa (Machiko Kyō) seduces Genjurō (Masayuki Mori) in *Ugetsu* (1953). © JANUS FILMS

TOP: The consul (Albert Finney) surveys his territory in John Huston's *Under the Volcano* (1984). © UNIVERSAL PICTURES

LEFT: Nick Nolte and Tuesday Weld star in *Who'll Stop the Rain* (1978), an adaptation of Robert Stone's novel *Dog Soldiers*. © MGM

BOTTOM: Chaos ensues as the walls crumble around the cast of characters of *WR: Mysteries of the Organism* (1971). © DUŠAN MAKAVEJEV

18

Jay Duplass
Joe Versus the Volcano

Even box-office bombs can be forgotten when they are replaced by bigger bombs. That's what happened to Tom Hanks with *Joe Versus the Volcano*, a quirky, stylized movie that didn't quite connect with audiences—but was quickly overshadowed by the larger flop of *The Bonfire of the Vanities*. But to director Jay Duplass, *Joe Versus the Volcano* is a perfect piece of cinema. "I see it as a weird-ass little piece of art that I've never quite seen anything like before—or after," he says.

In this first pairing of Tom Hanks and Meg Ryan, Hanks plays hypochondriac Joe, who is convinced he's dying and escapes his crushing job under fluorescent lights to sacrifice himself into a volcano. Criticisms aside, Duplass says, "I want to keep it sacred—so I honestly don't listen to people too much, because the movie means so much to me."

> **Jay Duplass, selected filmography, with codirector Mark Duplass:**
> *The Puffy Chair* (2005)
> *Baghead* (2008)
> *Cyrus* (2010)
> *Jeff, Who Lives at Home* (2011)
> *The Do-Deca-Pentathlon* (2012)
>
> *Joe Versus the Volcano*
> 1990
> Directed by John Patrick Shanley
> Starring Tom Hanks, Meg Ryan, Lloyd Bridges, Robert Stack, Abe Vigoda, Ossie Davis, Carol Kane, and others

How would you describe *Joe Versus the Volcano* to someone who's never seen it?

DUPLASS: It's about a guy (Tom Hanks) who is a hypochondriac who is led into taking a magnanimous journey to his own death and is reborn. It's a kind of amorphous movie that's not about the plot; it's about the spirit of it.

When was the first time you saw the film?

DUPLASS: My brother Mark and I saw this on a family vacation. "What the fuck is this?" That was my first reaction. "Is this even a movie?"

Meg Ryan plays three different characters in it, the movie is directed by John Patrick Shanley, and it feels like a play on some level. I thought, "I've never seen this before." It created a very stylized world unto itself that I had no problem buying into, because I knew they were using these devices to get into the head of this guy trying to get out from under this giant personal problem. It just appealed to me enormously, because it just felt different from all the movies that I had seen up until that point.

Let's talk briefly about John Patrick Shanley. He won the Oscar for writing *Moonstruck*, but this movie ruined his career for about two decades, until 2008's *Doubt*, which was adapted from his Pulitzer-winning play.

DUPLASS: I don't understand why people hate the film. But I can tell you some of the adjectives that come out when people start talking about it. One is "boring" and another is "lame." People just didn't connect with it. I think probably in my microcosm, I want to keep it sacred—so I honestly don't listen to people too much, because the movie means so much to me.

Vincent Canby of the *New York Times* said, "Not since 'Howard the Duck' has there been a big-budget comedy with feet as flat as those of 'Joe Versus the Volcano.'"

DUPLASS: Wow.

He also said, "The director's throw-away touches prompt occasional smiles while an overview of the film prompts only puzzlement. . . . [Hanks] never manages to be more than theoretically comic." Is Canby wrong?

DUPLASS: I can absolutely see that point of view. But to me, this movie is about magic. If you don't buy that magic and don't lock with Joe in those first moments of him being caught up in the rottenness of his existence, you're going to be disappointed. You have to completely buy into his hypochondria and want to see him grow and come out of it. If you're not on board, you want to shoot yourself halfway through the movie. If you're on board, it is a magical, brilliant ride that plays out in a really weird and stylized way. People who like this movie tend to love it, and people who don't like this movie tend to hate it. I think maybe one in fifty people like this movie.

One of those fifty was Roger Ebert. He gave it three and half stars. He wrote, "It is not an entirely successful movie, but it is new and fresh and not shy of taking chances." This is also Hanks coming off of two hits, *Big* and *Punchline*. But then this was a box-office bomb, and directly afterward, *The Bonfire of the Vanities* was an even bigger bomb. That's why it is a forgotten film, because it's overshadowed by *The Bonfire of the Vanities*.
DUPLASS: Right. Because if *The Bonfire of the Vanities* hadn't happened, then this thing would be on the map as the biggest steamer of all time.

It's also notable for another reason: this is the first Tom Hanks/Meg Ryan film, before *Sleepless in Seattle* and before *You've Got Mail*.
DUPLASS: I never thought about that, but yeah.

What is it about their chemistry together that made producers stick them back together?
DUPLASS: This is so cheesy, but I just have to say—there's magic there. It's not a sexual chemistry; there's no sex. It's almost like they're brother and sister, which is really weird.

Which is exactly what you want in a romantic comedy . . .
DUPLASS: Yeah, exactly. God, I'm going to sound like the biggest cheeseball in the entire world, but it really felt like they were soul mates in this film. I think they share that sensibility of just, like, playfulness and fun and, at the same time, are absolutely deeply concerned with the evolution of their souls and the purposes of their lives here and now, at least specific to *Joe Versus the Volcano*.

Let's talk about Meg Ryan. She plays three roles—a redhead, a blonde, and a brunette. This is her Peter Sellers movie, and she got raked over the coals for it.
DUPLASS: She totally did.

So why does she deserve notice for these roles?
DUPLASS: Because I fell in love with her when she did this film. That's why. No other reason. Each permutation, iteration of her character became more and more lovable for me. It's almost like each character is a different reincarnation of herself, you know? It's hard to explain, other than I fell in love with her.

In the first part of the film, Joe is a factory worker in this giant industrial factory, where he's under fluorescent lights and hates life. Have you ever held a job like that?
DUPLASS: Yes. It's called Catholic school. I felt like that. I mean, I've never had a job like that. I've had waiter jobs, but I never consciously made that comparison. It's weird, because you're tapping into all the stuff Mark and I have always talked about.

The reason we didn't originally make films like we do now was because we didn't think that our white middle-class problems were film-worthy. But to see this guy trapped in that industrial vibe, to me, felt like what it meant to be in Catholic school. We went to Catholic school in New Orleans, Louisiana, which is seventy years behind the rest of the country in classes with no air-conditioning, two-hundred-year-old buildings, and just getting Latin pounded into my brain—that's what it felt like.

And the characters were trapped in sets that could have been from a Terry Gilliam or Tim Burton film, which makes sense because Bo Welch is the set designer. He did *Beetlejuice*, *Batman Returns*, *Men in Black*, and *Edward Scissorhands*.
DUPLASS: Wow. I experienced it as an emotional expression. The stylization of it made the representation hit me on an emotional level. It made the circumstances come alive for me.

Have you encountered anybody, besides your brother, who shares your love for this film, or is it more random film fans?

DUPLASS: Random strangers. Random strangers cite it in their top five. And everyone else hates it with a passion or doesn't know what it is.

Could it be part of what I call the *It's a Wonderful Life* factor? *It's a Wonderful Life* did so poorly at the box office that they let the rights lapse, and it ended up on cable TV and became a classic. Did this film have sort of the same effect because it ended up on TBS over and over for ten years?

DUPLASS: Where it could start to seep in? Maybe it did. I don't know. I actually haven't talked to other fans of the movie as to whether their love of it happened in the movie theater or over the course of random subsequent viewings. I think it was subsequent viewing for me and Mark. We loved it from the beginning, but we fell more and more in love over time. So maybe it was an additive experience.

That being said, I do see similarities between it and *It's a Wonderful Life*. *It's a Wonderful Life* is interesting because there's a magic there that you have to, like, latch on to. And if you latch on to that magic, it's this incredible experience. But if you don't latch on to it, you're just throwing up at the hokiest movie ever created. And I feel like that's the key to *Joe Versus the Volcano*.

What's your favorite scene from the movie?

DUPLASS: Oh my God, I'm just such a cheeseball. My favorite scene is when he is lost at sea, sleeping on his luggage, and the moon comes up over the ocean, and he stands up and thanks God for his life. Which is just a straight-up, sheer spiritual experience. And for me it worked. It totally worked. And that's what's so polarizing about it, because if you do a scene like that and the audience isn't there, it falls so flat it's just cringe-worthy.

It also recalls another Tom Hanks film where he's lost at sea during the typhoon in *Forrest Gump*.

DUPLASS: Right. And *Cast Away*, too.

Tom Hanks said, "This was an opportunity to be quiet in a big movie . . . an opportunity for a degree of subtlety that I haven't had a chance to do in a while. Usually, I just yell a lot in movies."

DUPLASS: It totally makes sense. He was basically yelling and being goofy in movies prior to this, and I'm wondering if this is one of his first really kind of serious roles. I mean, this is a totally silly movie, but the arc of who he's playing is someone sincere, someone who's going through something.

But the studio did market it as a comedy.

DUPLASS: They did, right? They shouldn't have. It's not really a comedy. The interactions in *Joe Versus the Volcano* are almost not human. It's like it's operating on some weird metaphorical level the entire time. I don't see it as similar to other films. I see it as a weird-ass little piece of art that I've never quite seen anything like before—or after.

19

Steve James
Le joli mai

Confession time: neither Steve James nor I could find a complete copy of Chris Marker's *Le joli mai* (*Beautiful May*). During the eight years I took to write this book, interviews with Marker were scarce—as were descriptions of the film. But that only fueled James's desire to talk about it, to bring it to a modern audience.

And it was easy. James's vivid memories of the film sparked one of the most insightful, passionate interviews in this book.

"It's a very liberated film in every respect. It doesn't have a traditional story at all," James says. "There are so many unexpected twists and turns, and people say unexpected things. You have certain expectations, and the best films turn them on their head."

Steve James, selected filmography:
Hoop Dreams (1994)
Prefontaine (1997)
Stevie (2002)
Reel Paradise (2005)
At the Death House Door (2008)
The Interrupters (2011)

Le joli mai
1963
Directed by Chris Marker

How would you describe *Le joli mai* to someone who's never seen it?
JAMES: It's this documentary mosaic portrait of Paris and its inhabitants that runs the gamut from the political to the personal and from the ghettos of Paris to its version of Wall Street. And in between, it really captures the essence of a city at a certain time in history, after the Algerian War.

It's a hard film to characterize, because it's so eclectic in its aesthetic and what it's about. It's one of the first cinema verité films, and so its place in history is ensured because of that. But it's also a poetic rumination, like Cartier-Bresson photos brought to life.

The film itself, although it is political, seems to be about the different levels of happiness: about social happiness, about individual happiness.
JAMES: Yes, the conceit of the film is about happiness. In hearing that, people who haven't seen the film might think it's boring or trite, but it's Marker's way into getting at things far deeper.

The question of what makes you happy or doesn't is a really interesting question. I hope somebody selects *Inquiring Nuns* as one of their favorite underappreciated films, because that's a film, I think inspired by Marker, where filmmakers went around with nuns and asked people, "Are you happy?" And there's a confessional nature to it, where people are given permission by their being who they are, at least at that time in their lives. Today, it would be viewed as camp.

In *Le joli mai*, because of his way with people and his approach, Marker is able to get very quickly to the essence of who these people are. And one way to do this is to ask them: Are they happy? What makes them happy? What is happiness? It gets at class, it gets at race, it gets at politics, it gets very personal and political all at the same time.

Tell me about the first time you saw the film and its impact on you.
JAMES: The first time I saw it, I was in graduate school, studying film at Southern Illinois University. It was shown to me in a class where we looked at *La jetée* by Chris Marker, and we also watched *Le joli mai*. I was just blown away by it, because it is so freeing in its approach.

It's a very liberated film in every respect. It doesn't have a traditional story at all. The story is: I'm trying to get at the essence of Paris and its

citizens and who they are and what makes them happy. It has this seat-of-the-pants quality to it, where Marker lets one idea or person lead him to the next person. Young lovers who are full of all kinds of expectations of eternal love lead him to a wedding party where the groom and the bride already seem destined for divorce. The only people really having a good time are the drunken people attending the party. Then an amateur artist, who does a painting called *Cosmic Man*, leads him to an exhibit about space and astronauts and the Gemini capsule and John Glenn.

It has this sort of serendipitous quality about the way it's put together, where he really didn't go in with a preconceived notion about what this film was going to be. He really let the film and the experience of being in the streets of Paris dictate where it took him.

There was something quite moving and liberating about the experience of watching the film, because what it says to you is "You can make a film about anything, and you can make it in any way you want." Probably the most important lesson to me as a filmmaker—and it's not one that I necessarily realized at the time—is that you shouldn't go into a film knowing what you plan to come out with.

You have an idea—and he had a great idea—but then he let the film be this act of discovery about the city that he loved, clearly loves, and what is Paris at this particular juncture in time.

When it works well, does filmmaking work like that as the film unfolds?
JAMES: It's what I love about documentary. It can happen in fiction films too, this act of discovery, but it's part of the DNA of documentary.

There are different kinds of documentary filmmaking. I watched *Nova* on TV last night, which was really good and very informative and very interesting, and I'm sure it was totally scripted. They did the pre-interviews, they figured out who they needed to talk to and what that person was going to tell them, and then they roughed together a script, and then they went out and got it and came back and put it together. That's one kind of documentary filmmaking that can be very informative and interesting, and you can learn a lot, but it holds no appeal for me as a filmmaker.

So every film worth doing is one where you have this good idea, but that the act of making the film takes you places you never imagined, reveals

things to you that you couldn't possibly have known going in and shakes you up. It changes the way you look at it. Otherwise, what's the point of doing it, right? I mean, when you write a book, that's the whole point of it.

I wonder what my publisher thinks of this, but yes. It's discovery.
JAMES: Right. And I had a broadcaster once say to me about *Stevie*, "You go on these fishing expeditions. But the thing is, you don't worry about whether you're going to come back with a fish."

I said, "You're right, but I think the question isn't 'Will I come back with a fish?'—it's 'What kind of fish will I come back with?'"

And most filmmakers who work the way I work, your gut tells you. In other words, if you pick situations that are inherently dramatic and interesting, you're going to get an interesting film. What's great about it is you have no idea what that story is ultimately going to be, and that's the discovery part.

Coming back to *Le joli mai*, can you tell me about your favorite sequence?
JAMES: It's the passage where he talks to the woman about her new house. And she is so excited that she's moving into this new place, and she's thrilled, and she's full of excitement and anticipation. Then we get to see the place, and we see that it's basically a tenement house, government housing, and she's got a big family, and they're going to be squeezed into this very small place. But her enthusiasm is genuine. So the passage really operates on all these levels. She's not cynical about her life.

In retrospect, it reminds me of the moment in *Hoop Dreams* where Arthur's mother is making him this birthday cake for his eighteenth birthday and says, without a trace of irony or cynicism, she's just truly genuinely happy he made it to eighteen.

There's another very interesting sequence in which Marker talks to young stockbrokers, but he is interrupted by a senior stockbroker....
JAMES: When you're trying to do something and someone is bothering you and getting in the way, what you want them to do more than anything is just go away. But Marker, in his brilliance, realizes that this is part of the story.

This older stockbroker, in many respects, is jealous that he's not the focus of attention. Marker is talking to these young guys who, from his point

of view, don't really know anything anyway. So why are you interviewing them? So Marker both gives the man what he really wants, which is he lets him be in the film, but in the process, he also manages to expose him in a lot of ways. So it's just a brilliant filmmaking moment.

It's the kind of moment that can only happen when a filmmaker is completely in tune and comfortable with that act of discovery, of letting the film take him where it takes him.

Can you tell me about a time when that happened to you?

JAMES: This isn't exactly that, but there was this moment when we were doing *Hoop Dreams*. We realized that we had filmed Arthur Agee and his dad when we had first met them, playing some basketball together, and Arthur was just a little guy at that point. And his dad had spoken with pride of what he hoped for his son. He used to play basketball—the dad did—and he was passing that love down to his son.

Well, four and a half years later, when Arthur was soon to head off to college, we were over there filming one day at the house, and they mentioned that they occasionally go out and still play against each other. And we thought, oh perfect! It'll be a tender, sweet, beautiful bookend.

So we went to the court and they started to play, and frankly, it was boring. It's like something out of a Hallmark special, actually. It was boring. Then suddenly, the game got competitive. And as it got competitive, it got more interesting. It wasn't about a proud father seeing his son off to college at all; it was Arthur settling the score on old wounds. In those intervening four years, Arthur's dad had left home, hadn't been there for him, had been using drugs, and yet would still come back and expect to be dad and be listened to. It was a far more interesting moment than we could have possibly imagined. It became this vicious battle of wills, where all the old wounds that Arthur felt from his dad came to the fore on a basketball court.

Marker's most famous short film is *La jetée*, which was the basis for Terry Gilliam's *12 Monkeys*. Comparing *La jetée and Le joli mai*, how can you tell they're by the same filmmaker?

JAMES: What links them is the poetry. He is a truly poetic filmmaker, and both of those films are very poetic films in differing ways. One is composed

entirely of photographs and conjures up this science-fiction world, and the other is very much a film in the moment in the streets of Paris.

So they're very different, which speaks to his versatility. Because as I said earlier, *La joli mai* has all this versatility within it. It has all these things going on in it. It's not strictly verité. Not at all. I think Marker's goal is to comment on the world much more overtly, and the world he lives in, but to do it in this incredibly free and liberating way.

You just barely see Marker on the edges of the film, but his personality and voice are the driving force of the film. You also became a character in your own film, *Stevie.* **What was that like?**
JAMES: It's not something I ever thought I would do when I was starting out as a filmmaker or even when I began the project *Stevie*. I thought, at most, I would personally narrate it. And there are some real differences between *Stevie* and *Le joli mai*, obviously. As far as I know, Chris Marker doesn't have a history with any of the characters.

He knows some of them, and then some of them he just happens upon. There are 127 interviews, and he knows a few of them.
JAMES: Well, you're telling me something which is really interesting, which is not apparent in the film. He did not foreground that.

What would *Le joli mai* **lose if he had chosen to take himself out of the documentary?**
JAMES: It would lose some of that probing quality that it has, that desire to probe and push and cajole people, and that conversational quality it has, which makes it even more freeing.

In most documentaries, when we make them, we cut our questions out. I want it to feel like it's all coming from them and it's not prodded by a question. But sometimes, a question is part of what makes the answer poignant, and not just meaningful but poignant and powerful. So I think that his presence in it is great, because he strikes just the right delicate balance of being on the margins, but you hear his voice, you hear his intelligence, you hear his probing, you hear his interaction. And it allows the interactions to be more of a conversation instead of an interview. And there's a difference. There's a difference between a

conversation and an interview. I feel like the best interviews are conversations, whether your questions end up in them or not.

You're constantly having your expectations undermined and your stereotypes overturned about how people are, how they react, what they're going to do, what they're going to say. And that's really the beauty of it. And I think in Marker's film, that exudes from the entire film. There are so many unexpected twists and turns, and people say unexpected things. You have certain expectations, and the best films turn them on their head.

In four decades, Marker has done a handful of interviews. Stanley Kubrick gave more interviews, and they called him reclusive. Is there anything about Marker's filmmaking that shows why he might be that way?

JAMES: I wish I knew more about Chris Marker . . .

There are artists who feel like they don't really want to talk about the work. They really just want you to approach the work on its own terms and take away from it what you take away from it. He's not naive. He's not an optimist, but there's this humanist kind of open embrace of the world around him. So it's surprising in a way that a guy like Marker might be more reclusive, given the sort of spirit of those films.

And maybe it's because he is shy. And maybe it's because he feels like he doesn't want you reading about his films and deciding that you need to take what he has to say about them as any kind of gospel for anything. Maybe he would rather you just approach them on their own terms.

And that was my very next question. For you as a filmmaker, is there an allure to doing that?

JAMES: There is an allure to that, for sure. There are a number of great artists who are not comfortable with it or who have chosen not to talk about their work. I'm not one of those. Maybe it's because I get too excited about the work and love to talk about it, or I have more ego and love giving interviews.

But I like to think that the films I make present a complicated reality. They don't encourage you to view things in a very specific way. That's what I love about storytelling. And I'm always attracted to stories where the reality is complicated.

Why do you think *Le joli mai*, for lack of a better term, remains lost, and why do people need to rediscover it?
JAMES: I can't explain why it's been lost. Except for that maybe it's a film that's fifty years old. Maybe in France it's not lost. I don't know, maybe if you're in Paris, it wouldn't be so hard to track it down. So it could be our cultural ignorance here.

Except for the fact that I could find just one book with only one half-chapter about it.
JAMES: Well, then, maybe it's Chris Marker's fault. Maybe if he had been out there doing interviews about it, we would still have it [*laughs*]. I can't explain why.

And it's an odd film. Usually the films that survive, like most of the books that survive, have a certain level of clarity and entertainment value and conformity that make them more commercially viable over time. This is not a commercial film at all. I think a lot of people might see this film and go, "What the hell?" For me personally, I saw it at the right time in my life and it really impacted me. And I know there are other people who love the film. I've run across other people who love the film.

Why do people need to see it? Why is it an essential film?
JAMES: It's historically important, and he's one of the great filmmakers in the canon. And it's a historically important film for what it did at the time it did it. If you see this film now, it's still innovative; it still doesn't conform to what most films try to do, including documentary or narrative. It may be about fifty years ago, but its sensibility and artistry and insights are just as relevant today. I've always dreamed of trying to do something like it as an homage here in Chicago, but I was always busy with another film, and it just wasn't practical.

But I love the idea of trying to do what he did with any number of cities—in our case, Chicago—where you would do a portrait of a city, but you would go about it in this totally serendipitous way at a particularly significant moment in the life of that country or that city. That's an idea that should be done.

20

Brian Herzlinger
Killer Klowns from Outer Space

Killer Klowns from Outer Space is at once a B-movie and a sloppy wet kiss to B-movies—and that's exactly what Brian Herzlinger loves about it. "What we have here, wrapped up in the body of a B-movie, is a wonderful satire on American culture and pop culture and Chinese monster movies," he says.

The movie features an odd cast of characters: attack dogs made out of balloons, a killer T. rex shadow puppet, and blood-sucking cotton-candy pods. But the over-the-top special effects hold up, Herzlinger says. "There is not one moment in *Killer Klowns* that you want to fast-forward through."

Brian Herzlinger, selected filmography:
My Date with Drew (2004)
Baby on Board (2009)
How Sweet It Is (2012)

Killer Klowns from Outer Space
1988
Directed by Stephen Chiodo (also cowritten with brothers Edward and Charles)
Starring John Vernon, Grant Cramer, Suzanne Snyder, Christopher Titus, and John Allen Nelson

How would you describe this movie to somebody who's never seen it?
HERZLINGER: I describe this movie as Tim Burton's wet dream. The title says everything: *Killer Klowns from Outer Space*. The small town of Crescent Cove is invaded by killer clowns from outer space who want to use all the humans as food for their next interstellar travel.

Tell me about your experience with the film.

HERZLINGER: It was one of those beautiful moments when you're flipping channels and you catch a movie just as it begins. I was hooked from the opening graphic and the opening theme song.

Here's the thing about *Killer Klowns from Outer Space*—the whole thing is an homage to '50s horror movies, specifically *The Blob*. I hate to say it, but almost every horror movie is an homage to either *The Blob* or *Alien*—in structure, in character, or thematically. Basically, there's this unknown enemy that invades a small town or invades us as a society.

So, for this book, why defend an homage to a '50s B-movie as a classic?

HERZLINGER: This is one of the most creative, original movies based on a foundation of homage. First of all, it is hysterical in a way that's on purpose. When *Snakes on a Plane* came out, the distributor was so worried about how bad this movie was, how terrible it was, that they started to tell the press that it was *on purpose* made to be a B-movie. False. False.

B-movies are watchable; B-movies are entertaining in their own way. They know what they are, they know what they want to be, they know what their goal is, and they achieve it. Their success is extraordinary. *Snakes on a Plane* is a horrible movie. A-movie, B-movie, C-movie, D-movie, Z-movie, however you want to classify it—terrible. It's an offense to B-movies everywhere that New Line tried to use it as a marketing ploy to save their movie. Audiences, fortunately, weren't dumb enough to buy it.

How are the performances in *Killer Klowns*?

HERZLINGER: John Vernon, who plays Mooney, the grizzled sheriff—he's like Sean Connery in *The Untouchables*. Vernon should have been nominated for an Oscar for best supporting actor. The tragedy of him not receiving an Oscar nomination—let alone there not being any Oscar nod for this film—ranks up there with Tommy Lee Jones in *The Fugitive* beating out Ralph Fiennes for *Schindler's List*. This is what I compare it to; this is how seriously I take *Killer Klowns from Outer Space*.

How has the film aged?

HERZLINGER: There is not one moment in *Killer Klowns* that you want to fast-forward through. You know they went through a lot to get it done, especially on a two-million-dollar budget. The effects were pretty much done by the Chiodo brothers, who are puppeteers; these are the guys who did the puppets for *Team America: World Police*. If you look at the DVD, it has the three brothers making stop-motion animation movies when they were children.

The special effects are still phenomenal. They used stop-motion animation; they used matte paintings; they used animatronics, rotoscoping, forced perspective, puppeteering, optical printing, and miniatures. It is awesome. They hold up, and not just in making the movie look great—the clowns are terrifying. One frame of this movie is more terrifying than the entire miniseries of *Stephen King's It*. There's a sequence in this movie that I watched last night to refresh myself for this interview. It scared the crap out of me again.

Which scene was that?
HERZLINGER: The clowns have invaded but the town is unaware that the clowns are there. This little girl is in a hamburger joint with her parents and her parents' friends, and the parents aren't paying attention to the little girl.

Now, you're in adult territory, where they're playing into the fear of your child getting kidnapped from a restaurant or a mall. So this little girl looks through the window and she sees a clown waving at her. Creepily, eerily waving at her. She smiles, and she waves back, and she's shy, and the clown starts making faces. Then he starts to wait for her to come towards him. She starts to go out, and the clown is taking steps closer towards her. Behind his back, he's got a giant cartoon-type mallet that they used in the Bugs Bunny cartoons. Just as she's about to go through the door, the mother grabs her and says, "You're not going anywhere till you finish your food!" And the clown lets out a horrifying yell. That scene epitomizes, to me, why that film is so perfect.

The horror of this movie feeds off of what we as people find to be innocent and fun. It's a universal theme. In *Killer Klowns from Outer Space*, cotton candy is not something your parents buy you at the circus. Cotton candy is

a cocoon that they stick you in and stick one of those funny bendy straws into to suck your blood. In what other movie can you see four cotton-candy pods on a street corner under a loading zone sign, waiting to be picked up by a giant vacuum cleaner that looks like a clown parade car?

Not everyone loves this film as much as you do. There were bad reviews. What did they misunderstand?
HERZLINGER: Everything. What we have here, wrapped up in the body of a B-movie, is a wonderful satire on American culture and pop culture and Chinese monster movies. I'll have to use specific scenes to illustrate my points. The movie opens up, there are teenagers making out, they're all in the back of their cars, and you can find Christopher Titus in a starring role.

Something's gonna happen, and à la *The Blob*, a comet goes streaking overhead. The comet lands. Now, instead of it being a comet with a gross jelly-like substance coming out of it, it's a circus tent. This guy finds it with his dog and immediately says, "There's gonna be thousands of people! Thousands of people a-comin'. . . . We gonna be rich!" And he is immediately killed by the clowns. Now our two teenagers who are making out see this tent and go racing after it with some cheesy dialogue.

They go into the tent, they see that the cocoons are there, they realize this is not a normal tent, and they race out for their lives—at which point they are shot by popcorn. Funny, very funny. Stupid, but funny—how is that a threat?

They get out of the tent and now they're being pursued by clowns and—in one of the best moments in the movie—a balloon-animal dog. The popcorn that's clinging to their clothes—later we find out the popcorn kernels are pods for the clowns to grow. With the popcorn all over the teenage girl's bathroom floor—she's taking a shower à la *Psycho*—the popcorn grows into clowns and attacks her.

It's the combination of homage to classic horror movies and classic horror monsters, but it's also this satire, this commentary on us and what we find to be fun and innocent and important, if you will. This movie is about anarchy.

What makes a successful homage?

HERZLINGER: For me, a successful homage is when the story that you're telling excels and is original enough to create its own entity and be its own movie. You're not going to watch *Killer Klowns from Outer Space* and think of it ripping off *The Blob*.

It's a B horror movie with a story that we're familiar with overall, but it has got really fun characters and unique situations that you've never seen before or since. This movie is familiar but it's original, and I'll tell you right now it's the fastest ninety minutes ever. When you watch it, it goes by like *that*.

When you look at *Scary Movie*, for example, that's a parody of horror films. There's a difference between parody and homage, there's a difference between homage and copyright infringement.

Then what's an unsuccessful homage?
HERZLINGER: An unsuccessful homage is every serial-killer movie that was released after the original *Friday the 13th*.

How did you share your enthusiasm for *Killer Klowns*?
HERZLINGER: The next day after I saw it on cable, I told all of my friends at the playground and at school to watch this movie, and I actually drew illustrations of all the clown faces and passed them out to all my friends at school. That movie is so fun to watch by yourself, but then when you get a group of friends to watch it, it's a blast. It's like the *Rocky Horror Picture Show*, maybe. But I think more than that, for me personally, it's the movie that I've had the most fun watching on my own.

When you tell people about your love for this film, what are the reactions you get?
HERZLINGER: I've gotta be honest about it, it's the first time I'm actually speaking out about it. I've been a closeted *Killer Klowns from Outer Space* fan. For me, *Killer Klowns from Outer Space* and *Grease 2* are the movies that have always been my favorites of the bad movies. I feel that I've done justice to *Grease 2* with *My Date with Drew*, and *Killer Klowns from Outer Space* deserves its due.

Here's the thing: If I met Stephen Chiodo, the director of the movie, or actress Suzanne Snyder, who had great back-to-back years with this and

Weird Science, I would honestly tell them, not only is this some of the best puppeteering but also some of the best visual effects that I've ever seen on film. Thank you for inspiring me, I would say, and igniting my imagination and making me see that everything we see as children that's supposed to represent fun can also represent pure evil. I would say that to them in a heartbeat.

There is such a fine line in bad acting. There is excessive performance, there's overacting, and then there's bad acting. Every note in this movie—this is why John Vernon should have won an Oscar for this—every delivery in that movie works. The guy who plays the young police officer, the role of Dave, he's terrible. He's the actor that breathes heavily for no reason. He's the actor that in order to come off as cool, will refer to Mike, the main character, as "buddy" or "pal" at the end of every line. Watching it now, it makes me laugh, so it doesn't take away from it. As a kid, I didn't recognize it as really bad acting.

The movie's got two climaxes, and each one is better than the other. Not only did they escape the maniacal group of these things in the town where they're going from house to house killing everybody, but there's a clown-zilla! There's a giant clown that's the leader of these things. I wish that Frank Darabont or George Lucas would watch this to know what a climax is.

You talked a little bit about the visual effects. But is there something that hasn't aged well?
HERZLINGER: I am a fan of all that is animatronics, of all that is matte painting and all that is tangible. Computer graphics reached their peak when they began in 1993, when the first characters were really fleshed out.

Jurassic Park is the best, will always be the best use of computer-generated imagery, because they didn't overuse it; it was used to enhance the tangible animatronic creatures. You see the T. rex in front of them, roaring into the windshield of the car. That's a real T. rex, and they couldn't get the thing to run, so they used CG, which looked phenomenal and still does to this day.

Now when you see that and you compare that with the nonsense that is gracing the majority of our films today—I'm sorry, but the visual effects in *Indiana Jones and the Kingdom of the Crystal Skull*, the CG effects, are terrible.

It is enough of a challenge to get your audience to believe in flickering images of light and picture on that screen, to believe in it and get immersed in it. But when you get them engrossed, you kick them right out by using these effects that are cost-effective. All it does is take your audience right out of the movie.

What would you say to the filmmakers who think that's an elitist attitude?
Herzlinger: I will say this: Peter Jackson has become what Spielberg was to the '80s and the early '90s. Jackson's *King Kong* from 2005 is flawless. That is, he is the only filmmaker today that can make CGI feel tangible, and I hate saying that because Spielberg's my favorite director.

They've been talking for years, the Chiodo brothers, about doing a *Killer Klowns 2*. I would love to see that.

The Chiodo brothers thought that *King Kong* was real. Is there anything that you thought similarly as a child?
Herzlinger: Yes, Niagara Falls. I wanted to see where Superman saved the kid from falling over.

Did you find the spot?
Herzlinger: I found the spot, I got a picture taken at the spot, and I gotta say, it was actually exhilarating and disappointing at the same time, because yes, I found the spot, but I couldn't find the hot-dog stand that he flew behind and changed into Clark Kent.

So that was a day that canceled itself out in terms of my pilgrimage, but I will say that the first weekend I moved to L.A. to pursue the dream of being a moviemaker, they were shooting *Mighty Joe Young*, the remake, in Hollywood; they had a giant inflatable blue replica of the gorilla. They had all the cars already pre-crushed on the street along the side of Hollywood Boulevard, and all the actors were looking up—Charlize Theron, Bill Paxton—were all looking up at this blue balloon.

And all my friends, after watching the filming for about an hour, they were bored, and they went back to the room, and I'm like, "I'm not leaving, are you kidding?" and I ended up getting to meet Ron Underwood and

talking to him about movies and how much I love *City Slickers* and *Tremors*, and this and that.

That was the first weekend that I was in L.A., and that helped strengthen my bubble that surrounded me when I moved out here. I made a promise to myself—I knew that I had this bubble, and I would never let it get burst. I would let it get poked and prodded and scratched and bruised, but the day that the bubble popped and it wasn't fun for me anymore and I couldn't see the joy of the business—that would be the day that I left the business. And it hasn't, yet.

21

Kevin Smith
A Man for All Seasons

Kevin Smith was one of the first directors to say yes to *The Best Film You've Never Seen*, and his interview ranks among the most enthusiastic—and also longest. In a wandering conversation that inched over the two-hour mark, Smith talked about his Catholic upbringing, his admiration for Sir Thomas More, and his love of the language in *A Man for All Seasons*.

Smith also spent considerable time defending his choice. After all, I argued, a film that won Best Picture and five other Oscars in 1967 did not belong in a book about overlooked films. But Smith passionately defended his choice and I relented, including his argument in this interview.

Remembering his first viewing of the film, "I was *hooked*," Smith says. "I was so roped in, literally leaning over the arm of the couch, knees on the couch, almost in that face-in-hands, resting-on-elbows position, like a '50s schoolgirl would pine over Ricky Nelson."

Kevin Smith, selected filmography:
Clerks (1994)
Mallrats (1995)
Chasing Amy (1997)
Dogma (1999)
Jay and Silent Bob Strike Back (2001)
Jersey Girl (2004)
Clerks II (2006)
Zack and Miri Make a Porno (2008)
Cop Out (2010)
Red State (2011)

A Man for All Seasons
1966
Directed by Fred Zinnemann
Starring Paul Scofield, Wendy Hiller, Leo McKern, Susannah
York, Corin Redgrave, and Robert Shaw

How would you describe *A Man for All Seasons* to someone who's never seen it?

SMITH: It's the story of Thomas More, who was the lord chancellor of England under Henry VIII and who was a very strict Catholic. Henry kicks off the Reformation, where England switches over from Catholicism, rejecting Rome as the seat of their religious government, to Anglican, where suddenly the Church of England is established, and they disavow Rome and the Pope. [This was also tangled up with Henry's desire to marry his mistress, Anne Boleyn; the Pope would not annul his marriage to Catherine of Aragon, thereby blocking his plans. —ed.] And the choice that Thomas has to make is between his king and his soul as he struggles to stay alive in a climate where not going along with the king is tantamount to treason.

You saw this at age thirteen at the insistence of your teacher, right?

SMITH: Sister Theresa told me to watch it, because we were putting on a kind of truncated version of it for the school play that year. So she took [the original play on which the film was based, by Robert Bolt] and just kind of chopped out the narrator, who was the common man in the play, and shaved scenes down.

At thirteen, what was your obsession with it?

SMITH: The language and the concept—just the idea of somebody whose convictions are that strong that he would rather face the grave than switch to another religion—or just sign a piece of paper that really would have meant nothing to anybody else but him and meant nothing to so many other people. But to him, it was all the difference between his relationship with God and a lack thereof. So it definitely captivated me on that level as well, as it was my final year in Catholic school before I headed off to public school. But really, the dialogue was so wonderful. Everyone sounded so fucking smart.

You've said that *A Man for All Seasons* is "porn for somebo[dy] language." How does it differ from regular, missionary-positiou ~~~ logue in other movies?

SMITH: Because every line of dialogue is a close-up jizz shot to some degree or a really great close-up on double penetration. Everything is so insanely well written, and all the actors pull off the dialogue in the fashion that you feel like it's just rolling off their tongue. Arguments are countered and logic is splayed out for the viewer to sit there and realize that Thomas had absolutely no choice, as far as he's concerned. Everyone else in the film offers a counter to his argument that is completely valid. Particularly Margaret, his daughter, is just like, "Say the words of the oath and in your heart think otherwise."

And More responds with, "What is an oath then but words we say to God?" And, "When a man takes an oath, he's holding his own self in his own hands. Like water. And if he opens his fingers then—he needn't hope to find himself again."

Powerful stuff.

And for the school play, you played the role of Cromwell. How did you do?

SMITH: You know, my performance was pretty good. It was a little hammy. I was the only one who attempted the British accent. Even Sister Theresa was like, "Don't bother."

I said, "No, no," because Leo McKern's performance in the film was so influential that I was just flat-out parroting his readings. But I might have had a bit more Snidely Whiplash than Leo McKern did; I didn't have the subtleties of the craft then—or now. The Silent Bob performance is so insanely over-the-top, with the facial gestures and tics and whatnot and the wide eyes—the white Buckwheat, if you will. Now apply that to a role where I actually have to speak, and you pretty much get the picture. That being said, for thirteen it was good but probably a very precocious performance. I did win an acting award.

It's a pretty heady play for thirteen-year-olds. How did it go over with the other students?

SMITH: It went over really well. Of course, I'm tempted to say it was the best production. In terms of production value, it was OK. But the performance itself I thought was really good.

Michael Belicose, who was in *Clerks* as the guy to whom Dante says, "Thirty-seven! My girlfriend sucked thirty-seven dicks," and he goes, "In a row?" *That* dude played Thomas More. And Sister Theresa cast all the characters, she said, based on what she felt we were capable of and also based on personality. She cast Michael based on his personality, because he was so soft-spoken and such a gentle soul. And I always wondered why the fuck she cast me as a duplicitous headhunter. She swears that it was just because I was hammy.

Fred Zinnemann directed this movie and *High Noon*, *From Here to Eternity*, *Julia*, and *Oklahoma!* What defines Zinnemann as a director?
SMITH: Zinnemann knew how to stay out of the film. His camera work does not call attention to itself whatsoever. He is content to let the material and the actors do their jobs. Zinnemann, I always felt, was best at just staying out of the way.

But he doesn't show up on many top ten director lists. Do you think that's why he's not better remembered?
SMITH: Probably because he wasn't the guy who jumped around; there was no flash. He wasn't part of that *Easy Riders*, *Raging Bulls* generation of filmmakers who were knee-deep in the fucking yayo [cocaine] in telling these stories that were so insanely avant-garde. For *A Man for All Seasons*, he adapted a play.

How do you account, then, for his great success in doing a musical, a Western, and then a period romance?
SMITH: He was a versatile man; he was like what Ang Lee is today. Ang Lee, to me, has always been a very interesting filmmaker, because he jumps from project to project; there's no through line. You don't sit there going, "Well, this is the typical Ang Lee picture." He'll go from *Sense and Sensibility* to *The Ice Storm*. Prior to all that, he's doing *Eat Drink Man Woman*, then he jumps to *Hulk*. Whether movies are good or bad, you can't pigeonhole him. He's just a guy who's really trying to tell as many different stories as he can, and that, to me, is like what Zinnemann was.

Zinnemann said, "I've always been fascinated by the idea of conscience. To photograph that conflict expressed in the actions or choices a person makes is very photogenic." To me, that is such a paradox, because inner conflicts are the toughest to film. How does he accomplish that in a film with so much dialogue?

SMITH: That's a good question. I don't know, but he certainly pulled it off, didn't he? Give him credit actually where credit's due, but at the same time, the source material was pretty genius.

But yeah, how do you shoot a conscience? I don't know. He got it, but I would say a lot of the credit goes to Scofield [as More], who has the face and the demeanor of somebody with the weight of the world on their shoulders. Years later, we'd see a brilliant Scofield performance in *Quiz Show*, where he's not playing the same character at all, but there was also a guy whose morality and conscience define that character.

And also, intelligence. That was the beauty of More to me too, and it lends to shooting the conscience as well. More was not the strong, silent type— he was a lawyer, and he's portrayed as such in the play and in the movie. He's constantly thinking and talking, constantly looking for the angle. He's a demon with the words. The moments where you can see the internal conflict are represented by when he's not talking. Here's a guy who does have an answer for everything, and it's not even a half-hearted, thrown-out-there answer; it's a brilliant response, thought of from many angles.

But when he's not speaking, the courtroom scene, where he deflates, when Richard Rich perjures himself against More, I don't think I've ever seen that matched in a film. It's wonderful. Particularly against Robert Shaw's scenery-chewing performance. A great performance, but, man, that dude in that scene—it's his scene. And he really leaves very little breathing space, but you're watching Scofield's performance against Shaw, or watching More against Henry, and seeing that he is at an absolute loss. So I think it's in the quiet moments that you can find the battle of conscience.

What's your favorite scene? What made you a fan?

SMITH: It's that first scene with Henry (Robert Shaw). By that point in the movie, I was *hooked*. At thirteen, you're not really like, "All right, it's a British period piece." It felt like it was going to be a tough watch. But by that scene,

I was so roped in, literally leaning over the arm of the couch, knees on the couch, almost in that face-in-hands, resting-on-elbows position, like a '50s schoolgirl would pine over Ricky Nelson.

Robert Bolt, a history teacher turned playwright, wrote the play and screenplay. And his past credits included *Doctor Zhivago* and *Lawrence of Arabia*. He went on to do *The Mission*. He also gets a special thanks credit in your film *Dogma*. Why?
SMITH: Because I so admired that play and that movie, so I gave him the big shout-out. He'll always be defined for me as the guy who wrote the best screenplay I've ever seen put on film.

But why attached to *Dogma* in particular?
SMITH: I mean, obviously the parallels with religion. And ours wasn't nearly the trial of conscience that More had to go through, but Bethany has a bit of it herself.

It's been debated that *A Man for All Seasons* is not really a historically accurate portrait of More, that the idea of personal conscience dictating action and belief is very much a twentieth-century ethical worldview. But according to a biographer, More believed that "if parliamentary statute offends against the law of God it is 'insufficient.'"
SMITH: That is laid out there pretty clearly in the movie. He was largely known as being a very religious man. I think if there was any aspect trumped up for the play and for the movie, it's his playfulness. He wasn't really a fun-loving guy, a playful wit in person.

As a thirteen-year-old, did you even understand "divinely ordained conscience"?
SMITH: Yeah, but certainly not under that exact terminology. But again, I was in Catholic school at the time—very easy to understand. Particularly when you've got a teacher breaking it down for you. Because Thomas More was Sister Theresa's favorite saint. So of all the saints that we learned about, boy, she hammered More into us as a role model.

Oliver Stone is also a great fan of this film. After *JFK* and *Nixon*, he said that a non-literal-minded movie fan "would tend to view a movie as a first draft, would deepen his perception with reading around it." But is that skirting the issue? What do you think is a filmmaker's responsibility to history?

SMITH: Considering the source of the quote, obviously the filmmaker doesn't feel the need to be historically accurate. And it's based on a lot of conjecture. *JFK* is one of my all-time favorite movies as well, one of my top five, right up there with *A Man for All Seasons*. And you know, that movie was riddled with inaccuracy but presented in such an entertaining, thought-provoking, and authoritative package that I bought it hook, line, and sinker.

It wasn't until my friend Vincent read the Jim Garrison books after that movie came out that Vincent started debunking left and right: "Well, this didn't happen, this didn't happen, this was kind of thrown together . . ."

But I like the idealized version. I guess that's the filmmaker's job, right? To idealize the historical figure and distill their entire life down to these few moments in time that supposedly represent them. When or how could you ever possibly do that? For all we know, More was a wife beater. I hope not, but we don't have an entire picture. Bolt was working at an even greater loss, because his source material wasn't even alive.

The more you read about Thomas More, the more complicated he becomes. For example, he had people burned at the stake for heresy when he was chancellor.

SMITH: I've gotten into arguments with people, because I see him as something of a role model and a man to be admired, and people will point out very quickly that had he been in America in the early 1700s or 1800s, he would have been burning witches. But I tend not to lean too heavily on that. I tend to chalk it all up to, well, that was a time when everybody was deeply religious.

This book is an attempt to rewrite film history and open people up to new works, but my initial argument with you over choosing this film was: it's not overlooked, because this movie swept the Oscars in 1967.

SMITH: Right. But nobody remembers that. That was at a time before the Oscars became as fetishized as they are.

It beat out *Alfie* and *Who's Afraid of Virginia Woolf?*
SMITH: Right. But nobody remembers it, and particularly people in my age group. You know, a lot of people remember *On the Waterfront*. A lot of people remember classic movies that didn't win Oscars but are thought of as classics and have high rotations on television, even pre-cable. This was a movie that doesn't have high rotation on television, because the subject matter's so rarefied.

Why did you feel so strongly that this had to be your choice? I lost this argument with Richard Linklater, too, because his overlooked movie is *Some Came Running*, for which Shirley MacLaine was nominated for an Oscar. So slowly, Oscar movies are creeping into this book.
SMITH: I think the fact that it swept the Oscars makes it even more tragic, because you would imagine it would be a movie that would be remembered. But it's not; it's a multiple-Oscar-winner that barely anyone ever thinks about or talks about or cites as an influence.

I've been in many conversations with people who work within a studio system who have never seen that movie. People who work in the movie biz never saw that movie. When I would talk about it in my Q&As, people would be like, "I've never heard of that movie."

Your wife, Jen, doesn't like the movie, right?
SMITH: My wife loved *Howards End* and she loved *Sense and Sensibility*, and these are period pieces as well that are dealing with loftier issues—issues of character, conscience, and morality.

But I think my wife's block for *A Man for All Seasons* came because it was about a man's faith in God and she does not identify with that at all. To her, God equals religion, and religion is the worst thing that ever happened to humanity as far as she's concerned. It's tough to get her to watch that movie without her being like, "Well, he's giving up his life for an imaginary supreme being, and widowing his wife and orphaning his child."

Is *A Man for All Seasons* different for someone who believes in God, and how?

Smith: I think so. I think it's a far more powerful film if you have any sort of faith or sense of spirituality or belief in God. Yeah, I would have to say so. Because without it, this guy is facing a dilemma that's easily broached. People who don't necessarily believe in God or have some kind of deep spiritual background or religious background are just like, "Look, just sign the piece of paper. Who gives a shit?" Because this dude can't do it on peril of his soul.

Having done eight years of Catholic school, from first to eighth grade, we're kind of taught that there's no greater sacrifice man can make for God than to give up his life defending his belief in God. You know: the martyr or the hero. Which is kinda shitty, because it's one of the greatest ways to become a saint—one of the only ways to become a saint—but at what price? And I guess, to me, it's about releasing the corporeal and embracing the spiritual. Here's a guy who wanted to keep his life, but to him, his soul was far more important than his body.

So, having been raised with that belief and watching a guy who I could identify with more so than Saint Peter or Paul or any number of the other saints who got it real bad because they were preaching the word of God—this was a guy who was a layman and had a government job, for lack of a better description. And couple that with the fact that he was a fucking lawyer! And even at the age of thirteen, I knew lawyers were shitty and alleged to be duplicitous. I mean, the job of a lawyer is to defend at all costs! So to me, it ties in with all I was taught in Catholic school: God before everything else, including your own life.

When you were in England, you took time to see all the Thomas More sites you could find. What was that experience like?

Smith: Really cool. It was kinda like, I would imagine, the cats who come down to Jersey and go to the Quick Stop from *Clerks* or the park where Holden and Alyssa sat in *Chasing Amy*, or stand out in front of Jack's Music Shoppe where Holden and Banky's apartment was. It was kind of like that; I was in fanboy mode.

But it had deeper historical significance, because I could go to those places, like Chelsea or the Tower of London and realize that More actually walked there and died there. There was infinitely more power to it. But still, to boil it all down, I was just a fanboy.

Has your perception of this film changed as you get older?
SMITH: If anything, it's become even more watchable later in life, and that's coming from a guy who watched it multiple times when he was a kid off of that one tape. I wore that tape into the fucking VCR. It's even more enjoyable. It's one of those movies I totally love sharing. I'm married now, but back in the day, it was a real great litmus test for when I was dating. Pop that in—if a chick didn't dig it, I knew she wasn't long for this relationship.

Tell me, what's your interpretation of the title?
SMITH: Well, it comes from a quote in regards to More, but my interpretation of it really comes down to: it was about a guy who, it didn't matter when, or didn't matter at what point in his life, could always be counted on to be the same individual. No matter what the circumstances were.

What is your favorite line?
SMITH: "Why, Richard, it profits a man nothing to give his soul for the whole world. But for Wales?"

It's a really powerful, deep, sad sentiment, but it's got a fucking zinger on the end of it. Even in that moment of gravitas, this guy who had a singular wit was able to pull something out of the bag that was actually music, too, and biting. At least as he's portrayed in the movie, this is not a guy who is caustic with people; he was always very straightforward. So that's as close to insulting, or as close to a slap, as he gets. You know, by just kind of using his wit.

22

Antonio Campos
Murder by Contract

Claude (Vince Edwards) is an unusual hit man. He wasn't born to the life, but instead he made himself a resourceful, calculating contract killer with an existentialist worldview. "He is so committed to his point of view and his philosophy that he's developed—you respect that," says Antonio Campos, who champions *Murder by Contract*. Campos praises the stylized off-camera hits, the economy of shots, and Edwards's lead performance in this B-level noir film, shot in eight days.

That's not to say he thinks it's a perfect film. "What's also charming about the film is that it is kind of a diamond in the rough," Campos says. "Whatever rough edges *Murder by Contract* has are ultimately completely overshadowed by the brilliant dialogue and the commitment to a tone that was so ballsy."

Antonio Campos, selected filmography:
Afterschool (2008)
Simon Killer (2012)

Murder by Contract
1958
Directed by Irving Lerner
Starring Vince Edwards, Phillip Pine, and Herschel Bernardi

How would you describe *Murder by Contract* to someone who's never seen it?
Campos: It's a faithful noir film about a contract killer, from a time when not many films were made like that.

What made it special?

CAMPOS: I remember vividly, I'd seen it at the Film Forum, and I remember feeling like I hadn't seen anything like that in the program, and also I'd never seen anything like that outside of even contemporary film. Obviously there are contract-killer films now, but there was something about it, and the lightness, the light touch that it had, that really struck me as something very unique.

Let's talk about the star, Vince Edwards, who was best known as the lead in TV's hospital drama *Ben Casey*. Can you talk about him as a leading man?

CAMPOS: The first time I ever saw Vince Edwards was in Stanley Kubrick's *The Killing*. And I think he's one of these B actors from that period. I was thinking about Vince Edwards and I was thinking about Jim Carrey—they're very specific kind of actors but could never be the classic leading man. Vince Edwards could be the leading man in that film, but he couldn't be—he would never be—the movie star that he probably wanted to be. And I find those kinds of actors fascinating.

What does Edwards do in this role that makes him so magnetic, that pulls us through the film?

CAMPOS: It's his charisma as an actor. As a character, it's the fact that he believes in something. As fickle as it may be, he has this amazing control. He is so committed to his point of view and his philosophy that he's developed—you respect that.

If the film was made today, you'd have a little bit more violence to make the character a little more complex. You're kind of rooting for him from the beginning.

This is Edwards's first film with Irving Lerner, a former documentarian, and shot in eight days.

CAMPOS: What I find really interesting is that it isn't a perfect film. It's not a film that you watch and you think, "This guy is some brilliant unknown director!" What's interesting is, for example, the first scene where Claude meets the character of Mr. Moon, that long shot that plays out. That felt like

a very strong choice. It felt like Irving Lerner was in complete control of the way this film was made.

In *Afterschool*, many of your characters are also kept out of frame, especially in that first twenty minutes. Am I right to draw that parallel to *Murder by Contract*?
CAMPOS: It wasn't necessarily a direct influence. There was a certain kinship, I felt, with the way that he was approaching his composition.

My feeling about offscreen action and that fragmentation of characters is that you heighten the mystery and the tension because you're holding back someone who feels very important to the story. Those moments in which the characters are offscreen or, for lack of a better word, decapitated by the frame, you almost make the universe of the film larger. In terms of *Afterschool*, you always felt like there was a bigger world outside of the frame that you wanted to see and also a bigger world outside of the frame that you couldn't see. That, to me, is one of the things that can make a smaller film or a lower-budget film feel bigger.

And one of the other parallels is the solitary nature of Vince's character, especially inside his room—something it shares with the protagonist in *Afterschool*. Was that sequence influential?
CAMPOS: *Murder by Contract* definitely could've played a sort of subconscious influence on me. I find that there are the filmmakers whose body of work I've become very familiar with, but then I'm aware of them influencing me. And then there are those one-off films that I see that subconsciously have made a greater effect on me that I don't realize.

That particular sequence also influenced Martin Scorsese. Lerner's austere training montage is reflected in *Taxi Driver*.
CAMPOS: For Claude, it's a job, and he's had to train himself. He says many times that this is not the way he was born. He's developed a certain coldness intentionally so that he can be a contract killer. Obviously, film noir was so much about antiheroes, and this is about someone who is a very cold-blooded killer and so calculated. The other thing that struck me is his point of view of the world that was quite misanthropic and quite cynical, but

at the same time, he had a heart and he had certain principles that he was struggling with.

When you discover that there is something that he won't do—kill a woman—all of a sudden you realize there is humanity there. He can get away in the end, but there's the revelation of who he really is and what he's really capable of.

Why do you think we, as viewers, are drawn to the charismatic psychopath or sociopath?
CAMPOS: We're drawn to them when they're done a certain way. *Taxi Driver*, for example, has Travis Bickle, and Bickle is the charismatic sociopath. At first, you sympathize with the fact that he is so disconnected and confused.

I don't feel like they're completely sociopaths. They have sociopathic tendencies or something, but deep down inside, there is a heart and humanity. They've developed coldness, and the film is challenging that—and then reveals their humanity.

The murders have this *Godfather*-like quality, because each hit is very stylized even though, again, it takes place offscreen. How did that impact you when you first saw it?
CAMPOS: One of the things that I really loved about the film is the playful element to the very dark subject. That contrast creates a certain tension for the viewer. You're going along with this central character who is doing awful things, but you are fascinated by it, and at the same time, you're turned off by the character. You're excited because it's exploring a side of humanity that exists and is within all of us, but it's in a movie, which is the safest way to be the voyeur.

Afterschool is often referred to as a very graphic film, and for me, it's the complete opposite. I tend to avoid showing violence in close-ups or in a direct way, and I'm always more interested in finding ways of hiding the violence or presenting the violence in a way where there's so much more that your imagination fills in. And it's interesting, because I think the new film that I'm finishing right now, *Simon Killer*, is much more of a straight noir. And I would say that the noir film I've seen and literature I've read had a much more obvious effect on that film than *Afterschool*.

You were talking about the portrayal of violence. The cinematographer on *Murder by Contract* was Lucien Ballard, who later shot *The Killing* and *The Wild Bunch* and *The Getaway*. If he was the model of restraint on this film, he certainly overcompensated for it later in his career. Can you talk about what he brings to the film?

CAMPOS: The moments that I really love in the film are the restrained ones. The moments where they hold on a shot, but I don't think he delivers the kind of cinematography that you would expect from someone as accomplished as him.

Tell me about your favorite scene in *Murder by Contract*.

CAMPOS: It's a bit of a tangent. It has nothing to do with anything. But it's the scene between him and the room-service waiter, Harry. I just feel like that scene alone is worth the price of admission. The monologue he delivers in that scene should be taught in acting classes.

And he's basically berating him for bad service. But you don't think that's him confronting his former self?

CAMPOS: Absolutely. It is that recognition of something that disgusts him and was probably what he was like at some point.

What's so great about this character is that he confronts people in such a direct way, and in a way that's offensive but at the same time magnetic. He's confronting the waiter in a very aggressive way, but in a very honest way. I just find that scene to be hilarious in a lot of ways but also just shocking. And it's all dialogue. It's just two people in a room and one character calling somebody out.

There are also great one-liners as well, such as when he calls a gun store "a warehouse full of murder."

CAMPOS: I feel like in order to compensate for the fact that they couldn't be as graphic in terms of the violence, his aggression and their monologues really exposed the darker side of humanity.

And the whole gun store back-and-forth between him and George (Herschel Bernardi) is brilliant. George is all excited about this plan of getting military weaponry to basically blow up their target's house, and then Claude

draws a comparison between himself as the killer and any soldier as the killer. When a soldier doesn't kill, he's court-martialed and seen as a coward. Whereas if he does kill, he's a better citizen.

Later in life, Irving Lerner worked with Scorsese. He was Scorsese's supervising editor on *New York, New York*, and that film is dedicated to him. But if there's any legacy that Irving Lerner has, what do you think it is?
Campos: When I was watching the film, I felt like Quentin Tarantino must've seen this film at some point. The way that he treats Claude reminds me so much of the way that Tarantino is so playful with his killer characters. There was a certain kind of cynicism in that film that I feel like is much more present in films today, that he was doing something very much ahead of his time. The contrast of that playful, almost Fellini-esque music against such a story that could've been treated very heavy-handedly.

That is the very spare guitar score by Perry Botkin. It was influenced by *The Third Man*, and Scorsese said it was this score that led him to the guitar score in *The Departed*. What is the effect of this very interesting, spare score?
Campos: For me, I feel like it's such a misdirection of the film. The score actually allows for you to go along with that character in a much easier way than if the score were heavy-handed. They are playing two very different ideas against each other. Just the playfulness of it draws you in and gives the film a levity that then allows you to keep going on this journey with this guy who's killing people cold-bloodedly.

But also what's brilliant about it is that at the end, you have an amazing moment of humanity. I mean you see him not kill Billie Williams, his female target. And there's that beautiful shot of her picking up the tie. The commitment he made to that score throughout the film makes that last moment resonate in such a beautiful way.

I had a strange reaction against the ending of the film, because it felt so abrupt. I realize it's only eighty minutes long, but it seemed abrupt to me. When you first saw it did you have a similar reaction, or am I alone?

Campos: I just watched that film again, and I, alone in my room, started applauding. That's the life that Claude has chosen. I mean, there was no other way—he was gonna get shot, he was gonna get killed. And I love when they don't glorify a death. Someone's gonna shoot you in the back. He was killed by two random policemen.

I feel like so many of those B noir movies end like that. They just end. They're literally just, "The End," and then in the Film Forum, the lights go on and you're like, "Whoa. I didn't realize the film was over." But I do appreciate that.

And some of the other rough edges are trademarks of the time: a lot of rear projection, a lot of stock footage.
Campos: I kept thinking, "Well, someone just took the master of that film and fixed the glitches." Because there are so many glitches. Sound drops out in places where it doesn't make sense for sound to drop out. What's also charming about the film is that it is kind of a diamond in the rough.

I made a film called *Buy It Now*, and the film was made for a thousand bucks in film school. When we played it in Cannes, we were up against films that cost eighty thousand dollars with big crews and big production designs, and we made this little movie on video with a crew of four. There was one shot in which you actually see the boom pole come in and out of frame.

At the end of that screening, I thought, "Well, we're fucked," because no one's gonna see past that. But the film won the prize, and I think that what the jury thought was that there was something unique about the film, and there was an approach that was unique and daring and that you looked past those mistakes, the rough edges.

Whatever rough edges *Murder by Contract* has are ultimately completely overshadowed by the brilliant dialogue and the commitment to a tone that was so ballsy.

23

John Woo
Le samouraï

John Woo is a man of few words. It's easy to understand, then, why he has such an affinity for French star Alain Delon in Jean-Pierre Melville's *Le samouraï*. Delon's quiet, trench coat–clad assassin left such an impression that Woo modeled his own killer Chow Yun-Fat in *A Better Tomorrow* on the performance.

Woo talks about something action movies aren't generally known for: characterization. As he puts it, "In one shot, you tell the whole story." Below, Woo recounts meeting his matinee idol and reveals which parts of his films were direct homages to Melville. There are more than you might think.

John Woo, selected filmography:
A Better Tomorrow (1986)
A Better Tomorrow II (1987)
The Killer (1989)
Bullet in the Head (1990)
Once a Thief (1991)
Hard Boiled (1992)
Hard Target (1993)
Broken Arrow (1996)
Face/Off (1997)
Mission: Impossible II (2000)
Windtalkers (2002)
Paycheck (2003)
Red Cliff (2008)
Red Cliff II (2009)

Le samouraï
1967
Directed by Jean-Pierre Melville
Starring Alain Delon, François Périer, and Nathalie Delon

How would you describe *Le samouraï* to someone who has never seen it?
Woo: It's about a killer who has great honor. The Chinese translation for the movie was *The Lonely Killer,* and Alain Delon is so cool. He doesn't even say anything, he just watches. There's a lot of language on his face.

How did you see the film?
Woo: It was in a pretty commercial theater in Hong Kong. At that time, Alain Delon was extremely popular. People were crazy about him—he was number one.

When I watched the film, I just kept my mouth open. From that movie, I found out about director Jean-Pierre Melville. It was very unusual to make a movie like that. Not much dialogue, very quiet, and very stylish. It's the coolest movie [*laughs*].

Let's talk about style. Delon made trench coats look cool.
Woo: That's why, when I made *A Better Tomorrow,* I put Chow Yun-Fat in a trench coat. It's like Delon. In Hong Kong, it's so hot. People would never wear, even in winter, a long coat.

But after *A Better Tomorrow,* Hong Kong people did wear long coats. . . .
Woo: Yeah, yeah. And sunglasses.

As a director, what is your favorite scene in *Le samouraï*?
Woo: One is the opening scene, in his room. He's lying in the bed, and there's a birdcage in front of the camera. Remember the birdcage? And the bird is bumping around and jumping around. It's a long, long shot, just holding the camera, seeing him lying in the bed. And that was the title scene.

So in one shot, you tell the whole story. I mean, it tells who he is, how lonely he is. His only company is the bird. That's why in all my movies, I like scenes with birds.

You actually met Alain Delon a few years ago, didn't you?

Woo: A friend of his told him how much I liked his movies. He had seen my movie *The Killer* and he liked it a lot. And he knew that movie was an homage to Jean-Pierre Melville.

He said how much he loved my movie, and he hugged me, and then he told me a story: Melville owned his own studio, and in the middle of the movie, all of a sudden, the studio caught on fire. It burned everything. Melville went to the studio, still with his pajamas on. It was the middle of night, and Alain Delon also went there. He saw Melville standing in the door of the studio. He's looking inside, and there's a lot of fire. Alain was so curious about what he's looking at, because people were so nervous, so panicked about the fire. Melville turned to Alain and said, "The bird, the bird." He saw the birdcage in the corner. The fire kept coming, and all he was concerned about was the bird he used in the movie.

Delon is not doing any more movies; he works some in television. He said, "It's hard to find a good director, like in the old times." That's why he's not interested in movies anymore. But he still has the same kind of passion, a lot of great energy. He doesn't seem old. He was so kind. He said if I needed him, wherever I am, if I just give him a call, he'll come help right away in my movie.

Are there any other lessons you learned from that film?

Woo: I just made a similar scene, the homage in *The Killer*. Chow Yun-Fat is walking into a nightclub, and in the nightclub, there's a singer, Sally Yeh. She was singing, and they have a little eye contact. And the song, the lyric, was about loneliness, love, and looking for love.

The song seemed to bring them together. They are both lonely and need love. And then he walks past her without saying anything. He goes into the room. The guy he is going to kill is inside the room. He put on gloves, takes the gun, and knocks on the door. He kicks the door in and shoots.

That scene was pretty much like *Le samouraï*. Alain Delon walks into a nightclub, sees the black singer singing, playing the piano, and then he walks past her, goes inside the office, and kills the guy. And Alain walks away.

What made Melville a great director?

Woo: Because there was no one like him at the time. [*Laughs.*] It's hard to explain. Just see more of his movies. Go buy *The Red Circle*. It also has some behind-the-scenes material. The movie was released in 1970. That's the movie I dreamed of remaking for a long time. Have you seen *Hard Boiled*?

Of course.

Woo: There was the moment there where Chow Yun-Fat and Tony Leung are trapped inside the hospital tunnel. They need to blow it up, to find a way out. So he puts the bullet in a hole in the wall.

　　Then he aims his gun at the bullet. His hands are shaking, and all of a sudden, he fires without looking. He shoots it, and the bullet blows up the wall. That idea came from *The Red Circle*.

What did you like about Melville? Why did his movies resonate with you?

Woo: I think we have the same kind of philosophy. We believe in the same kind of code of honor. In the old times, in Chinese society, people who had the true spirit of chivalry were admired so much. Helping people, sacrificing for others. It's the same.

24

Richard Linklater
Some Came Running

As an aspiring artist growing up in small-town Texas, Richard Linklater immediately felt a bond with Frank Sinatra as Dave Hirsch, the struggling writer home from war, torn between a world of debauchery and a world of respectability in Vincente Minnelli's *Some Came Running*.

The film was overshadowed, in part, by the success of Minnelli's light-hearted musical *Gigi*, released the same year. The difference in the style and tone of the two films is just further evidence of Minnelli's talent as a director and his diverse gifts. Here, Linklater discusses Minnelli's penchant for divided characters and why he considers *Some Came Running* the ultimate Rat Pack film.

"So much of what I like about this movie, I can't articulate. It's just a feeling, like looking at a painting, the way the colors and the camera just all add up," Linklater says. "It's just something to be experienced."

Richard Linklater, selected filmography:
Slacker (1991)
Dazed and Confused (1993)
Before Sunrise (1995)
Waking Life (2001)
The School of Rock (2003)
Before Sunset (2004)
Fast Food Nation (2006)
A Scanner Darkly (2006)
Me and Orson Welles (2008)
Bernie (2012)

Some Came Running
1958
Directed by Vincente Minnelli
Starring Frank Sinatra, Dean Martin, Shirley MacLaine, Martha
Hyer, and Arthur Kennedy

How would you describe *Some Came Running* to someone who's never seen it?

LINKLATER: It's a story about Dave Hirsch (Frank Sinatra), the prodigal son returning to his hometown, post–World War II. The movie came out in '58, but it really depicts a period ten years earlier. So the movie itself really is a period piece.

Sinatra plays a drifting soldier and writer who is blocked, who hasn't written in a while. He's cynical and drinking more, but he returns to his home in Parkman, Indiana, where all his colliding, contradictory impulses are played out—his mixed feelings about his hometown and these two worlds that he seems to inhabit simultaneously: both the world of respect, culture, and smart English teachers and then another world of booze, broads, and gambling.

These worlds are embodied by different people, most pointedly his drinking buddy, gambler Bama Dillert (Dean Martin), and Ginnie (Shirley MacLaine), the floozy who he's kind of taken up with. His other world is the hypocritical, social scene of Parkman with his phony older brother—played by Arthur Kennedy in one of the great depictions of a phony—and his frigid wife and all these frigid and false society ladies. The movie just rips the cover off the mannered '50s era of America—just that whole mind-set of conformity. It's a wonderful melodrama.

Do you remember where you saw the film?

LINKLATER: I saw it on campus in '84, at the University of Texas. I was just starting to make films for the first time. This film affected me. I remember the next few days thinking about it constantly; it was so much more than I expected. It was a big eye-opener.

It had something to do with Dave Hirsch's character and something personal with me. I think we're all torn, in a way, between both worlds. I felt

that way personally. I'm from a small town in east Texas. As an aspiring artist at that time, I was moved by his story. He's a writer and nothing's come of it yet, so he gives in to his lower impulses with the gambling and the broads. He can hang out with that world, but he really craves some sort of respectability. Ultimately, Dave inhabits both these worlds, but he's not really at home in either of them.

He was a failed novelist. He had one novel that no one had read. . . .
LINKLATER: The artist out of work is a dangerous thing. He's attracted to these two different women.

Speaking of which, a twenty-four-year-old Shirley MacLaine plays Ginnie, the "loose" girl who follows Dave around. She was nominated for an Oscar for the role.
LINKLATER: Deservedly so. She'd only been in a few films then: *The Trouble with Harry* and probably most importantly *Artists and Models*, the Frank Tashlin movie. She'd also been in *Around the World in 80 Days*, as the Hindu princess.

I always think of Shirley MacLaine as the title character in *Sweet Charity*. I think of Charity as Ginnie come back to life and moved to the big city. I just feel a connection between those two characters for her. She's so great in this movie.

And Sinatra, the story was that he had a print of *Some Came Running*, and it was a film that he would watch over and over. He would invite people over to see it in the screening room, usually under the premise of "Come see how great Shirley is." And she certainly is. I've shown this movie to a lot of people and they just go, "Oh my God." She was the babe of her day.

I think all three of them are fantastic. It's my favorite film of all three of those people: Martin, Sinatra, and MacLaine.

Depending on whose biography you read, Minnelli brought them together—according to his version—but I think it's more likely that Sinatra got his friends a job, making this the first Rat Pack movie.
LINKLATER: This was the first Rat Pack movie, and to me it is the best Rat Pack movie. It's the ultimate Rat Pack movie, although it lacks Sammy Davis

Jr., Peter Lawford, and Joey Bishop. Those guys were always kind of minor players anyway. To me, it was always about Frank and Dean, and Shirley MacLaine as the mascot. But this is unique because these guys are—in a big way—sort of playing themselves.

There are definite parallels between Dave Hirsch and Sinatra. Pre–*From Here to Eternity*, Sinatra was sort of washed-up, not in favor, probably close to being an alcoholic bum, kind of a has-been, and that's where Dave finds himself right at that moment.

This was filmed just after Elvis hit it big in 1956, so Sinatra had been outshined or replaced by the advent of rock 'n' roll.
LINKLATER: Yeah.

It's interesting that you bring up this thing about Shirley MacLaine as the mascot. It's been written over and over that she was the mascot of the Rat Pack. In this film, that's exactly her role. I'm wondering if that was informed by their actual relationships, if you get a sense of that on-screen?
LINKLATER: They couldn't have nailed it so well if there wasn't something personal there. I think they were all buddies.

The thing for me that was off-putting was Bama constantly calling Ginnie and the other girl "pigs"!
LINKLATER: Even she knows she's a pig. There are charges of misogyny. But how can you look at this and not think it's Dave and Bama who are the pigs, clearly? But it is a sad portrayal of a woman's masochism, certainly. Bama is ultimately a piece of shit, but a charming one. But see, Bama never would have responded to Ginnie and her pure love the way Dave does. Dave is an artist. Bama would be incapable of what Dave is capable of.

When you first saw the film, what was it about for you?
LINKLATER: It's a great depiction of a guy dealing with conflicting impulses, a typical Minnelli character, an artist who's divided against himself.

You saw the same guy over and over, whether he's Gene Kelly as *An American in Paris* or Fred Astaire in *The Band Wagon*, Kirk Douglas in *The*

Bad and the Beautiful—an artist who's trying to come to grips. He's trying to reach out to other people. You see these people yearning for some kind of human connection, but there's something within themselves that makes it difficult. It is a depiction of how people come together or don't come together. How your needs really can't be fulfilled by one person.

And in *Some Came Running*, Sinatra is torn between two women—Gwen, the respectable schoolteacher, and Ginnie, the floozy.
LINKLATER: When these women do meet, there's that one just unnerving scene where Ginnie visits Gwen (Martha Hyer) at the school and they talk. In a movie with opposites colliding, they are so opposite that they shouldn't even be in the same scene. It's just unnerving, like they shouldn't be in the same frame together. Opposites colliding everywhere—stylistically and thematically.

According to James Jones, this is what his novel *Some Came Running* is about: "the separation between human beings—the fact that no two people ever totally get together; that everyone wants to be loved more than they want to love." There was some tension about the movie adaptation, so Minnelli's response to that quote was "Why you would take 1,266 pages to say that is debatable." But do you see that theme come to life in the film?
LINKLATER: I think the adaptation of *Some Came Running* is one of the greatest adaptations ever. I'll admit, I haven't made it all the way through the book. I read about three-quarters of it, got interrupted, and never picked it back up. It's dense, it's lengthy, and actually, to Minnelli's credit, the movie's depiction of Ginnie is much more sympathetic than in the book. I just think Minnelli loved women and had a feel for her. She's a great depiction of someone giving unconditionally, and when Dave responds to that, when he asks her to marry him, to me, that's such a moving moment.

Is there a particular scene that closed the deal for you, that made you a fan?
LINKLATER: I love all of it; so much of it's so funny. I love it when Dave first meets Bama; you see him sitting in the background. It's a tremendous use of Cinemascope, one of the best ever, in the way Minnelli frames the shot. You

see his hat before you see him, on the right side of the frame [*laughs*]. Bama and his damned hat. The way those two come together is sort of a seduction between them.

How do you interpret the title?

LINKLATER: I just love it. I find it very moving. I know it's biblical—I think of it as a life metaphor. There are some people walking through life or strolling through life, but people who are really passionate come running. To me, it's about passion.

This movie was quite a departure for Minnelli. What about this film lets you know it's a Minnelli film?

LINKLATER: It's almost impossible to describe; you just have to feel it. I always call it a musical without the numbers—the way it was shot, the colors—and yet it was filmed on location, so it has this realistic quality.

Billy Wilder was quoted as saying that Minnelli was "a decorator." And he certainly was, but I think at the service of something. Visually, he was one of the most interesting directors ever.

That last sequence where the guy is chasing Dave with a gun. The music swells and there's this blast of red—you're getting lighting and things that you would see in a musical on a sound stage, and *boom!* It's real. I just love the way he can amp it up.

There are two great Hollywood stories that came out of the production. The first one is in reference to Shirley MacLaine and Frank Sinatra. They were on set, in his trailer, and the assistant director comes over and says, "Mr. Sinatra, won't you please come out? We're two weeks behind schedule. Please come out." And Sinatra says, "Come in. Is that a script in your hand?"

"Yes that's a script in my hand."

"Let me have it."

So he takes it and flips through it, rips out twenty pages, and says, "OK, we're not behind now."

LINKLATER: That's a takeoff on John Ford doing the same thing when some studio person visited him on the set. I've almost tried that myself.

According to Shirley MacLaine, he had accidentally ripped out one of her scenes. Sinatra's character was supposed to die at the end of the film, not Ginnie. So, according to one story, he said, "Why don't you have her get shot and maybe that will give her more exposure or boost her credibility, maybe she'll win an Oscar"—and that one gesture made her a star.

LINKLATER: How could it be any different? This movie ends at Ginnie's funeral, at a tombstone. Bama takes off his hat. Something he'd never do for anyone, he does for Ginnie. Maybe there's hope for Bama after all. But he's going to die from alcohol and probably of diabetes. He's on the way out. It's grim. . . .

Sinatra was famous for doing one take and then leaving. In fact, Billy Wilder said he would never work with him just because of that tendency. But Minnelli went head to head with him on the set because of this.

LINKLATER: Sinatra felt that his first take was his best take. But yeah, Minnelli had his famous "That was great, darling; let's do it again" kind of direction. And he drove people crazy, because it was often not only the performance but it was "The Ferris wheel in the background has to be in that part of the frame." It was all about the shots.

Well, that's the other famous story: Minnelli is setting up the carnival scene, and he's looking through the lens, and then looks up from the camera and says, "OK, move the Ferris wheel."

LINKLATER: That's a great story and no doubt true.

Minnelli said it was. Sinatra was so pissed that he got in his limo and went back to L.A. But Minnelli's point about this was "Well, if we didn't move the Ferris wheel six feet then it wouldn't be the focal point. You couldn't see it in the background."

LINKLATER: And you know what? He's right. It is beautiful. I heard years later Minnelli asked Sinatra for a song for a movie, and he gave it to him because they were real buds.

They did bend the shooting schedule to suit Frank. From noon to 8 P.M. How are those for hours? Sinatra is just so great in this movie. I think it's

the pinnacle of his acting career. To me, it's the peak of his vibrant middle period, if he has a three-act acting career. . . .

He had a great run in the '50s, *From Here to Eternity* on, but this is the best Rat Pack movie of all time. I think this depiction of him is a guy just like himself, like Sinatra. He was never a soldier; he played them. But here, he is an artist.

Shirley MacLaine said of Sinatra, "Oh my goodness, think of what that man could do if he really worked." She thought he was afraid to see what might happen if he worked up to his full potential. It might destroy everything he's done by playing it casual, which was his screen persona. Right about this time in his career, he was an artist in crisis.
LINKLATER: Or he had been. Certainly, I don't know where he was at this moment . . . it might have been a crisis over Elvis, maybe thinking his singing career was at an end.

In *All the Way*, his biographer quotes Sinatra saying, "I wasted ten years trying to do everything at once and getting nothing really done well." But from your perspective as a fan of this film, what does he do well?
LINKLATER: I think he plays himself incredibly well. Just as the way he would put himself into a song and just interpret it, I think he's so aligned with Dave Hirsch. I think probably this is so close to him and who he was at that moment. And it was a lot of the way he saw himself too.

I'm not surprised that he would watch this film later in life and look back. It's him: that's the guy on the album cover, that's the guy on the lamp-post alone, the cigarette burning. He's forlorn, and other happy people are walking by—but he's conflicted. Maybe if he had a shot of whiskey? There might be some floozy nearby. But fundamentally, he's alone. Maybe, in his heart of hearts, he was that kind of lonely, conflicted guy. I always imagined Sinatra as hugely torn and ambitious.

I think the contrast is between Martin and Sinatra . . . that's where you really not only depict these two characters Bama and Dave, but you see also Martin and Sinatra. While they're friends, I just think that for Sinatra, things meant more. He held grudges. He was aggressive. He was ambitious.

Look at how their lives turned out. When Sinatra died, I felt he had worked hard for his legacy—he sang until the day he dropped, practically. He was on tour as an old man. He was going for something. There was some internal demon in him that needed something in his performance, in whatever it was: adulation, his place in history. He wanted to be more than he was, he wanted to be a tough guy, he wanted to be a gangster. The best quote I've ever heard about these two guys was: "Sinatra wanted to be a gangster and all the gangsters wanted to be Dean Martin." That tells you everything.

What distinguished them?

LINKLATER: Let's look at Martin: a truly gifted singer—maybe not quite Frank, but he's truly gifted. He was a natural actor, a charming, wonderful person but just wildly underachieving, ultimately.

Just go into a record store and look under *Martin*—and then look under *Sinatra*. With Sinatra, you get eight thousand albums of every kind, and Dean Martin, today, you would find his greatest hits. That's all you would find. When they died, Dean Martin got a cursory treatment, but it was nowhere near the outpouring for Frank Sinatra. It was almost like Sinatra had earned that; it meant something to him. Dean Martin, on the other hand, didn't give a shit, you know? His attitude would be, "Why? I'm not going to be around to enjoy it." He never pushed himself—but that was his charm.

I heard that on his TV show Martin got paid like $15 million a year to do this show, and he put it in his contract that he wouldn't rehearse. He didn't need to. He was so smooth, you know? Everything came really easy to him. He was the master of getting the most out of the least amount of effort.

He exuded that character, and that's who Bama is. He says it very clearly in the movie, why he is a gambler: his father "used to gamble when he was plowing up his fields, hoping for a crop. . . . So I figure if a man's gonna gamble, he might as well do it without plowing." It's very funny. He states it very clearly, but he's the kind of guy who's going to confidently wing it through life—just be himself and that's going to be *plenty*, you know? That's going to get all the girls, and it comes easy to him. He's not conflicted; he's happy with who he is.

With Sinatra, you get the feeling he wasn't totally comfortable with his place. He never totally settled in. That's why he's so interesting to look at. His interior is so conflicted. So I know Sinatra didn't do a lot of takes, but that's probably because he knew in the first one he could be himself, and it probably was his best.

Let's get back to Minnelli moving the Ferris wheel. What do you think that illustrates about him as a director?
LINKLATER: He was the top stylist of his day. He couldn't just say, "I've had it in my mind for six months that this shot would be in there" and then go, "OK, well, I don't want to upset anybody; it's not that big of a deal." He had that in his mind: "That's the way it should be. That's the way it's gonna be." If I were working with Vincente Minnelli, everyone would bend over backwards to do anything he fucking said, because he deserved it.

I've been thinking a lot about him lately. I just don't think he's ever gotten the credit he deserves. I think maybe because he was a studio guy completely, whereas Wilder and the other guys were seemingly more independent. But I think Minnelli had the greatest career. I would trade anything to have that. It's a fantasy of mine to be a studio director at MGM for three decades. It just sounds like heaven to have a career like Minnelli.

I'm probably the only guy who flew across the country to see Liza Minnelli perform the songs of her dad on Broadway. There was this great show *Minnelli on Minnelli*. It was wonderful, because she never sang her mother's songs, but she did in this revue. She sang songs from her dad's movies and she did a slideshow and just talked about growing up.

She said, "Most kids go to camp, I went to MGM for the summer." She just talked about her dad, and it was this loving tribute to her father. I just think he had one of the great twenty-year runs. I would say between '45 and '63, arguably, he made more good movies than anybody else in that period. By definition, musicals and some of these melodramas aren't taken as seriously. He just pulls you in; he has a real feel for his characters.

What made you so drawn to him, and why do you think he's so overlooked?

LINKLATER: Well, I think that he could take on such a vast array of material. Like all the great studio directors, he had a huge range. All the guys back then—that was just the way you made movies. With Minnelli, you have the musicals, you have the melodramas, you have comedies, *The Long Long Trailer*; you have *Cabin in the Sky*. You have so much. Yet he found his way into all of these and personalized them.

I would rate him in the same breath as Hawks and Wilder. I think it was his personality. He wasn't very articulate. He personally didn't make a legend of himself. He didn't have a lot of crazy stories to tell. He wasn't that big a character. You feel like he was kind of a quiet guy, the sensitive artist-type dude. He wasn't a notorious person, just kind of an artistic perfectionist.

I see him as the quiet craftsman. He saw the studio as an apparatus to work for him. When the studio system was falling apart in the '60s, he was old, but that was pretty much the end of his career, too. So his fate was MGM's fate, more or less. I don't think you could find a director whose career so paralleled the studio system, the ups and downs.

Speaking of downs, the review from *Newsweek* read, "Despite its lack of thematic purpose (or possibly because of it) [it] shows flashes of brilliance." *Time* wrote, "The spectacle of Director Vincente Minnelli's talents dissolving in the general mess of the story [is] like sunlight in a slag heap."
LINKLATER: It's almost the same thing they would say about Douglas Sirk or anything that's melodramatic. It's why *It's a Wonderful Life* didn't work in its day. It's just too much; it's just too raw. Time has a great way of shaking out a film's core, what it's really about.

When you first watch a movie, you pay your money. Maybe you're on a date. I mean, movies have two lives, obviously. Their short-lived economic life is just how you hook up with an audience at that moment. If you're breathing the same air and it fits into the culture, then you're lucky that the planets have aligned and people respond to your movie at that moment.

Once it's an artifact from the past and you go see it in a repertory theatre or watch a DVD, then it's something else. You see it on its own merits for what it is. You can see more clearly the artist's intentions and the depth in there.

It's always fascinating to see the reviews. Pull out the *Raging Bull* reviews from when that came out and they're all over the place. There's something

unlikable about that film. I'd say, in a similar way, there's something just fundamentally unlikable about Sinatra and Dean Martin in this. Do you really want to pay money to see an artist dig through his own shit? Is that worth your money? And at that time and date, it probably is a little much, even though it is Frank Sinatra. It's misogynistic.

And that comes to the core question of why this movie was overlooked. Certainly Shirley MacLaine and Martha Hyer were nominated for Oscars for it. But it was also up against Minnelli's own *Gigi*, which swept the Academy Awards. Minnelli was against himself.

LINKLATER: See, that's what's exciting, too, in Minnelli's career, to have in the same year made this dark melodrama and then make *Gigi*, one that we all can rally around and say, "We love that."

Some Came Running, on the other hand, audiences seemed to say: "This depicts a world I don't love. In fact, I wish it didn't exist. So thanks for rubbing my face in it and reminding me that we're all kind of phonies. We all want what we can't have; we all are conflicted."

Did you ever have any association with people who worked on the film?

LINKLATER: A buddy of mine, Nicky Katt, an actor I've worked with several times, he was in a movie called *The Limey*. He got up at an awards show to accept an award on behalf of Terence Stamp, and Shirley MacLaine was in the audience.

Nicky got up and said, "Not to be too Ving Rhames about it, but I'd like to dedicate this to Shirley MacLaine for *Some Came Running*," and she came up onstage. In her mind, it was a forgotten film, too. No one hits her up on the street and goes, "You know, you were really great in *Some Came Running*."

Everyone knows Shirley MacLaine from *The Apartment*, and that's a great movie, but *Some Came Running*, to me, is *as good*. It's funny the way the canon exists. I think some of the depictions in it make people a little squeamish.

I forgot to ask, but what were you haunted by that week after you saw it?

LINKLATER: Just a feeling, just an emotion like when someone depicts something dark and personal. I woke up thinking about it the next few days after I first saw it.

I've shown it a lot in the film society that I run. If I can get the good 35mm Cinemascope print, I'll show it to some people who haven't seen it. It's a real eye-opener for people. It's not what you expect; it's deeper and richer and more nuanced.

It's far darker than I expected it to be.
LINKLATER: That's what I think is so ballsy about it. It's getting below the veneer of '50s America. It's creepy and just amazingly current. It's amazingly not dated in a certain way. Things change, but the way guys refer to women behind their backs is not that different. That milieu of gambling, drinking never changes. To me, its cup runneth over. So much of what I like about this movie, I can't articulate. It's just a feeling, like looking at a painting, the way the colors and the camera just all add up. It's just something to be experienced.

25

Edgar Wright
The Super Cops

There's a pretty direct line between the obscure '70s cop film *The Super Cops* and Edgar Wright's *Hot Fuzz*—he swiped a line of dialogue from it. But that's not all. More than anything, Wright said, *The Super Cops* taught him about tone—finding comedy in a deadly serious situation.

The Super Cops, directed by Gordon Parks (*Shaft*), also has a lead performance that Wright hasn't been able to shake: Ron Leibman as rookie cop David Greenberg. "He careens through the film with this absolutely unwavering confidence. It's like watching a film with Groucho Marx as the cop lead," Wright says. "He just made me totally fall in love with it."

> **Edgar Wright, selected filmography:**
> *Shaun of the Dead* (2004)
> *Hot Fuzz* (2007)
> *Scott Pilgrim vs. the World* (2010)
>
> *The Super Cops*
> 1974
> Directed by Gordon Parks
> Starring Ron Leibman, David Selby, Sheila Frazier, Pat Hingle, Joseph Sirola, and others

How would you describe *The Super Cops* to someone who's never seen it?
WRIGHT: Well, *The Super Cops* is very much in that same kind of genre of '70s films based on real-life cases, along with *The French Connection* and *Serpico*. It's based on the real-life exploits of David Greenberg (Ron Leibman) and Robert Hantz (David Selby), two officers in not the best area of New York.

It has the same gritty edge as *The French Connection* and *Serpico*, but there's a slightly more absurdist comedy element to it. It has a hint of Joseph Heller or even the Marx Brothers. There's something about the tone that is very appealing. It has one foot in the gritty '70s cop genre and another foot in that kind of absurdist comedy. It's very interesting to see a real-life story played with a raised eyebrow.

Tell me about the first time you saw the film.
WRIGHT: I saw *The Super Cops* on TV when I was very young, probably when I was six. I remembered the title, I remembered that the cops were nicknamed Batman and Robin, and the lead wore a Batman T-shirt. I remembered the end of the film, where it featured a *Batman*-like sound effect—there was a *Pow!* like in the Adam West TV *Batman*, of which I was a fan.

Actually, *Starsky & Hutch*, ironically, was influenced by, if not *The Super Cops* the film, then the story of Greenberg and Hantz. So *Starsky & Hutch* is a TV show that kind of grew out of the story of these characters.

Now, cut to more than thirty years later when I was writing *Hot Fuzz*, and I was rewatching every cop film that I liked and cop films that I'd never seen. I was in Mondo Kim's in New York, and there was an illegal bootleg of *The Super Cops* that somebody had done straight from VHS. I immediately recognized it as the film I'd seen as a little kid, and I knew it was directed by Gordon Parks, who'd done *Shaft*. And I'm going to admit to buying a bootleg copy of the film.

In fact, the only trace of its existence pre-Internet was that it was in Leonard Maltin's guide. I don't think I'd seen it in any other guide, but Leonard Maltin had given it three stars. So I knew I wasn't imagining this film. When I watched it, I was pleasantly surprised that it was actually really good fun.

How has it aged?
WRIGHT: I was struck by a couple of things as I watched it again. It's not a particularly brilliantly made film. It's very episodic, although it's quite fun. It's got a kind of breakneck pace to it. It's a more lighthearted version of *Serpico*.

This movie is from a screenwriter who I'd really loved: Lorenzo Semple Jr. And until I watched the film again, I didn't realize that he'd written it, but I was quite astounded. Semple had always been intriguing to me as a

writer, because he had written for both the *Batman* TV series and *Flash Gordon*, the 1980 movie version, which I'm a big defender of. Both are, in some circles, derided as camp, but they have an amazing sense of humor and are both incredibly arch and done with a big wink. Both of them are really funny in a sophisticated way. I think that neither of them gets enough credit for how funny they are.

Semple had an interesting career because he straddled the line between camp and more serious material. He also wrote *The Parallax View* . . .
WRIGHT: . . . *Three Days of the Condor, Papillon.*

Yes, these very paranoid, straight films. And then he wrote a James Bond film, *Never Say Never Again*.
WRIGHT: Lorenzo Semple Jr. has a very schizophrenic career. *The Super Cops* is sort of slap-bang between *Three Days of the Condor* and *Batman*.

There's actually a line from *The Super Cops* which we outright stole for *Hot Fuzz*, because it struck me as such an amazing line. First a little setup: David Selby and Ron Leibman are two extremely overzealous cadets basically taking matters into their own hands. They immediately make a bunch of arrests before they've even started. When they take the drug dealers into the station, the desk sergeant says, "When did you start working here?" And Leibman says, "Well, to tell you the truth, we started working here tomorrow."

And there's a line in *Hot Fuzz* where our desk sergeant says, "When did you start?" And he says, "Tomorrow." And that comes straight from *The Super Cops*. That line is totally from *The Super Cops*. So thank you, Mr. Lorenzo Semple Jr.

Let's put this in its proper context. This was Gordon Parks's fourth feature-length film, his last film before *Leadbelly*, which flopped and drove him into television work. He directed *The Super Cops* directly after *Shaft* and *Shaft's Big Score!*, and it's an anomaly in his canon, because most of his films dealt with strong, usually African American characters. Did that seem unusual to you at any point when you were watching it?

WRIGHT: I hadn't really thought about it in that context. I have to admit that the only other film I've ever seen of Gordon Parks's is *Shaft*.

It's really pretty ahead of its time. It took a real-life case and was funny in very serious circumstances. I imagine if the film was made today from real-life cases—especially a controversial case like Greenberg and Hantz—it would be completely ripped apart in terms of its accuracy and the tone.

The thing that's incredible is, at the beginning, you have the MGM logo, and then you have news footage of the real Greenberg and Hantz being awarded a medal of honor by the district attorney. And then you see Greenberg and Hantz holding a press conference and talking publicly, and the real Greenberg is wearing a Batman T-shirt on TV whilst getting a medal. The real Greenberg actually looks like Russell Crowe in *American Gangster*. He's kind of beefy and manly, and he's wearing that T-shirt on TV whilst being decorated.

Later in the film, they show the dramatized version of the opening scene. The press conference is a brilliant narrative trick where immediately before you see them getting decorated, you see the DA, played by Pat Hingle, screaming at them about how much he hates them and then cutting to the same press conference where they're being decorated.

I thought that's an amazing thing to do with a film—to start your film with real-life footage and basically building up to the message of: "Oh, see the start? Yeah, that was complete bullshit. Everybody hates them." These two are loose cannons breaking all the rules and getting into hot water.

I just thought it's something that you probably wouldn't be able to get away with in this day and age. It's funny how a controversial subject matter is dealt with so lightly, and it's got really funny texture. It is going for that same Marx Brothers irreverence and devil-may-care attitude toward authority, like taking *Duck Soup* and actually applying it to a real case.

Let's talk about the performances.
WRIGHT: No disrespect to David Selby, but Ron Leibman is the entire show in *The Super Cops*.

The thing that I really love, love, love about the film—aside from their exploits as Batman and Robin—is Ron Leibman's performance. After having rewatched this, I've become slightly obsessed and been in an ongoing Leibman festival.

He hasn't made that many films and apparently for good reason, as I discovered a bit more about him. Apparently he's very principled and very argumentative and famous for either being fired or walking off films. And then there's a line in a story I read which I found absolutely fascinating. I found out that Leibman was the model for Michael Dorsey, Dustin Hoffman's role, in *Tootsie*.

Really?
WRIGHT: That's what they said, that they had based the character on him. He was infamous for walking off films, getting his name taken off films, being fired from things—and Ron Leibman is an incredible actor.

It's amazing, this Tony Award–winning [for *Angels in America*] actor turns up in a lot of things now. Weirdly, when I showed the film to Simon Pegg, he said, "It's Rachel's dad!" He recognized Ron Leibman as Jennifer Aniston's dad from *Friends*. And then it became the cop film starring Rachel's dad.

But I went on a little mini Rob Leibman crusade, watching *The Hot Rock*, *Slaughterhouse-Five*, *Where's Poppa?* I looked at Ron Leibman's IMDb page and then tried to find every Ron Leibman film. He's also in *Garden State*, briefly. But what an amazing performance! He's sort of like the missing link between Al Pacino and Dustin Hoffman. He's just the most unlikely looking badass in the cop genre.

He doesn't have that same tough-guy thing, yet I believe him more as an undercover policeman than I believe some of those other actors. He careens through the film with this absolutely unwavering confidence. It's like watching a film with Groucho Marx as the cop lead. He just made me totally fall in love with it.

Let's talk about Gordon Parks himself, who had an interesting career. He was better known as a photographer. In fact, most of his obituaries mention his photographic work for the Farm Security Administration, and he did a very famous photo titled *American Gothic*. He was *Life* magazine's first black photographer. What are his strengths as a director?
WRIGHT: Some of the location work is really good in this, and there are really fun, really breezy episodes. I like the bit where Greenberg and Hantz

are in action—they've got white sneakers on, and they're scampering about on rooftops.

There are obviously scenes shot on the stage, but what's shot on location is gritty and kind of madcap at the same time. That definitely really resonated with me.

I wouldn't say there's anything visually that I took to *Hot Fuzz*. It was all really about the tone—the tone of the performances and pacing, which is not something to be underestimated. A lot of '70s films have a different pace to them. Even *Dirty Harry* has a deliberate kind of pace.

The Super Cops feels more like a sort of modern TV show. It's very snappy, and a lot of the gags come from the transitions.

Another shot that really sticks in my mind is when they beat up an undercover officer—not realizing he's an undercover officer. Out of nowhere, Leibman's character drop-kicks this guy and puts a garbage can over his head. And there's one shot where Leibman appears into frame doing this kind of flying karate kick.

What's really interesting to read about is Greenberg and Hantz's exploits afterwards. [Hantz resigned in 1975 after being caught with marijuana on vacation. That same year, Greenberg released a sequel to their story in his book *Play It to a Bust: The Super Cops*. Greenberg was eventually elected to the New York State Assembly but was sentenced to four years in prison in 1990 for insurance fraud. —ed.]

How have people reacted to your recommendation of this film?
WRIGHT: When I was on the *Hot Fuzz* press tour, I did these little festivals of cop films, and I got to show *The Super Cops* to an audience. It played really great! That felt very good to get a good audience reaction from that film. There are very few people who have seen it. It was a very difficult film to see, and so I feel very protective of it.

I'm going to put it in my top ten of classic cop films. It's very memorable, and it deserves to be seen. It's got a great script, the central performance is fantastic, and it really deserves to be celebrated a lot more. No, wait, let's put it in my top five. It keeps going up. I won't be shy about singing its praises.

26

Bill Condon
Sweet Charity

Musicals have long been an interest and a refuge for director Bill Condon, perhaps none more so than Bob Fosse's directorial debut, his flawed but beloved adaptation of *Sweet Charity*. Speaking about the impact the film had on him, Condon says, "Maybe it's being gay, but I think it's the way *Star Wars* was, believe it or not, for kids ten years or eight years later."

The following interview makes a nice companion to Richard Linklater's chapter on *Some Came Running*, in which he also praises *Sweet Charity* and the powerhouse performance by Shirley MacLaine.

Bill Condon, selected filmography:
Gods and Monsters (1998)
Kinsey (2004)
Dreamgirls (2006)
The Twilight Saga: Breaking Dawn - Part 1 (2011)
The Twilight Saga: Breaking Dawn - Part 2 (2012)

Sweet Charity
1969
Directed by Bob Fosse
Starring Shirley MacLaine and John McMartin

How would you describe *Sweet Charity* to someone who's never seen it?
CONDON: *Sweet Charity* is the first movie Bob Fosse made. It's an adaptation of a Broadway musical about Charity (Shirley MacLaine), a dancer who has several romantic misadventures in her quest to find somebody who's going to love her.

Tell me about the first time you saw it.

CONDON: *Sweet Charity* was a communal experience. I was thirteen, in an all-boys high school, and gravitating toward other people who had similar interests. We got ourselves tickets for a matinee of *Sweet Charity*. It was a 70mm film played with surround sound—that whole notion was new that year. Absolutely every seat filled, and your specific seat was ushered. The lights would go down, and then there was a three-minute overture. Then the curtain rose, and the movie went on.

There was intermission and then the second act. They did it like going to the theater. It was a contemporary New York movie, and that was part of what made it accessible. It was something that was so artificial, this musical-comedy form with people breaking into song and dance in a very familiar place. It started me on a lifelong interest in "orphan movies," movies that are unsuccessful or reviled in their time.

I think we had gotten these tickets in the third week of its run; the reviews had come out and they'd been pretty bad across the board. It was thrown on the same junk heap by critics as these sort of overblown, out-of-touch studio musicals like *Star!*, *Finian's Rainbow*, and *Camelot*, and later that year, *Hello, Dolly!*, *Paint Your Wagon*, and *Goodbye Mr. Chips*. None of them made money; a lot of them really just died. In an era of revolution, they were emblematic of a studio system that was basically going to collapse. *Sweet Charity* is fascinating because it really does have one foot in both worlds. Here it is: a G-rated musical about a prostitute.

Why, specifically, did *Sweet Charity* hook you the way it did?

CONDON: There are a lot of things just as it's starting: the bigness, the excitement, the color of it. Again, you can't explain this, because maybe it's being gay, but I think it's the way *Star Wars* was, believe it or not, for kids ten years or eight years later.

Are you telling me *Sweet Charity* is the gay *Star Wars*?

CONDON: I have to say I'm surprised by how many people I meet for whom it means something, this movie. But it was a great big, exciting, sensual experience. You know, it was the red of her hair. It was that intense color scheme that was part of the appeal of it. So, there were lots of little things.

About ten minutes into the movie comes the "Big Spender" number, which I think still holds up as one of the best musical numbers in movies. It's women in this dance hall. That number is part of the coded thing that makes movies of another era so interesting. These are whores, and they're funny too. You want to have fun, and then they stamp their feet at you like they are completely terrifying dominatrixes or something. It's really witty.

Just that line, "Fun, laughs, good time!"—try to get that out of your head after you've seen it.
CONDON: The cuts on those words, the incredible dissolves—they all seem like one organism, one big sexual being. It's incredible. Right when the number builds, the camera just pulls them toward you.

Also, the stylization of it; Fosse didn't embrace the realism of movies entirely, and that's what made it such a thrilling movie compared to these other adaptations. Basically, they're on a stage, and he has you believing that there is a sophisticated lighting technician who is changing lighting cues throughout this whole performance. But it doesn't matter.

He's throwing realism away, and thank God for it. It was a number that was included in *Fosse*, which was then taped for television and shot the same way. He found the perfect way to shoot that number, and that doesn't happen that much with film.

Also, *Chicago* is very much built on the *Sweet Charity* model. *Chicago*, the play, and the movie in many ways, too. Roxie is the Charity figure, and after an overture, she has one number, solo, and then the first big step we have is without her, without the star, and it's a big dance number. In that case, it was "Big Spender," and in *Chicago*'s case it was "Cell Block Tango." "Cell Block Tango" works in a very, very similar way to "Big Spender." There's no question that was a viscerally exciting number that really kind of cemented my feelings for that film.

Bob Fosse's wife Gwen Verdon originally starred as Charity, but what is your assessment of MacLaine as a singer?
CONDON: About as good as Gwen Verdon, frankly. Gwen Verdon didn't have a strong voice. That's not what she was known for. I didn't see Gwen Verdon;

I was too young for that. I had seen her do little numbers and snippets on *Ed Sullivan* shows, and there is no doubt that she was a better dancer.

And it's interesting, because it's the exact same steps. *Sweet Charity* is a very good record of that show, because Fosse didn't reconceive it, and he made MacLaine do the steps that had been built for Verdon. Her voice is limited and thin, as is MacLaine's.

MacLaine's voice is sweeter, probably. I don't think that Verdon's extremely broad Chaplin-esque performance would have translated on film as well. There are scenes in which MacLaine reaches levels that resonate with other roles in her career, certainly *Some Came Running*. It's an incredible bookend to *Some Came Running*.

Did you see the recut version in the theater?

CONDON: A number of times. You know, they say for a great performance, you need a great telephone scene. That scene when John McMartin can't go through with the wedding, and she's forced to call her girlfriends and pretend that he's in the bathroom shaving, is a really heartbreaking scene. When *Sweet Charity* flopped, it flopped big. It was cut and reissued [with several scenes removed, including the telephone scene], so it was a scene that I saw three times and then never saw again. It took on extra resonance for me because it had been lost. Again, it was at a time when you never expected to see that scene again, ever—before cassettes and any sense of movies as something that might be preserved or restored.

Those scenes were so powerful, especially this telephone scene. You needed some cleverness to figure out how to get her out of this, and just the power of love wasn't enough. But I have to say that [the alternate, "happy" ending], the scene in McMartin's apartment that leads up to him finding her in the park, seemed really, really cheesy to me. Universal had a certain look in the '60s: the bad sets with the blond wood, that kitchen set and that theatrical monologue that he had. It sort of makes it hard to embrace it at all. You like them winding up together, but it didn't solve anything.

You talked about how the film didn't have a chance because of reviews. Did these lower expectations play into your love for the film?

CONDON: It could have been, absolutely, and also the fact that the two friends that I was with didn't like the film.

What's interesting about that is it truly was a hopeless cause. You'd never meet anyone who felt this way. It's been fascinating to watch. I think there's a moment when the star count in Leonard Maltin went up one year, and suddenly the verdict had changed. You know, there was a real sense around ten years ago that people were taking it more seriously.

It's not quite *Gigli*, but it's not far from the way that Ben Affleck was thought of right after that film.

Fosse said, "When I finished it, I thought it was very, very good," but responding to the criticisms of it, he said, "I guess I had too many cinematic tricks in it. I was trying to be kind of flashy."

CONDON: It's a movie that is almost impossible to watch without wanting to get in there and just edit it. Just when you think he's about to pull off a number, there comes that zoom right when you don't want it. It's the most zoom-happy movie I think was ever made. There was also this technique of taking stills. This use of stills montages with underscore was very pretty but stopped the movie cold.

It was always a little part of Fosse, a little desperation to appear to be with it when he was always a little out of it because he was a Broadway theater person. That's always true of those theater people. You know they are always just a little behind. So, even as you hear that overture and the curtain came up, they had pit girls singing "*Ba-dop-bop ba-dop-ba*," which Burt Bacharach had introduced into the vocabulary, but by 1969, that already seemed dated.

That's how quickly things were changing. When you are young, you are so sensitive to that. I remember watching it the first time with my friends who didn't like it, and agreeing on the horror of Sammy Davis Jr. [who plays a hippie guru] and his monologue, because he was just so deeply wrong and a cultural joke.

We talked about other misfires, but what does *Sweet Charity* do really well? When is it spot-on?

CONDON: When it's good, the staging and filming of the musical numbers is among the best that we've had in movies, and that's what endures about it.

Also, Shirley MacLaine's performance. I think there are a lot of good people in the movie, but it is a vehicle for her, and she pulls it off. Those two things are the major achievements of that film. But to talk about the first one, I think there are six or seven great numbers that are very well filmed, if you could cut out those zoom shots.

Other than "Big Spender," what numbers stand out in your mind?
CONDON: "Rich Man's Frug" is a brilliantly filmed number.

And all those Edith Head costumes as well.
CONDON: Again, a sharp Broadway satirical number of 1966 gets right to the heart of a certain kind of East Side club restaurant and the kind of posturing that would go on in places like that. That, in the three-year interim, had become completely irrelevant.

It seemed like they might as well have been on Mars. It didn't connect to anything, which made it a chore to sit through, but in later viewings, there's something very pure about the dance and the way it's presented that is thrilling. Movies are such an ephemeral thing, and in this case, this movie got swept aside in the cultural sea change that happened between 1966 and 1969 when it opened.

I was amazed by the quick cutting and multiple camera angles. In at least this way, the movie is ahead of its time. Are there other ways that this movie was ahead of its time?
CONDON: You make a really good point, because that's one of the major criticisms, how jarring it was. Again, I talked about the sound; in "Big Spender," you'll see something very similar in "Cell Block Tango"—with all those sounds turned into music. Then the final note is a client closing his Zippo lighter. And the sound of that lighter—there were people I remember first seeing it, who first gasped a little because it was behind your head in this cavernous theater.

As a kind of visceral experience, *Sweet Charity* was looking to the future, in the cutting style, the camera movement, the sound design, all those things.

There is a big sea change between it and *Cabaret*, because *Cabaret* was the new vocabulary of concept musicals where musical performances and numbers are actually intercut with reality and commenting on that. *Sweet Charity* is still very firmly planted in the Rodgers and Hammerstein tradition of book musical and midcentury style. There's something very, very conservative about that. It is sort of a last gasp of that. So in other ways, I would say no. It was not all that ahead of its time. It was very much living up to its very sad advertising tagline, which is "The musical excitement of the '70s." Which was sad, because the '70s were the end of the movie musical.

How did this film influence you, either as a writer or a director?
CONDON: I don't know if it's explicit, except in *Chicago*. It was an explicit model for both Rob Marshall and me.

But in general, there's a warmth to *Sweet Charity* that *Chicago* didn't have that I think we kind of brought to the film a little. There are basic principles that you return to, and there are ways of shooting numbers that Fosse uses— it's always worth looking at. He did it as well as anybody, I think. I think he got better at it. I think *Cabaret* is better, and I think some of *All That Jazz* is even better than that. So this is seeing his style in its primitive form, but there is some appeal to that.

Of that original production, have you ever run into anyone who was a part of it, and did they illuminate it for you?
CONDON: Absolutely. Chita Rivera. John McMartin was in *Kinsey*. I've actually had a chance to meet Shirley MacLaine a few times, too.

They did illuminate, to a degree. John McMartin is very shy, so it was very hard to get him to talk about it much. Chita Rivera had funny stories, hatred of the little-old-lady wig that he made her wear, and the fact that she looks older in that thirty-five-year-old movie than she does now. She's still resenting the fact that she had to play older than she was.

Shirley MacLaine was just interesting on what it was like to work with Fosse. She remembered the perfectionism and the attention to detail that were really amazing to her and made her feel so secure. I could be wrong, but I got a sense that there's still a scar there because the rejection of *Sweet Charity* was so complete. Those things can't help but throw you into confusion.

27

Alex Proyas
The Swimmer

The Swimmer, based on a story by John Cheever, is about more than what it initially presents. Given Alex Proyas's films, which improve on multiple viewings, it's easy to see the kinship. In what has been called Burt Lancaster's first film noir, he spends most of the movie in swimming trunks (or out of them)—a man disconnected from his past, trying to piece together his life.

"I'm fascinated with perception and memory and keep coming back to those themes," Proyas says. "This film feeds beautifully into that. It's about a man changing his reality. Memory affects reality. If you have different memories in your head than the experiences you actually have, the world is a very different place for you."

Alex Proyas, selected filmography:
The Crow (1994)
Dark City (1998)
Garage Days (2002)
I, Robot (2004)
Knowing (2009)

The Swimmer
1968
Directed by Frank Perry (and Sydney Pollack, who was uncredited)
Starring Burt Lancaster, Janet Landgard, Janice Rule, and Marge Champion

How would you describe this film to someone who's never seen it?

PROYAS: Well, the plot is essentially about a man who makes a plan to swim to his house via all the pools that are in his friends' backyards. He lives in a fairly affluent neighborhood, so all the neighbors possess lavish pools and houses. Through his journey back to his house, he discovers himself. He discovers the truth of his past.

It's sort of an exercise in delusion. He's convinced himself that he's lived a very different life than the one that he finds that he's lived. It's not really memory repression; it's memory fabrication. He's fabricated a very different existence of himself from reality.

When did you see the film, and under what circumstances?

PROYAS: I saw the film when I was very young, and what struck me at the time is I think it was the first time I became aware that a film could be about a terribly flawed individual. Up until that stage—I must have been about ten or twelve—I thought movies were about heroic guys who achieved heroic deeds, and this was the absolute opposite of that. In subsequent years, I learned more about classic film structure and the hero's journey, and this is the absolute flipside of the coin. It's about a guy who, rather than becoming a hero through his quest, self-destructs through his quest. It's still very rich in that respect.

Do you remember the specific circumstances?

PROYAS: I would have definitely seen it on television. I don't remember it very specifically, but I'm sure it would have been late-night television in Australia. I'd switched on the television, there was this interesting film playing, and it drew me in. I probably came into it well into the story and had to pick up the pieces. For a while, I was trying to track it down and see the whole thing.

This is based on a story written by John Cheever for *The New Yorker*. Burt Lancaster called it *"Death of a Salesman* in swimming trunks." Does that parallel stick?

PROYAS: It does. I'd give it the subtitle of "The Crucifixion of the Modern Man." The way Lancaster plays it is really interesting. He plays it as a guy

who's a dreamer, an optimist, and anything but the character he actually is in the movie. What's fascinating is that the Ned Merrill we see on-screen and the Ned Merrill who he really is, who we discover, are two diametrically opposed people. I can't work out whether that's just by chance or whether they were trying to say we all come into the world naked. That parallel is very specific in this movie, because he is naked all through the movie.

I thought maybe they were trying to say that underneath it all, underneath all the lies we create for ourselves, there is another person. The true person. The soul. The character we sometimes create for ourselves can be entirely different from the true person. I felt that was a flaw, in a way, with the film. I felt like the two characters didn't quite come together. You could also view it as a choice that they made.

He remains this closed character throughout most of the film. What we know about him, we only truly know from other people. Can you think of any other film where that's true?

PROYAS: It's pretty unusual. It's a very brave movie, in that respect, and it's a brave role. Actors and directors want characters that the audience can identify with and sympathize with. There are certain rules and tricks that we use to do that, and this sort of breaks them all.

I think *The Swimmer* is similar to a film called *Seconds*, which was made close to the same time. That's a John Frankenheimer film starring Rock Hudson. Again, a very unusual role for him, and the film is very, very dark. It's about a man whose life is in crisis, and he decides to go to an organization that can change your persona. They perform plastic surgery and furnish you with a completely new life. The one caveat is that you cannot ever go back. They pretend you've been killed in a car accident so that your family thinks you're dead, and if you ever try to go back and reconnect with your past, there will be terrible repercussions.

Talk to me about Lancaster. What was so appealing about him, and why was he right for this role?

PROYAS: I think he had this utter optimism. He's almost childlike in the film. When people on-screen are telling us he's a real asshole, we realize he's this affluent guy who's clawed his way to the top, hasn't paid his bills, and has

caused all sorts of people grief. He's probably slept with every woman in the neighborhood, by all indication. But Lancaster doesn't play that character at all. He is totally charming and has this eternal optimism that makes you really like the guy. At the end, you feel as crushed as he does.

What's your favorite scene?
PROYAS: The scenes that always struck me were the ones where I understood the theme of the story. When this kid comes to one of the pools and the pool is empty, it brings everything together. For Lancaster's character, if you believe in something hard enough, then it makes it true. He's desperately believing something other than the truth.

He takes the kid and they pretend to swim across the pool. The great thing about the scene is at the end of the scene. When he walks off and is going to continue his journey, he hears the kid bouncing on the diving board. He runs back, terrified, thinking the kid is actually going to dive because the kid now believes there's water in the pool. The kid looks at him like he's crazy and says, "You thought I was going to dive? There's no water in the pool."

In his mind, he's created water in the pool and believes that there is water, but at the same time, there's something that makes him feel that the kid's going to hurt himself. It's sort of indicative of his past sneaking up on him, tapping him on the shoulder and saying, "You're going to find out eventually."

Some people describe this picture as Lancaster's first noir film. Is noir even a proper term to apply to *The Swimmer*?
PROYAS: I guess it is. One of the characteristics given to noir is that all the characters have something to hide, have a dark past or are flawed in some way. To me, film noir is always intrinsically linked to a style—a visual style, as well. Like the way classic film noirs looked, with the landscape and the wardrobe. I guess the idea that you can do a film noir in broad daylight in people's backyards is an intriguing notion.

It didn't have a studio that believed in it. One writer suggested that "*The Swimmer* crossed a line into a hallucinatory zone where the work

of art—the film—is so much the reality of its times that . . . it seemed unbearable, almost unwatchable." Does that resonate to you?

PROYAS: I agree with the first part of the statement, but I think that's what makes it so watchable. What's fascinating is that it's all about deception, and you start to wonder who's actually crazy in this world. The characters' world is painted with a great deal of disdain.

It's quite openly satirical about these people. They're all obsessed with the trappings of their lives, and they're all horrid people. There's a lot of humor in it I wasn't aware of when I first saw it.

For example, what?

PROYAS: The nudist couple, for example. It starts out with them trying to convince their daughter to come to their house and bring her kids, and she doesn't want to because they're going to be naked. They're these terribly eccentric people who live in this big mansion, and yet they're nudists.

There's one guy who's going on about this horrid skylight he's built over his pool, and now he sits there even when it snows outside and enjoys his pool in the middle of winter. The people in the movie really aren't that nice, and the filmmakers are obviously poking fun at these rich people who live for their material possessions.

What I am interested in is the difficulty of filming a story or a novel. What is the clash between the two techniques of screenwriting and novel writing?

PROYAS: That's a tricky question. They're very different mediums. Film can say so much in a very subtle way that the written word can't, and vice versa. They have their different merits. I'm coming into this film in the best way, because I haven't read the story. If you know a story well and you watch a movie—and certainly, as a filmmaker—you go in saying, "I wouldn't have done it that way."

What are the inherent difficulties?

PROYAS: I think it is that notion that the audience comes in with preconceived ideas, and often when you translate one medium into another, you change things, because as a filmmaker, you think it's going to be better. People may disagree with you.

I think short stories are often more successful as movies because it becomes about the big story. The details can often be filled in a different way. With a novel, it often feels like you're culling something, like you're taking away some of the stuff people like so much about the original work. With a short story, you often have to elaborate. To me, that's often more interesting and results in more successful film.

What I like about the movie is it makes you think. It asks that the audience becomes an active participant. I love films where you're constantly surprised. Things fall into place, and you go, "Aha! That's what's going on." To me, the film sustains that throughout its entire running time. It's quite a clever thing, really.

Has that influenced your work in any way?

PROYAS: I think it has. I'm fascinated with perception and memory and keep coming back to those themes. This film feeds beautifully into that. It's about a man changing his reality. Memory affects reality. If you have different memories in your head than the experiences you actually have, the world is a very different place for you.

Here's a man who's consciously tried to alter his past. He refuses to see he's been such a dismal failure. He changes his memory. He alters his past and tries to inhabit a new world. That's something I've always been interested in, and I imagine, when watching it as a wee lad, it would have had an impact on me.

Is there anything that is quintessentially Perry? How did he make his mark on film history?

PROYAS: I think he's a pretty edgy filmmaker, really. This and *Mommie Dearest* [which Perry also directed] certainly have a very disturbing view of life.

But I think this one more than *Mommie Dearest* has a connection. I understand this guy. He makes sense to me. Maybe that says something about me. To me, he's not just being disturbing for the sake of it. He's finding some sensitive nerves and hitting them so the story resonates with people.

When this film came out, it was roughed up by critics. For a modern audience, how do you think this will play, and what should they know going in?

PROYAS: I think the film has its flaws. The characterizations are a little broad at times. The acting is melodramatic at times. You're aware of those things, but the film is, thematically, so rich.

It was released during a time when Lancaster was habitually saying, "Two more years, and then I want to quit acting." Have you ever thought about how you'd like to check out of the film career? Or are you like Studs Terkel, who wanted to die at his typewriter, working?
PROYAS: I'm pretty much Studs Terkel. I've always said I'm going to die on the set, and hopefully not before my years. It's a tough business. There are days when I have a very different attitude toward that, but you always come back to it. It's the best time in the world. I often say I wish real life would be more like the movies.

28

Sean Durkin
10 Rillington Place

"Claustrophobic" and "dark" are two words that describe Sean Durkin's directorial debut, *Martha Marcy May Marlene*. Those words also serve as an apt description of *10 Rillington Place*, Durkin's choice for this book.

This unconventional true crime story of a serial killer in Notting Hill stars Richard Attenborough in the lead role, as a seemingly meek man hiding a murderous double life for two decades. The case helped abolish capital punishment in Britain.

In the interview below, Durkin says what he likes most about Attenborough's performance is that "his tactics of manipulation are so subtle and believable and quiet and calm. And it's that subtlety that makes him all the much more terrifying."

Sean Durkin, selected filmography:
Martha Marcy May Marlene (2011)

10 Rillington Place
1971
Directed by Richard Fleischer
Starring Richard Attenborough, John Hurt, and Judy Geeson

How would you describe this film to someone who's never seen it?
DURKIN: It's about a young couple who rent an apartment in a townhouse in post–World War II England. The owner of the home, John Reginald Christie (Richard Attenborough), is renting rooms, which is a front for his MO as a serial killer.

It was being screened in a film series at Film Forum in 2007, and I'd never heard of it before, but I wasn't able to see it there. I couldn't find it anywhere on DVD at the time, but my friend Antonio Campos was able to track down some European copy.

Why was it important for him to find it so you could watch it?
DURKIN: I was interested in films about serial killers and films based on true stories about serial killers. I also spent my childhood in England and am interested in making films in England and English crime films. And so it was the combination of all of those things that initially attracted me to it.

A little background about the film: It's directed by Richard Fleischer, who did films such as *Tora! Tora! Tora!*, the original *Doctor Dolittle*, and *20,000 Leagues Under the Sea*—he had a long, storied career. This is one of his least-known films, and his memoir, *Just Tell Me When to Cry*, never even mentions it. Why do you think this film fell through the cracks?
DURKIN: It's relentlessly dark, such a brilliant piece of filmmaking. I've only seen two of Fleischer's other films: *Violent Saturday*, which I was impressed by, and then I saw *The Boston Strangler*—but they are all so different. *10 Rillington Place* felt like it got into realism in a whole other way. There's a card in the beginning that says, "Whenever possible the dialogue has been based on official documents" from the case.

So that should immediately put you in the mind-set. You should completely disregard any standard for trying to create any character who you can really follow—or any character who you can really like or follow through any sort of character arc. It really just depicts this story the way that a piece of journalism might, as opposed to worrying about preconceived notions of what a film should achieve. But I feel like it's so dark. It's too dark.

It's not like Fleischer shied away from dark material. He directed Kirk Douglas in *The Vikings*, Orson Welles in *Compulsion*, and Charlton Heston in *Soylent Green*. But *10 Rillington Place* is a particularly bleak film. The *Los Angeles Times* called it "a model of restraint" in its storytelling. What was your initial reaction to it?

DURKIN: I was struck by the performance, Attenborough's performance. First and foremost, it is one of the best serial-killer performances I've ever seen.

Attenborough's biographer, Anthony Dougan, called the role "possibly his finest screen performance" and then never mentions it again in his book. Why did it so affect you?

DURKIN: It's so singular. It's so convincing and methodical and consistent. He's obviously a complete maniac, but his tactics of manipulation are so subtle and believable and quiet and calm. And it's that subtlety that makes him all the much more terrifying. Then he has these strange moments—like in court, after they announce the verdict, he just lets out that yelp and starts crying. It's totally unexpected.

Why do you think he cries in court after helping convict another man of his murders?

DURKIN: Well, it struck me as a release of human emotion rather than a sign of sadness and remorse. There's another point like that before he kills John Hurt's wife (Judy Geeson). He looks at her in a way—it's this complicated moment when you feel like he genuinely cares for her and has almost fallen in love with her.

He looks at her differently than he looks at the other victims and almost feels sadness for doing it, but it's like this insatiable thirst he has that he can't control. It's that little moment that's so complicated and so impressive.

As a serial killer, Christie is unusual—a man who seems almost afraid of his victims. In most cases, he tricks and drugs his victims into unconsciousness before killing them.

DURKIN: That's a really interesting observation. He's such a weak little guy. He doesn't have the presence you think of serial killers having. But he has a cunning that's so specific and calm. One of the most interesting moments, for me, is when they out him on the witness stand for his shady record.

Up to that point, you develop a respect for him. Not respect as a person, but you are almost impressed by how calmly he handles the whole situation and the manipulative powers he has. And then, all of a sudden, he's outed in court as a thief and petty bully with a criminal record. You just look at him

differently: "Wow, he's just a little weasel." He pulls the wool over your eyes, too, in a way.

You were talking about his tactics. It reminds me of a line from the American remake of *The Girl with the Dragon Tattoo*: "Why don't people trust their instincts? . . . It's hard to believe that the fear of offending can be stronger than the fear of pain. But you know what? It is. And they always come willingly."

DURKIN: Absolutely. That's a great comparison. That's exactly what it is. The red flags are going off. John Hurt's character, Timothy Evans, just goes along with Christie's explanation that his wife died during the abortion and then agrees that Christie should dispose of the body! And he leaves his infant daughter with Christie. It's just insane that he goes with it. It's almost impossible to feel bad for him, because it's ridiculous that he keeps going and going and going.

I saw this movie when I was starting to write *Martha Marcy May Marlene*. There's some definite overlap in the manipulation of John Hawkes's character, a cult leader in my film, and that calm approach Christie has talking people into things. They go along with it in a way that is not violent until that final moment when it is.

Was it an influence? Both films share a sense of claustrophobia.

DURKIN: Yeah, absolutely. When I was setting out to write my first screenplay, I had to give myself some restrictions, such as: how do I create something that is contained to one or two locations without feeling like it's for budgetary reasons? It's definitely one of the things that was attractive about *Rillington*. You are completely restricted, and it's completely natural to the world. That definitely had an influence, and there's definitely a relentless tension that played a part.

***10 Rillington Place* was one of John Hurt's first roles. In the tabloid-like trailer, the voiceover says, "If ever there was an actor to walk in a dead man's shoes, it was John Hurt." Can you talk about his performance a little bit?**

DURKIN: He's so great in it, because you can't believe that his character is doing what he's doing, but you are given enough information—seeing little glimpses of his personality—enough to believe that he is doing it. Does that make sense?

The fact that he's lower-class, uneducated, and illiterate?
DURKIN: You also don't figure out he's illiterate until twenty-five minutes into the movie. It's a really subtle way of revealing that. He has to sign his confession with an *X*.

I love all the little moments in it. Like when the construction guy checks out Judy Geeson as she walks up the stairs, Attenborough sees him and starts chastising him silently. It's this fake display of morals. There are those little interactions, moments of playfulness and humor.

I was wondering, why do you think this film went so unnoticed?

I think it's forgotten because, one, it is relentless and dark, but, two, it is about history people wanted to forget. It had huge implications in Britain. Because the wrong man was executed (and later, posthumously pardoned), the case itself helped abolish the death penalty in Britain. Lastly, an infant is murdered offscreen. I think all of those elements make it something you watch only once.
DURKIN: I think you're right on. I really admire the film for what it achieved. It's not something you want to see again, but at the same time I think it's such an accomplishment. It's so groundbreaking in its lack of form, its lack of following any sort of structure. I think it's an important film.

When you think of *10 Rillington Place*, what is the image that comes to your mind?
DURKIN: The moment after he sells the house and the new people move in. They find the hole in the wall and open it. There are bodies wrapped up, fully wrapped so you just see the form of them—it was so sort of stunning and shocking.

Even though you've watched him kill several people over the course of the film, there's something about this image, the hole in the wall and the

way the bodies are positioned and piled that, it's an hour and a half in, it's a whole new feeling of "Oh my God, what did he do?" With that one image, it just makes you realize it's even worse than you thought it was.

Ultimately, why did you choose to champion this film?

DURKIN: It's such a unique film in how relentless it is and how true to the terror and the fear of the situation. When I make a film, I think about things that scare me. My exploration of those things is to try and wrap my head around them and confront them. And this film confronts fear and the horror of this event in such a real way that it forces you to fully be in that place, be claustrophobic with it—with none of the trappings of filmmaking that let you off the hook. It forces you to fully confront and wrap your head around horrible things that actually happened.

Why do we have a particular fascination with serial killers?

DURKIN: I try to stay away from analyzing society or thinking in terms of that. I try to think about things on a personal level and what affects me. I think there's just a fascination, and I think it comes from fear. It's difficult to comprehend that these things actually happened when you've never witnessed or experienced anything firsthand. The fascination comes from that—trying to understand something that seems so inhumane but it's such a huge part of humanity. I think that's so hard to comprehend. I also think that people like to be scared of movies.

I've seen recently an English miniseries called *Appropriate Adults*, in which Dominic West plays a serial killer. I think that actually is the best portrayal of a serial killer that I've ever seen. That's what I was thinking of when I watched *10 Rillington Place* this time around. What draws me to it is that desire to confront and explore something that seems impossible but is very real and very much a part of our society.

29

Frank Oz
The Trial

"I think he was extraordinarily successful in creating a nightmare," says Frank Oz of Orson Welles's *The Trial*. And a very compelling nightmare at that. Anthony Perkins stars as Josef, a young man caught in a bureaucratic hell after being accused of an unknown crime by an oppressive system. Though written by Franz Kafka in 1923 (and posthumously published in 1925), the story carries overtones of Jewish persecution and a haunting premonition of the Holocaust, which influenced Welles's ending.

Oz, who knew and worked with Welles, defends his friend's artistic choice. "The film is better than the book. It reflects the showmanship of Orson," Oz says.

> **Frank Oz, selected filmography:**
> *The Dark Crystal* (1982)
> *The Muppets Take Manhattan* (1984)
> *Little Shop of Horrors* (1986)
> *Dirty Rotten Scoundrels* (1988)
> *What about Bob?* (1991)
> *The Indian in the Cupboard* (1995)
> *In & Out* (1997)
> *Bowfinger* (1999)
> *The Score* (2001)
> *The Stepford Wives* (2004)
> *Death at a Funeral* (2007)

The Trial
1962
Directed by Orson Welles
Starring Anthony Perkins, Jeanne Moreau, and Arnoldo Foà

How would you describe this film to someone who's never seen it before?
Oz: A nightmare about a man being lost in the system.

When did you first see the film?
Oz: I must have seen it in New York in the '60s when it came out. I'm pretty sure I did. At that time, I was very much into film with Jim Henson and the Film-Makers' Cinematheque. It was an extraordinary explosion of new ideas in film. When I saw *The Trial*, I was stunned. The elements of the movie are just stunning to me. The atmosphere, the nightmarish atmosphere, he created was just extraordinary. In a way, I feel bad because I'm not talking about this film as a filmmaker. I'm not being smart enough, because all I know is that it just fucking affected me.

Welles has been quoted everywhere saying, "When you do a play, you make it for an audience; when you do a movie, you make it for yourself." When he was interviewed in 1962 on the BBC, he said he had not considered audiences for this. He said, "*The Trial* is made for no public, for every public, not for this year, for as long as the film may happen to be shown. That is the gift of gifts."
Oz: I think that totally makes sense. I think he totally believed that he made the film for himself and said "Fuck it," but I don't believe that for film in general. I think the criteria are that you make it for an audience, otherwise you get indulgent, and, to a degree, *The Trial* is indulgent.

It's like Welles's *Touch of Evil*; it stews on top of his ass all the time. If you look at *Touch of Evil*—that's one I studied—the extraordinary locking to create tight shots and medium shots and wide shots on a master. Welles did that for economic reasons, and it turned out incredible. That was not the case in the nightmare. He still had masters, but he didn't create his own close-ups and medium shots and wide shots. The wide angle he used a great deal. Towards the end, that gave it that ominous feeling.

What advice would you give a modern audience?

Oz: I'd say experience it and feel it viscerally as a man giving you the gift of experiencing a nightmare for not a few seconds, but an hour and a half, and that feeling of being lost in life.

Had you seen Anthony Perkins in *Psycho* by the time you saw *The Trial*?

Oz: Anthony Perkins just seemed like an alien in that movie to me. The word that describes him most is "lost"—so lost. The pattern, the dialogue there is just so unrhythmical. It seemed to stop and start. It also seemed that when he spoke, it seemed to be halting. I know that was partly his looking back on something he did, but it just made it seem more alien.

When Josef dies in the book, he just lies down and allows himself to be stabbed, but Welles has Perkins play Josef as defiant until the end. Here's the reason he gives for that—again, this was written in 1923 and filmed forty years later: "I don't think Kafka could have stood for that after the deaths of the six million Jews. . . . It just made it morally impossible for me to see a man who might even possibly be taken by the audience for a Jew lying down and allowing himself to be killed that way."

Oz: It's striking, because it does contradict what he said there—because he's talking about how it affects the audience. He was talking about that film being made for himself. But truly, he did care about the audience and how it affected the audience. I believe it is important to him. As an artist and an entertainer, he always had to care about what the audience thought.

The film is better than the book. It reflects the showmanship of Orson, who was extraordinary in that way, knowing that the audience doesn't want to follow this journey, and then all of a sudden have the main character allow himself to be killed and leave unsatisfied.

Tell me about meeting Orson Welles.

Oz: It's so odd, because I didn't want to ask him about movies. I didn't ask him one question about movies, because that's what everybody does. We were doing *The Muppet Movie* and Orson came in for a day to shoot. Everybody was scared of him. I just started talking to the guy, and it was delightful. He invited Jim Henson and me to dinner the next night, and that was quite wonderful.

He was a very big fan of ours; he was so taken with our characters. He was trying to sell his own talk show, so he asked Jim and me to be guests on that show. I didn't want to be a fan talking about his films.

He did say one thing about *Citizen Kane*, but I wish I could have talked to him about *The Trial*. He was telling the story that a student came up to him once and said, "Mr. Welles, can you answer a question?" He said, "What is it?" "When Charles Foster Kane dies, he says 'Rosebud.' How do they know he said that, because no one was in the room?" And Orson said, "I told him, 'Never tell a living soul, because it's true.'"

Tell me about a particular scene in *The Trial* that you're drawn to.
Oz: The scene where he wakes up and the guys come in is extraordinary. The scene that I'm drawn to is where there's Orson with Romy Schneider. I always remember her parting her hands and having the web between her fingers. The scene that strikes me more than anything else is the actual trial scene. That's absolutely stunning to me. Again, I'm totally aware that the film doesn't work as entertainment but, boy, does it work as a hit in the stomach. I think he was extraordinarily successful in creating a nightmare.

In *This Is Orson Welles*, Peter Bogdanovich said, "I've always felt that, unlike the rest of your films, *The Trial* is not really entertaining—just on that simple level." That brings me to a very central question about filmmaking: are we meant to enjoy everything? If it's not enjoyable, should it be engaging, and where do we draw the line in this age of test-marketing movies?
Oz: Movies are made for people, and they should either be enjoyed, or people should be compelled by them, or they should be touched by them in some way. You're not making it for yourself or a friend of yours; you're making it for a lot of people. There are movies that don't work, like *The Trial*, but there are extraordinary things about it that have tremendous value.

Why, specifically, does the movie not work?
Oz: It doesn't hold up. As a filmmaker, I can see now that there are very long scenes. The scenes themselves are not compelling, dramatically. The conflict is not evident. The individual scenes, certainly, and the accumulation of scenes

are not, I guess, entertaining, because they go on too long. There's a master shot all the time. You can't see people's faces. The dialogue repeats itself a lot. It's almost like Orson said, "Okay, just ramble on," and that's *not* entertaining. The reason you have a cut in a movie is because you want to show emotion or build tension or build action. I think because of economic reasons, he didn't use the cuts very much. That didn't help the movie.

What it did help, on the other hand, was the nightmarish quality. On the one hand, I think it was not as successful as entertainment, but it was extraordinarily successful with its own limitations—because of its limitations, possibly—as a nightmarish feeling.

The project nearly fell apart when financing fell apart. And so Welles had to go to Paris, and they couldn't build sets, but he found this huge abandoned train station. There's a quote from Welles that seems to reflect that: "The great danger for an artist is to find himself comfortable. It's his duty to find the point of maximum discomfort, to search it out."
Oz: To a degree, I think comfort is an enemy. Maybe satisfaction is, too. Matisse once said something like, "Please tell people I'm a happy man." You can still be happy or feel good about your life, but there's got to be something inside you that you're trying to work out, some conflict. You don't have to be Tennessee Williams, where you're creating characters to be different aspects of yourself.

One more thing about being comfortable—I've always felt that "comfortable" was a dirty word. If I was in a wagon train, the last thing I'd want to do would be stay with the women and children. I'd want to be out there alone as a scout and scouting ahead.

How has this film changed for you? How has your perception changed in subsequent years?
Oz: Well, before, it hit me in the face. In fact, I was a peasant in a village coming for the first time to see a film; it was that kind of experience. This time I saw it, having made some films, totally that are different from Orson—I'm only an entertainer, he was an artist—now I see why he did the masters like that, in my opinion, why economically he did it, why for this vision he did it.

What are its enduring virtues?

Oz: The tone, the ambience, the atmosphere, the visceral feeling of being lost in the world. I think the nightmarish tone, the mood—it's like smoke that seeps across the audience.

Why do you think this film still hasn't found its audience?

Oz: I don't think it ever will. I think there's a reason why it hasn't found its audience, because it really isn't entertaining. To be entertaining you have to be aware of the audience more and how long they'll accept a scene, how long they'll like a character, what conflicts in a particular scene that lead to the next scene really build the story. He wasn't thinking about that. He just didn't give a shit. He said, "Fuck it. This is what I want to do."

30

Peter Bogdanovich
Trouble in Paradise

Famously, director Billy Wilder kept a sign in his office that read, WHAT WOULD LUBITSCH HAVE DONE? Straddling both the silent and "talkie" eras of motion pictures, Ernst Lubitsch (1892–1947) moved effortlessly between Mary Pickford melodramas and lush musicals and later directed Greta Garbo (*Ninotchka*) and Jack Benny (*To Be or Not to Be*) in unforgettable, against-type performances. But Lubitsch is remembered as a director's director, which is a kind way of saying, "Brilliant but forgotten."

But not by everyone. In 1998, Hollywood remade his Jimmy Stewart vehicle *The Shop Around the Corner* into the Tom Hanks/Meg Ryan romance *You've Got Mail*. Later, in 2003, the Criterion Collection started to rerelease his films in lavish DVD packages, and aided by outspoken praise from directors such as Peter Bogdanovich, Lubitsch was introduced to a new generation of film aficionados.

In this interview, Bogdanovich calls *Trouble in Paradise* that "high point of sophisticated comedy, yet it's as light as a soufflé."

Peter Bogdanovich, selected filmography:
Targets (1968)
The Last Picture Show (1971)
What's Up, Doc? (1972)
Paper Moon (1973)
At Long Last Love (1975)
Saint Jack (1979)
They All Laughed (1981)
Mask (1985)
Texasville (1990)

The Thing Called Love (1998)
The Cat's Meow (2001)

Trouble in Paradise
1932
Directed by Ernst Lubitsch
Starring Herbert Marshall and Miriam Hopkins

How would you describe this film to someone who has never seen it?

BOGDANOVICH: It's a very sophisticated romantic comedy. It's a story about a couple of jewel thieves, con artists, who meet. They have a date, and then they fall in love when they find out who each of them is.

I saw it first in the '60s and a couple of times since then. I thought it was brilliant—one of the best I've ever seen. It keeps getting better.

Why do you think that is?

BOGDANOVICH: Well, most things improve, if they are any good. Ernst Lubitsch is one of the great directors. As his work ages, it improves—most of them, not all of them.

This tale was taken from the true story of George Mondeau, a career thief who had two silent films made about his life before this. But Lubitsch took this obscure Eastern Bloc tale and adapted it.

BOGDANOVICH: It totally has a European sensibility.

And don't forget, Lubitsch is the director who changed Hollywood. In the mid-1920s, it went from totally influenced by D. W. Griffith to being totally influenced by Lubitsch. Everybody wanted to make a Lubitsch movie. They all wanted to figure out what he was doing by indirection.

I once asked Jean Renoir, "What do you think of Lubitsch?" And he said, "Lubitsch? He invented the modern Hollywood." Modern Hollywood, by those standards, when I was talking to Renoir in the '60s, would have been way back in the '20s. That was the modern Hollywood, what happened after Lubitsch. He brought a whole kind of European sophistication to movies that hadn't existed before.

The *New York Times* wrote, "The tale it tells is scant and innocuous, yet, because it was fashioned by . . . Lubitsch, it is a shimmering, engaging piece of work."

BOGDANOVICH: That's the whole point. It's all gloriously done, but the characters are the plot, in a way. It's sort of the high point of sophisticated comedy, yet it's as light as a soufflé. Yet you could eat a lot of it.

Especially intriguing is that the jewel thieves are picking one another's pockets as foreplay. What do you think about the sexuality of the film?

BOGDANOVICH: That's what it is, and they really fall in love when they realize how good the other is. This film is raw in its sexuality. Even a year and a half after this film was released, it could not have been made due to the production code. These two people are both degenerate crooks, and they get away with it. There's no retribution. They all go off happily laughing. They would have had to go to jail, or the film wouldn't have been made. It would have had to have some insufferable, different kind of ending.

Tell me more about the European vs. American approach to sexuality in film. What exactly are the differences?

BOGDANOVICH: Films were much less puritanical and much more laissez-faire about affairs and sexual games—much more open about that stuff, as Europe is. No country in Europe would have made an issue about Monica Lewinsky, nor would anybody in a Lubitsch movie. I'm afraid we've lost "the Lubitsch Touch."

How would you describe "the Lubitsch Touch" to someone?

BOGDANOVICH: It's really a style, how he approached things, which is basically through indirection. He never hit things on the nose.

In *Trouble in Paradise*, he needed to begin in Venice. They wanted the audience to know they were in Venice, Italy. He didn't want to have a title that said, VENICE, ITALY, and he didn't want to have a shot of the lagoon, of the canal. So Sam Raphaelson, the writer, spent quite a lot of time—a few days—trying to get a good beginning, because Lubitsch never wanted to go forward unless he had a good beginning for a shot.

He didn't want it to just begin. He wanted it to begin with a bang. They finally came up with this shot: A dog is rummaging through some garbage, it's night, and a heavyset man comes up. He picks up the garbage, walks, and we pan with him, and it reveals a canal in Venice at night.

You realize he's a garbage collector, and he's got a garbage gondola, into which he pours the garbage and starts to sing in Italian. That's typical Lubitsch, to go to all that trouble to tell you that you're in Venice. And then he connects this guy singing to the next scene, which is in a hotel, where we realize there's a robbery taking place. All of this is done in a few scenes.

Prior to this movie, he had done four musicals. So this is his first "talking picture." Do you see any of his musical sensibilities carrying over?
BOGDANOVICH: Not just that, but look at the silent-movie sensibilities. All the transitions in *Trouble in Paradise* have that sensibility—they are all silent. If you look at the work of virtually every great movie director that started out in the silent era, and even a couple who didn't, you'll see that all the big moments are silent. The big moments are all visual, and there's a kind of poetry to that.

In terms of his musical sensibilities, it seems to me that almost all of his dialogue is always very sing-songy and lyrical.
BOGDANOVICH: All the great playwrights have a certain style. You could say that of certain filmmakers. Yes, there is a musicality, but there's a particular kind of rhythm that is very Lubitsch and hard to describe. It's a rhythm—a way of building up to something, then deflating it. It's always indirection.

For example, at the beginning when Herbert Marshall says, "It must be the most marvelous supper. We may not eat it, but it must be marvelous." "We may not eat it"—that's very Lubitsch.

Or the line where Marshall says, "Waiter, you see that moon?"
"Yes."
"I want to see that moon in the champagne."
"Moon in champagne."
"And as for you, waiter . . . I don't want to see you at all."

There are a lot of examples of directors being influenced by Lubitsch. How did movies change after him?

BOGDANOVICH: There was more inference to things; things became a little more subtle. He was considered by almost everybody as the master. Even Hitchcock admits to having learned some things from Lubitsch.

If you look at Hitchcock's *To Catch a Thief*, it's certainly a version of *Trouble in Paradise*. It's about a thief, and he's attractive and all that. There's the whole thing with the jewelry—it's very Hitchcockian. Nevertheless, I don't think it could have existed without Lubitsch. He changed movies from being rural to being cosmopolitan.

What did you learn from him?
BOGDANOVICH: I think the question of rhythm is the big thing, pacing within the frame, as opposed to cutting. A lot of good directors did that. A sense of indirection, trying to do things around the corner a little bit.

I did it more in a picture that wasn't successful called *At Long Last Love*. I was trying to do a Lubitsch musical. Everybody thought I was trying to do Fred Astaire and Ginger Rogers, because they'd never seen Lubitsch! The released version was not the good one. The one I cut for television was better. The point is, that was my attempt to do something Lubitschian. It's very hard to do Lubitsch, so I'm not surprised that I had a big flop.

Why do you think Lubitsch and his work aren't better remembered? Why isn't he among the big ones like Howard Hawks and John Ford?
BOGDANOVICH: He sure is for me. Who knows? Nobody in this country remembers anything beyond last week. In Europe, he's remembered, and in places where there is some kind of cultural heritage. We don't even know what that means here. People have no sense of history, and they haven't seen the movies. Ignorance, that's all. It's simple ignorance.

31

John Dahl
Twin Peaks: Fire Walk with Me

"This is not a film that I would recommend to most people," says director John Dahl about David Lynch's *Twin Peaks: Fire Walk with Me*.

It's a strange way to begin an endorsement but also a challenge, a dare—one affectionately made. Lynch's *Twin Peaks: Fire Walk with Me* is, of course, the prequel to his cult TV show (1990–91) that had America asking, "Who killed Laura Palmer?" By the end of the series, everyone already knew the *who*—but Lynch expanded on the *why* and *how* in this moody, esoteric exploration of mass and small-town psychosis.

Be warned: there's a lot of Montana in this interview. David Lynch is a Montana native, as is director John Dahl, who attended Billings Senior High—the same halls I wandered as a teenager. That connection, Dahl suggests, is an essential influence on Lynch's work. "I like this idea that there's this dark, dangerous, seductive presence lurking behind the veneer of small-town America," says Dahl.

> **John Dahl, selected filmography:**
> *Red Rock West* (1993)
> *The Last Seduction* (1994)
> *Unforgettable* (1996)
> *Rounders* (1998)
> *Joyride* (2001)
> *The Great Raid* (2005)
> *You Kill Me* (2007)

> ***Twin Peaks: Fire Walk with Me***
> 1992
> Directed by David Lynch
> Starring Sheryl Lee, Ray Wise, Mädchen Amick, Dana
> Ashbrook, David Bowie, and others

How would you describe *Fire Walk with Me* to someone who's never seen it?

DAHL: It details the sad life of Laura Palmer. It begins a week before her death, which you discovered at the beginning of the *Twin Peaks* series.

Under what circumstances did you see the film?

DAHL: I went and saw it when it was released. I loved it, and everyone else I knew hated it and probably still does. I like a lot of David Lynch's films for various reasons, but this movie is very uneven.

I was a *Twin Peaks* fan. I've never really watched that much television, but I had a friend, Lori Eschler, who's also from Billings, who was the music editor on *Twin Peaks*. I was always a big fan of David Lynch, but I had never seen television like that before. It was covering very bizarre material. You were seeing characters like the Log Lady. Even today, it's hard to imagine anyone running that series on television. It's very esoteric, almost surreal. The FBI agent who is always drinking coffee and eating cherry pie. It's just so untypical of what you see in mass entertainment.

I love the world that he created. Maybe it's because I'm from Montana. I like this idea that there's this dark, dangerous, seductive presence lurking behind the veneer of small-town America. Growing up in a small town, in rural areas, it always seemed that there was that lurking presence out there. I guess I can kind of relate to it.

Did you learn any secrets from *Fire Walk with Me* that you hadn't gleaned from the original *Twin Peaks* series?

DAHL: I kind of watch it as one of his movies rather than a continuation of *Twin Peaks*. What he did, for me, was make Laura Palmer a real person and take me into this hell that her life had become. That's why I thought that this was a pretty apt description: she was looking for love in hell.

Lynch called this film "My cherry pie present to fans of the show— however, one that's wrapped in barbed wire." But people weren't expecting how nasty it was going to be. Series star Kyle MacLachlan was even critical, saying it had none of the comic relief that had come with the original *Twin Peaks* formula.

DAHL: I was thinking about that today as well. Basically, you have a woman who's a high school girl who is sexually molested by her father and then murdered by him. That's an incredibly dark, bleak, black story. To think about it, for an American audience to sit through a year of television, a third of the way through the second season to have it revealed that Laura Palmer's dad killed her.

It wouldn't be quite as shocking today, because I think we've seen more incidents and horrific stories of people who have abused their own children and murdered them. It's probably not quite as salacious today as it was in 1992 when it came out. It was pretty mind-numbing stuff then for a major-release Hollywood film.

The film had a troubled debut. It was held for release and not screened for critics, which is indicative of a film that a studio doesn't believe in. And then it was savaged by critics.

DAHL: I doubt that most people who are fans of David Lynch would pick this as their favorite movie, but it's a really interesting culmination of a lot of things that he does that are so stylized. For one, I think the music is one of the best collaborations between Angelo Badalamenti and David Lynch. The music's really seductive and lush. I also really liked the woman who plays Laura Palmer, Sheryl Lee. She really put her heart into the role.

But the movie is very uneven, and the first twenty or thirty minutes are almost laughable. It's just really crude. What I like about David Lynch is that he has an idea that he's trying to convey and he tries to find a way to convey it that works for him. It's pretty unconventional, and it doesn't seem like he really cares if it works for anybody else, in a strange way. I don't know how you arrive at "Well, there's a room and it's got this zig-zaggy floor, and it's got these red curtains around it and everybody walks and talks backwards." I don't know what his process is.

Parts of the filmmaking are very uneven. As a friend of mine described him, he's really the only surrealist working in American film today. What does it mean to David Lynch to have a little boy jump around in a suit coat with a white mask over his face?

***Dune* was a bona fide flop, and this was the second major disappointment of Lynch's career. I think your film *Unforgettable* probably didn't do as well as you would have liked. Are there career lessons to be learned from films, and is the second time any easier?**
DAHL: I can only speak for myself. I don't think people who make movies think in those terms. I hope they don't. I can only imagine that he's making a movie, and he's making it to the best of his ability, and to me, this film certainly stands with the rest of his work as a good example of the powerful story elements that he deals with and the cinema that he puts together in terms of the performance, the sounds, the music. It's powerful filmmaking to me.

Is there some sort of Montana aesthetic that informs your worldview or connects you to Lynch?
DAHL: I'm not sure. He was born in Missoula but moved when he was like twelve. There are things like, he cuts to a shot of trees blowing in the wind and puts music under them, and all of a sudden it's just kind of creepy for me. When I'm in Montana and I see trees blowing, they mean something different to me now. That's a sign of a film that's impacted me in a way. It makes me look at things slightly differently.

What does David Lynch do that other filmmakers can't?
DAHL: When I think of David Lynch films, more so than anything else in his movies, I think of images. I think that the pictures and the moments are really powerful. Is it the title sequence of *Blue Velvet* where there's somebody waving to the fireman as they're going by?

It's such a surreal image. Like the ear in the grass [in *Blue Velvet*] or Laura Palmer's face being revealed in the opening of the TV series. The images are so evocative in a way that they're more something that you experience. When I think of David Lynch movies I think of moments, I think

of sounds, I think of music, I think of pictures. For me, those moments where some image just gets emblazoned in my mind to the point where it's just part of a vocabulary for me. Not that I would try and imitate that, but certainly, every now and then you sort of experience what I would say is a Lynchian moment.

In your film *Joyride*, one of the victims loses his lower mandible in one of the most disturbing film moments in recent memory. Am I right to call this a Lynch-influenced moment?

DAHL: I remember thinking, "Oh, gee, is this too much of a David Lynch movie?" Also, in *Joyride*, when they're listening to the wall and the camera dollies in on the painting, you hear these grotesque sounds next door. That whole roadside motel-like sequence . . .

Stylistically, both *Twins Peaks* the TV show and the movie have had a great impact on my work—not so much so with *The Great Raid* but with the other ones.

How did your perception of the film change as you saw it again?

DAHL: It was more disturbing to me watching it again. I found it quite tragic and hard to watch. It seemed to me like he set out to make a very dark movie. The first image you see is someone bashing a television. I imagined that was probably a reaction to working on a television show. That frustration and the fact that this wasn't going to be a television show. That's one of the things that I like about it. This woman, this high school girl, is leading a double life and being abused and how that just destroys her life.

Does the film work if you've never seen the series? How does it work as a separate entity?

DAHL: My only recommendation would be to do a chapter search up until the point when *Twin Peaks* music starts. Before that, it's almost twenty minutes of Chris Isaak as Chester Desmond and this whole FBI thing leading up to Philadelphia, and I'm not really sure what it has to do with anything. They find a *T* under someone's fingernail.

Really the movie begins when you see Laura Palmer and she's walking around Twin Peaks and then you go into this progressively darker and

darker world of what her life has become and those days leading up to her murder and demise.

I don't really know how the beginning connects to the end. I like seeing Kyle MacLachlan at the end with Laura Palmer in the red room. He solved her crime, and he allowed her to be released, in a way. That was a satisfying conclusion. She's in her room and the angel disappears out of the painting. She's put through this horrific ordeal, and Kyle MacLachlan's character is there to usher her into whatever her new peace is.

I would say that chances are, it's probably the most bizarre movie that people have ever seen if you haven't seen foreign films or you don't go see small independent films. It's incredibly dark, and parts of it are extremely violent and extremely disturbing. It's really extremely upsetting. I was surprised watching it yesterday by how dark it was.

Why do you think this movie has not been given its due?
DAHL: I don't know that this is one of those movies that most people would appreciate. This is not a film that I would recommend to most people. I understand how people would object to it and find it flawed, but there's something about seeing Laura Palmer and hearing that music and seeing those images that I just found to be pretty compelling and powerful filmmaking.

32

Kimberly Peirce
Ugetsu

To call Kenji Mizoguchi's *Ugetsu* a precursor to M. Night Shyamalan's *The Sixth Sense* would be correct, but also a misdirection and a disservice to both filmmakers. While *Ugetsu*'s ghostly story shares elements of *The Sixth Sense*, there's little supernatural horror in his ethereal tale of love and loss.

Though some critics consider director Mizoguchi to be on par with Japanese master Akira Kurosawa, he's still less well known to American audiences. But Mizoguchi's interest in whom people choose to love made his work, and *Ugetsu* specifically, appealing to director Kimberly Peirce. "I keep going back to this movie because I love its sense of possibility and its magic and the intensity of this love," she says, adding that if she hadn't seen *Ugetsu*, "I think my understanding of love would be different. Slightly."

Kimberly Peirce, selected filmography:
Boys Don't Cry (1999)
Stop-Loss (2008)
Carrie (2013)

Ugetsu
1953
Directed by Kenji Mizoguchi
Starring Masayuki Mori, Machiko Kyō, Kinuyo Tanaka, and others

How would you describe *Ugetsu* to someone who's never seen it?
PEIRCE: It's the story of this guy Genjurō and his friend Tōbei and their two wives during a time of wars in Japan. Genjurō is interested in pursuing

money, and Tōbei would like to be a warrior, a samurai. In the pursuit of their dreams, they both end up losing their wives.

Mostly, the story focuses on Genjurō, who is selling his pottery. One day he goes to one of the towns that sells his wares, and he's approached by somebody who represents Lady Wakasa, who lives in Wakasa Manor. He goes there to sell her some pottery, and she buys it, and he's affected by her. What ends up happening is he falls in love with her, and after a little bit . . .

. . . the story takes a supernatural turn. It's based on short stories by Akinari Ueda, and there's a little bit of influence from Guy de Maupassant. What makes this film notable is that this and *Rashomon* put Japan on the map, postwar Japan. Tell me about how you experienced the film.

PEIRCE: I think it was when I was living in Japan. I lived there for two years. When I saw it, what struck me was the intensity of the ghost story. I love ghost stories, and it's probably one of the greatest ghost stories I've ever read or seen. So I was just kind of blown away by the mastery of storytelling—the fact that it was set during a war, the intensity of the love story, and just how wonderful the ghost story part of it is.

To me, it is a ghost story that does not feel particularly ghostly or particularly supernatural. Is that because I'm American, or is that because that is the way it's supposed to be?

PEIRCE: You're dealing with such a masterful storyteller, who really believes in realism. What's really wonderful is when he gets to what we would call the superreal or the surreal stuff; he's making it very realistic.

It's unlike what you have now as the contemporary horror film, where everything is overdone, the sound is very ghostly, the effects are huge—the whole point is just to overspectacle it. Mizoguchi really is a great storyteller, so he's relying on drama. It's not about, "Woo, the ghost, let's scare you!" It's more about trying to bring you into a story.

Actually, the reason that Lady Wakasa is a ghost—I mean, that she comes back, is really, really moving. Just to give it away, she died before she had a chance to fall in love, and so her nursemaid comes back with her, and

they're seeking a man for her to love. You don't want to telegraph that she's a ghost. You want to make her beautiful, ethereal, perhaps haunting, but definitely an alluring figure. Mizoguchi has such a respect for storytelling and for character. It's only going to work if it's not a huge spectacle, but you're being seduced into it the same way he's being seduced into it.

More like *Rosemary's Baby*. It's very much a Japanese equivalent of *Rosemary's Baby*, because it's the idea that ghosts or witches . . . that they can exist with us, and it takes a while to figure out that that's what they are.

And unlike *Rosemary's Baby*, it's a ghost story without being horrific. Am I being fair? Or, to Japanese audiences at that time, would that have been an element of horror?

PEIRCE: Yeah, it's not horror in the same way *Rosemary's Baby* is, but so much of *Rosemary's Baby*, the fear is psychological, it's what could happen to her. It's not that there's blood being spilled, and there's not people fighting

To Japanese audiences of *Ugetsu*'s time—I certainly think that the moment that the priest warns him and says, in essence, "If you stay here any longer, you will die. Lady Wakasa is a spirit from the dead"—it's scary. You're going to lose your life, which is sort of what Rosemary is facing as well. But then when they put the code on him, the symbols, it's pretty intense. Lady Wakasa is horrified when she realizes that he knows that she's a ghost.

In the original text, Lady Wakasa is much more of a villainess. Do you think, because Mizoguchi built a reputation as a, quote, "women's issues director," he makes her less of the villain?

PEIRCE: Maybe he just knows that it's a better story if there's more dimensionality and she actually has a reason for coming back. When you realize that she's never loved, and that there is something so pathetic to her doing this, it gives it much more resonance. I think that if you had made her just evil and you didn't empathize with what she wanted, it would have much less resonance for us.

Whereas I think if you give her something that's deeply human, and it's really affecting—"Wow, what if I had died without loving or without hav-

ing some really important human experience? Then I might come back as a ghost"—it just makes it so much deeper. That's probably why he ended up being considered a feminist filmmaker, simply because I don't think that he reduced characters in general to these clichés. And since he didn't reduce women to that, he ended up making more dimensional women than people were used to seeing.

When you saw it, what scene or sequence gripped you? What made you a fan of this film?

PEIRCE: A few of them. I certainly love when he first sees her and she's sort of floating, so you're kind of like, "Is she a ghost or isn't she?" I really love when they make love by the hot springs. It's a spectacularly lit scene. She's got the kimono on.

I also really love when the priest puts the protective symbols on Genjurō's body and he goes back, and Lady Wakasa realizes why he has the symbols. She asks him to wash them off and he won't. And when he's fighting, what's amazing is he's hitting at air with a sword, but he's engaging in a fight, and then he realizes that the ruined manor is just burnt embers. It's just such a beautiful cinematic representation of this thing having been a dream, or something that wasn't part of the real world.

There's also a fantastic shot at the very end—again, it's Mizoguchi's genius of being able to take a story, figure out the ways to represent it cinematically. I don't know if I remember it exactly right, but I know he comes home, and he thinks that he sees his wife.

He comes into the house, and there's no one in the house. As he goes through the house, there's a reveal, and his wife is there next to a fire. So where there was no fire and no one before, on the second turn of the camera, there she is.

PEIRCE: Mizoguchi is always making sure that you're viscerally experiencing the love story and the ghost story even in the ways that he's filming it, which I think is really important. I think really great films do that; they're not just about the text. The story is actually woven in the very making of the film.

He was a proponent of one scene, one cut. He also made famous what's been called "the scroll shot," in which he pans across the landscape. How effective is that in his storytelling technique? What does that achieve?

PEIRCE: You mean the lack of cutting? I think it engages you more in the story. I think you're more engaged for longer. First of all, there's a narrative sense, so you're moving from A to B to C to D; the world is coming into you. By not cutting, you're holding onto the tension.

You're aware. Even if you're not fully aware, it creates suspense, because you're holding on to where you've been and you're anticipating where you're going. I think that's what a lot of filmmakers gain by not cutting. So I certainly think he does that. It brings you more deeply into the mood and the atmosphere because it's being written on you. And I think for a ghost story, it really is important, because when you cut, the audience then thinks, "Well, did you just do a trick on me?" Whereas if you're able to unfold these things through pans and dollies, the audience feels more that you're being up front with them, even though you aren't.

I've just watched it many, many times on my own, because it spoke to me in such a deep way. I had to decode it. I had to say to myself, "Why is this affecting me so much?" It was in those early days when I really was breaking films down every day, and I broke it down. I drew the scenes, I drew the shots, I figured out the camera angles. That was just how I got to know movies.

How did it specifically affect you?

PEIRCE: It's very emotional, and it gave me permission to do certain things. Most of the stories that I make are love stories. I thought it was transgressive in a way that was very exciting—that he's married, and then he goes with the ghost. Then he realizes it and he's got to go home. I love the idea that he was infected with this love and that he was seduced. They said he was drunk with love.

He was "in thrall." I always love that part, don't you?

PEIRCE: Yeah. "I never imagined such pleasures existed." Those are just scenes and topics that I'm really drawn to, and they resonate deep within me. Like *Rosemary's Baby*, or I think *Rouge*—it's a Chinese ghost story—is

another one around that time that I saw. So *Ugetsu* just affected me in that it opened up the possibilities for what film could be. It's literal in that love stories are literal, but it's literal within a surreal world. It breaks down very nicely, which I really love.

In your films, or in any of your scripts, can you draw a direct line from the influence of this film? Do you have an overt homage in either of your films?

PEIRCE: Certainly. I think *Boys Don't Cry*, when they enter into the landscape of their imagination. There's a moment when the family sends Lana and Brandon into the bedroom. Lana says, basically, "I'll check and tell you guys what I see," about Brandon's anatomy and goes in there, and then Brandon's ready to take down his pants, and Lana says, "Button up your pants. Don't show me anything. Think about it. I know you're a guy." I interviewed the real Lana. What I loved was that she entertained a reality and a fantasy about Brandon because she loved him, and certainly this movie was a direct influence on that.

What effect did seeing this in Japan have on you?

PEIRCE: Well, I was young. I was nineteen. I had left America and gone to Japan, quit college, just kind of growing up a little bit. It was interesting, because it was a period when I started really longing for America, longing for American stories. But to see it in Japan—I guess anything I saw there just allowed me to get closer to the culture. It allowed me to connect more to the people. It allowed me to try to see art as they saw it.

It's hard to say, because living there in Japan has had a huge influence on me in general. I think I just was very enamored with their stories. I was just starting to read their literature in translation. It was just another element of something that to me was just really brilliant and very beautiful. I tended to go for the stuff that—I wouldn't say had a Western feel, but that I could grasp the storytelling. I think that's why some of those modern filmmakers really spoke to me, like Kurosawa, Mizoguchi, like Ozu—there just was such an emotional depth to them, and their ability with execution was phenomenal. The kind of stories they told and their look at the human drama was really extraordinary.

You say that you've seen *Ugetsu* a lot over the years. As you see it from one year to the next, what do you notice that's different? How do you experience it because *you're* different?

PEIRCE: I think early on the thing that hits me is the visual stuff. Right away I'm completely taken with the hot springs scene and the scene by—is it Lake Bima?—where they make love, and then him fighting. Those are the things that will immediately get me, because they're so intense and vibrant.

But then I think over time, I can kind of see a bigger picture, which is just amazing to me. The narrative of "love what you have when you have it, or you will lose it." Because both the men, they have these wives that they love, but the one wants to become a samurai, and then his wife ends up becoming a prostitute. She says, "I'm a defiled woman. . . . How many times I've wanted to die, but I had to see you first." She was waiting, and then he rescues her and gets rid of the samurai equipment.

With Genjurō, it's the same thing. Here he has his wife, and he's going and selling his wares, selling his wares, and people are saying, "Don't focus on money too much." But he can't help himself. Well, he ends up with this love affair with this ghost. He manages to save himself, but of course, he loses his wife.

I've cried a couple times when they cut to the end scroll and the wife is speaking to him from above. She's basically saying, "You've finally become the man I had hoped for." And he's just so full of grief, because he only became that man by not being that man and by giving up his wife. So I think that as I get older, I see the brilliance of the overall story beyond the images, because the story's what really sticks with me.

One of the reasons *Ugetsu* may not be better known is because it's in the shadow of *Rashomon*, which came out two years earlier. Why do you think American audiences or Western audiences have not embraced it as much as Kurosawa?

PEIRCE: Well, that's interesting. Number one, I think Kurosawa became the Japanese filmmaker for most people. So I think if you weren't going to get to know a bunch of Japanese filmmakers, if you were going to know one, you were going to get to know Kurosawa. That's number one.

I think number two, just the body of Kurosawa's work. Because he's very Shakespearean, and he's been reading Shakespeare's stuff—*The Hidden Fortress* and *Seven Samurai*—I think that there were just many more famous titles that he made, so therefore you were bound to see his films. And if you were going to see one—*Rashomon* has that, I wouldn't call it a gimmick, but it's the movie that's cut up into three parts. I think that if you're going to look for something unusual, you look for that movie. Probably mostly Kurosawa's name recognition would be the main reason that *Rashomon* was more famous than Mizoguchi.

This film has some very significant biographical elements for Mizoguchi, because when he was a boy, his father had huge economic troubles and lost a business. They had to move to a ghetto, and his fourteen-year-old sister, Suzu, was put up for adoption and was sold to a geisha house. Film critic Roger Ebert wrote, "So perhaps the sins of the father were visited upon Mizoguchi's two heroes." It's an interesting fact that we have here, but is there something inherently dangerous about that? Are there dangers of people reading too much biography into your films?
PEIRCE: I don't think so, because my movies are very inspired by personal experience, both of them so far and certainly this third one. People often say to me, "Well, don't you feel frustrated because there's all this different press on you? Multiple stories are told of you in the press and no one's really getting to know the real you." And then I always say to my friends, "But really it's the proliferation of stories, and people can piece together what they want to piece together."

For instance, you're telling me this about Mizoguchi. It adds a wave of emotional resonance for me. To know that his fourteen-year-old sister was put up for adoption and sold to a geisha house and that the sins of the father might be being visited upon the two heroes, to me just adds another layer of possible understanding. I already have a read on the movie. I already have a deep love of it and an appreciation for the way the narrative works and the way he shot it, so for me, to find out something about him and to find out that part of him is in the movie, to me that adds intensity and makes it more compelling.

The flip side of that is: you can be misunderstood. After *Boys Don't Cry* came out, there was a whole bunch of press about you, talking about how this was the product of your own struggle for sexual identity. Is that dangerous for you, personally, as an artist, as a filmmaker?

PEIRCE: Well, I think in my case, I'm very articulate and very expressive about the role that my personal life played in making the movies. For *Boys Don't Cry*, I make it really clear that I've dealt with gender issues: I've been gay, I've been straight; that I've traveled with transsexuals to understand the story; a lot of my friends were butch lesbians. That way, there's a lot of information out there if it interests you to piece together what role my personal life has played in the movie and what role the movie's played in my personal life.

For me, the work has to stand on its own. I feel like me going in and telling people what the personal connection is—I feel like it's another story. I don't think it's the film. You know, it's funny, I'll do these Q&As, and people—particularly younger people—will say, "What did you mean in that scene?" And then I'll say to them, "Well, what do you think I meant?" because I don't like to tell them. I think, like most filmmakers, I just think that either you got it or you didn't. And then they tell me what they think it was about, and I'm like, "That's exactly what it was about." The extra-narrative that goes on with the director and the personal thing—it almost has nothing to do with the movie itself. It's like another spectacle.

The *Village Voice* named *Ugetsu* among its top 100 films, but why do you think it's still—in modern times with modern audiences—largely unknown?

PEIRCE: Well, why it hasn't found a big audience is because, think about it, until it's on DVD, you have to be a bit of a film fanatic to have heard about it and go see it. I mean, most people I know have never heard of it. I tend to watch a lot of different films, like people like us who are very interested in the movies.

It's like you said, because it's not Kurosawa, because it's not *Rashomon*, because it hasn't been on video until recently, how would you have even heard of it, how would you have seen it? A Japanese film in black and white from 1953, a ghost story from a director who doesn't have a lot of other huge hits? I'm not surprised.

How would your life or work be different if you hadn't seen this film?
PEIRCE: I'm so in love with the way that he deals with superrealism or sur-
realism, and the sense of magic, and the sense of an afterlife, and the idea of
unrequited love, and the girl's suffering and the spell that's cast upon them. I
think a certain amount of magic would be missing. I keep going back to this
movie because I love its sense of possibility and its magic and the intensity
of this love. I think my understanding of love would be different. Slightly.

33

Rian Johnson
Under the Volcano

Although Rian Johnson admires John Huston's adaptation of Malcolm Lowry's novel *Under the Volcano*, it's really Albert Finney's performance as a self-destructive, alcoholic British consul that hypnotizes him. "There's something very self-indulgent about it, where you feel like you're watching a man be very theatrical and play to his inner demons," Johnson says.

Under the Volcano follows the descent of a British consul in Mexico into his own personal hell as he fights his own alcoholism, crumbling relationships, and self-destructive patterns. The novel, thinly masking Lowry's own alcoholism and sexual conflicts, was the last Lowry published. "I think the film is incredibly worthwhile to engage with, because that self-destructive mechanism exists in all of us," Johnson says.

Rian Johnson, selected filmography:
Brick (2005)
The Brothers Bloom (2008)
Looper (2012)

Under the Volcano
1984
Directed by John Huston
Starring Albert Finney, Jacqueline Bisset, Anthony Andrews, Ignacio Lopez Tarso, and Katy Jurado

How would you describe *Under the Volcano* to someone who's never seen it?

JOHNSON: The film is set in Mexico on the Day of the Dead in the late '30s. It's the story of a British consul, played by Albert Finney, who's a drunk and living in this small town in Mexico. It's about his wife coming back to him; she's had an affair with his half-brother, and it's about the storm that ensues between the three of them. But really, it's a character study about this consul and his descent into the hell of his own mind, if you want to get dramatic about it.

Tell me about the first time you saw the film.
JOHNSON: This is a film that my dad loved. My dad was not in the film business—he was a home builder—but he was a huge movie buff. This was one of the films that he had on his shelf, so I saw it when I was in high school.

But then I didn't see it again for years, and it was only when the Criterion Collection released a beautiful DVD of it, that I was able to pick it up again and watch it. The thing that struck me then was that it's tonal. It's more than tonal, but it really does draw you into this feeling; it almost feels like you're sinking into a swamp through the course of watching the film. You really feel yourself sinking deeper and deeper along with Finney into a mire of jealousy and a web of that place where love and loathing intersect.

And for me, that's essentially what the film is about. It's about a man who, in the same way he indulges with drink, indulges those—and almost plays up—those feelings and lets himself belly flop into the swamp of these feelings.

When I first watched it, I didn't really understand a lot of it, but I knew that I was going on a trip to a really dark and dangerous place. The film always had this mystique to me; it always felt like an unknown country that I had seen through the window of our car when our family was driving through it. It felt like something mysterious and dangerous that I had just glimpsed. And watching it today, the main thing when you talk about the film is you're really talking about Finney's performance in it. That just knocked me flat on my ass when I saw it this time.

My father's side of the family is Swedish, so when our family gets together, there's a lot of drinking that happens. I don't have anyone in my family who has even close to the problem that Finney's character has, and they tend to

be happy drunks, but I have seen a lot of men under the deep influence of alcohol in my time.

And from my memory, this is the best drunk performance I've ever seen. Finney understands that with this role you can't underplay it; you have to go for the throat. He's so "big" in this part, and every single thing he does is so huge in terms of the choices that he makes. Yet it all works to create not only an incredibly subtle but also an incredibly realistic portrait of a man lost in a deep haze of alcoholic stupor, who has been there so long he's learned to function under it.

That's one of the conceits of the film, which is the drunker he becomes, the more clearheaded he becomes. The line is actually, "The more drunk he gets, the more sober he becomes."

JOHNSON: Exactly. There's the other classic line, "Hell is my natural habitat." It's undisputed, even by Lowry, that this was autobiographical. Lowry was an insanely drunken man, and this is very much a chronicle of his own interior state of mind. There's an amazing documentary of Lowry that's on the Criterion disc. He was a deeply troubled and deeply unhappy man. He really lived *Under the Volcano*, and I don't think he ever published another novel.

It was the book that destroyed him.

JOHNSON: I think that's very much present in the book itself. It's also present in the movie. The film is very much about man indulging his demons. Drink is the obvious metaphor of the demons, but more than that, it's this kind of fiery, deep-seated resentment and feeling of betrayal from his wife. He lets those waters kind of rise in his mind over the course of the film.

Much of Finney's performance, there's something very self-indulgent about it, where you feel like you're watching a man be very theatrical and play to his inner demons. You're watching him throw out a handful of crumbs for these demon birds. I think when Finney delivers that line "Hell is my natural habitat," he might as well be a painted King Lear on the stage. He delivers it with all of the theatricality of someone that's speaking to an audience of two thousand people, even though the camera is three feet from his face.

Another of the lines, which actually begins the film, is "Some things you can't apologize for." Is forgiveness possible for that particular brand of infidelity, do you think?

JOHNSON: Yeah, it is. You mean in terms of story tone? Absolutely. You can find salvation at the end of anything if you work at it. Story-wise, there's a way to redeem this character and to even do it honestly, I think.

But not redemption, forgiveness. Is he boxed in by this betrayal?

JOHNSON: I don't think that he's at all boxed in by circumstances outside his own head, if that's what you're asking. I think for him, it proves to be impossible to forgive his wife (Jacqueline Bisset) this past infidelity, but that's part of what's striking about the film—the contrast of what he's offered when she comes back. It's a sunny day, and they're sitting on the veranda. It's obviously over between her and the half-brother, and she's almost an angelic presence descending and genuinely offering to be his, to save him and to move forward.

The duality of the way it's presented is very much like the virgin and the whore—the way she is in the sunlight when she's actually there with him and in his head, the split side of that, characterizing her as the harlot. That's what he indulges, what he can't get past at the end of the day. I think that's what makes this a fascinating character, but it's also deeply fucked up.

Let's talk a bit about the background and the casting. This is Jacqueline Bisset's third film with Finney. They were in *Murder on the Orient Express* and my favorite Finney film of all time, which is *Two for the Road*. Do you think there's resonance of that history on film?

JOHNSON: It's tough, because for this particular performance, Finney's character is a man who's so encased inside his own head, and the point of it is that they're completely missing each other. One of the beautiful things about her performance is that you can see that in her eyes. You can see the pain at just not being able to connect with this man at all anymore while genuinely trying to.

In many ways, it's a film about two lives that never intersect, in terms of these two characters. That in itself is something that requires a base of intimacy, so in that way, I guess you could say that the fact that they have

chemistry on-screen, maybe that's a part of what makes it so potent when
they don't.

**It seems that there's this self-fulfilling prophecy in that she leaves
him and cheats on him because he's a constant drunk. He's a constant
drunk because she left him and cheated on him. From your perspective, how did you interpret that relationship? Does she leave because
he's a drunken asshole?**
JOHNSON: It's hard for me to watch this with a clear head and place the
blame anywhere, especially given the fact that this film captures a moment
in which she does come back, offering him something good and pure, but
through indulging these demons of his, he can't grab on to it. I think the
success, definitely of the book and of the film, is presenting this indefensible
man and pulling you into the workings of his interior world.

**Why does this film not loom larger in Huston's canon? Is it simply
because it's in the wake of his last two films, *The Dead* and *Prizzi's Honor*?**
JOHNSON: I think it is, and for all the reasons we've talked about. It's not a
pleasant film. It's a film about, for lack of a more complicated word, a bas-
tard. I think the film is incredibly worthwhile to engage with, because that
self-destructive mechanism exists in all of us. If I'm honest, I can recognize
it in myself, albeit on a much smaller scale. But the seeds of it are something
that I think every man has, to some degree, within himself.

**The book is about somebody's interior life, but Huston chose to make
a linear film about the exterior of someone's life with no flashbacks,
very little exposition, and very few close-ups. How is he able to achieve
insight into this man's struggle?**
JOHNSON: Well, compared to the book, he doesn't. The book and the film
are two very different experiences. I saw the film before I read the book.
But having now read it, I feel like I'm somehow tainted from really analyzing the film in that way. While I was reading the book, I did kind of
reanalyze the film and was a little bit surprised at that approach to it.

There's something kicking underneath the surface of Finney's character, and there's something kicking throughout the course of the film.

There's no open door inviting you into his head; it is very much all of these exterior events that you have to witness and find your own way into. I don't think the film approaches the same interior life as the book; it's a very different animal.

Is there a scene you'd like to talk about?

JOHNSON: One of the beautiful scenes in the film—well, the entire first night is amazing, but the morning after when Finney is sitting, still in his tuxedo, in this little dusty cantina, and Bisset shows up. He keeps asking the bartender if he's listening to him, and there's a long moment where he regards his wife and is genuinely not sure if she's a hallucination or not. On the one hand, it's very theatrical; on the other, it's incredibly beautifully played by him. That moment stood out to me, and there are a lot of others.

This film really does break down into, not even scenes, but tiny moments, like when he's in the back garden searching for the liquor bottle or when he's walking on the street. I can literally see in my head his gait, the way that he's stepping. Or, in a dialogue scene, just the pause between when somebody says something to him and when he reacts and speaks back. Not even a specific line, but just the fact that there's a second and a half too long of a pause between his absorption and his reaction tells you more about exactly what's happening inside this man's head than what he actually says. For me, the film is composed of moments like those, most of which are entirely based on Finney's performance.

34

John McNaughton
Who'll Stop the Rain

It's difficult to discern whether John McNaughton's love of Karel Reisz's *Who'll Stop the Rain*, based on the novel *Dog Soldiers* by Robert Stone, stems from his experience with the film or his deep admiration and respect for the novel's author. "All I remember is going in prejudiced against it, and sitting down, and after five minutes I was hooked," McNaughton says.

Who'll Stop the Rain is an intricate narrative made up of morally ambiguous characters who fall prey to the internal destruction that war creates. The result is a genuine, emotional, and complex piece of art, McNaughton says.

John McNaughton, selected filmography:
Henry: Portrait of a Serial Killer (1986)
The Borrower (1991)
Mad Dog and Glory (1993)
Normal Life (1996)
Wild Things (1998)
Speaking of Sex (2001)
Shoedog (2013)

Who'll Stop the Rain
1978
Directed by Karel Reisz
Starring Nick Nolte, Tuesday Weld, Michael Moriarty, Anthony Zerbe, and Richard Masur

How would you describe *Who'll Stop the Rain* to someone who's never seen it?

MCNAUGHTON: Morally complex [*laughs*]. It starts with a journalist (Michael Moriarty) in Vietnam, in combat, and he's sort of a very mild guy.

The war is so horrific to him and so strange. He's a guy from Berkeley from kind of a hippie-culture background. The war, in the term of the day, just blew his mind. He's connected to this elegant woman who's very politically connected in Saigon and Washington, and somehow she gets him to agree to run two kilos of heroin back to America. They're all going to make a ton of money. But he's really a babe in the woods. He's being set up.

Moriarty's character can't personally do it, but he has a friend Ray, played by Nick Nolte, who's the very opposite of him and very much a man of action, a former marine and now a merchant marine. Because of his merchant marine status, he's able to actually do the deed of running heroin back to the United States, and he's going to get paid a couple thousand bucks.

It turns into kind of a road movie, which is very interesting, again, for me to revisit the period and the ideas of the period. When I saw first *Who'll Stop the Rain*, it was within a year of its release. It was during Vietnam or right after Vietnam. When I'm now seeing it twenty years later, I find that quite interesting.

Did anybody direct you toward the film?

MCNAUGHTON: No, that was the interesting thing. I'm from the South Side of Chicago, and I was living in the [working-class] south suburbs at the time. There was a second-run movie theater in Hammond, Indiana, that would run double features for a buck and a half, back in those days when I was lucky to have a buck and a half.

I remember walking into the theater and there was a poster, and there was Nick Nolte—and Tuesday Weld, I imagine—and there was the title, *Who'll Stop the Rain*, and I thought, "What a stupid fucking title." Because it was the name of a Creedence Clearwater Revival song—and I love Creedence Clearwater, but I just thought, "What could this stupid movie be?" I don't know if it was the first movie on the bill or the second movie on the bill. All I remember is going in prejudiced against it, and sitting down, and after five minutes I was hooked.

I knew who Robert Stone was but I had not read him yet. After I saw this movie, I went out and bought *Dog Soldiers*, which is the book it was based upon. The movie just hooked me and never let go. It's morally complex, it deals with issues—it's not just your standard movie plot where everything turns out swell in the end, morally unambiguous, and with clear good guys and bad guys.

I think the casting is superb. I've always loved Richard Masur from the time he played the mentally challenged bag boy on *All in the Family*. He was wonderful then, and I just actually read him for a pilot a few years ago and he just blew me away.

Do you remember how the book jibed with the movie? How were they different, in your mind?
McNaughton: It was pretty true to the book. And I know Robert Stone. He's sort of a mentor to a writer friend that I often work with, so I've had dinner with him numerous times, and I like him very much. I've read pretty much everything he's written.

I know that there were a few grumblings from him somewhere along the way about the adaptation, but Stone's language is just fabulous. But the film isn't as complex as the book, because it doesn't have all the thoughts of the character and the interior monologue and the beauty of language, although the dialogue in the movie is wonderful, because Stone has a wonderful ear for dialogue and a wonderful gift of language. But story-wise, it was pretty faithful.

He cowrote the script, although he was just as pissed off as you were about the name change.
McNaughton: [*Laughs.*] I would imagine.

I think where Stone split with the film is when they made Tuesday Weld's character an innocent. She no longer slept with Nick Nolte's character; she no longer worked at the porn theater.
McNaughton: That's funny, because when I went to watch the film again, I had a memory of her having an affair with Nick Nolte. And as I watched the film last night, I sort of went, "Where did that come from?" It never occurred to me. I thought I just had a mistaken memory.

Stone was himself a writer in Vietnam.

McNaughton: Yes, he was sent by *Esquire* to cover the fall of Saigon. This movie led me into the life of Robert Stone, which is a very ambiguous and morally unclear universe [*laughs*].

How would you describe Stone to someone who has never met him?

McNaughton: Oh, he's a tremendously interesting man. He's an incredibly mild-mannered and courteous man who can rise to the occasion. But it's easy to make that sort of identification between Stone and Moriarty's character. Watching the film yesterday, for the first time I was astounded at how limp he was morally. He was just at the whim of whatever happens is fine with him, just adrift in the world. Stone is more complex than that [*laughs*].

What makes him a compelling character and a compelling writer?

McNaughton: Incredible depth of humanity. He's been to a lot of places, done a lot of things, and was fortunate to be of age in that period. You know, he rode the bus with author Ken Kesey [who wrote *One Flew Over the Cuckoo's Nest* and led a psychedelic bus trip across the United States] and Neal Cassady; Stone's really been there and pretty much done it all. When he speaks, I listen, because he's incredibly well read and well spoken and a very kind and gentle man but also very crazy.

Nick Nolte plays Ray, who dies counting railroad ties, like Cassady—Jack Kerouac's friend and muse for *On the Road*—is purported to have died. Did you later make this link?

McNaughton: Yeah.

It's also strange that Nolte played Cassady two years later.

McNaughton: Many times I go into a movie prejudiced and then it completely turns me around, which this one did. My first impressions of Nick Nolte were of this big dumb hunky guy, and I was not at all a fan of his until I saw this movie. Which brings me to the point: *Heart Beat*—that was another movie that I didn't know what to expect when I saw it, but I loved it. Because it very much humanized the Beats. They were these mythic characters. I thought Nick Nolte was wonderful as Neal Cassady.

Who'll Stop the Rain **got really mixed reviews when it came out. Pauline Kael hated it; Kenneth Turan wrote that it was a "lean film with a nasty, nervous edge." It bombed.**

McNaughton: I think it got caught in some executive turnaround. [The leadership of the studio changed.] There was no support for the film. I think any complex picture's going to have a hard time in the marketplace.

Your point about it being morally complex reminds me of a line in the movie: "No more cheap morals to draw from all this death."

McNaughton: Yeah, I think once you actually commit to wars—and you have to commit to survive—you could theoretically commit incredibly morally horrific acts. And once the dogs of war are unleashed, nothing good can come of it.

Tell me about your favorite scene.

McNaughton: I really like when we get to the two moron thugs; it was a brilliant performance by Ray Sharkey. I was just watching it. The chess game between the two of them is wonderful. But when they break into Tuesday Weld's house and Nolte just dispatches them, I thought that was a great scene.

How did your perception of the film change?

McNaughton: Just the mind-set of those years, you know. It made me realize how much things have changed, and of course in some ways the human condition hasn't changed, but ideas and attitudes that were so prevalent then, widespread, how different things are now.

What did it capture specifically? What did it get right?

McNaughton: It got a lot right, I think. Something that I like very much about the film is it wasn't shot in Canada. It was shot in the right location. When they were in Berkeley, it looked to me like they were in Berkeley and that place out in the end, Mexico or Arizona, that was all wired up for the hippie lifestyle, that nonmaterialistic hippie lifestyle that seems to be missing today. It just brought back memories of ideas and attitudes that you believed in that had been beaten out of you, you know?

What could have been done differently?

McNaughton: The ending. This is where taking out the affair between Tuesday Weld and Nick Nolte comes in. I think without having the affair, the ending doesn't quite work anymore, because her connection to him is weakened. The relationship is very touching, but without the actual sexual contact, it's all weakened.

When he was politely warring with Stone, director Karel Reisz said that you don't do the novel or the novelist a favor by being faithful to the little details of the book. Do you think that's true?

McNaughton: I would say it depends on the details. But the film has to be more focused. You can't digress nearly as much, or you lose the audience. There's a point where the screenplay has to have its own birth. When I've worked on adaptations, there are always little details and descriptions that I try to leave in because they will be so valuable for the actors and for perhaps the production designer or the costume designer. On the other hand, in less fine writing, you're much more likely to get rid of a lot of it—to focus on that core story that's dramatic, which the writer of the book will have no perspective on.

He said that an adaptation was not a translation but a variation on a theme. And that seems parallel to what you're saying as well.

McNaughton: I make a distinction, I'm sorry to say, between what I call "real writers" and screenwriters. I tend to work more often with real writers who have written books or plays or made a living writing essays or whatever. Because so many people who write screenplays are just pastiche-ing movies.

I read five or six screenplays a week written by kids who, you know, nine out of ten times it's their first screenplay, and usually by half a page I can tell you the rest of the movie. Why? Because I've seen that movie a hundred billion fucking times before. And I can also tell that they're very young, because they haven't really experienced life or lived life. They're just writing movies about movies. This was cool. And cool is the criterion for making it into the screenplay. And it seems to bear little or no connection to life as it's lived by human beings in our time.

How do you deal with forceful personalities and difficult writers when you're filming their material? Do you have a strategy or advice you follow?

McNaughton: I have been very fortunate to work with wonderful writers who I usually invite to rehearsals—I usually try and get two weeks of rehearsal, and the second week I usually try and get the writer in, because the actors are going to want to change dialogue and often rightfully so. Once the actor really finds the character, they know the character better than the writer in many cases, because that's all they're concentrating on, that one character.

But do you follow any guidelines when you deal with writers, because it's material that they've sort of given birth to?

McNaughton: I remember an interview with a writer in which he was asked, "Are you disappointed with the way Hollywood ruined your books?" He happened to have a shelf behind him and he said, "No, my books are fine; they're sitting right there on the shelf."

35

Alex Gibney
WR: Mysteries of the Organism

Alex Gibney saw Dušan Makavejev's *WR: Mysteries of the Organism* while in college, an experience that he says "knocked me out." The film is a collage-like mix of both real and created footage that features such moments as a woman's head being cut off with a figure skate. Gibney went on to make use of real and invented footage in his own documentaries, notably in *Enron: The Smartest Guys in the Room.*

Of Makavejev, Gibney says, "This guy had something that he wanted to say, and he realized that saying it required an anything-goes approach to filmmaking."

Alex Gibney, selected filmography:
Enron: The Smartest Guys in the Room (2005)
Taxi to the Dark Side (2007)
Gonzo: The Life and Work of Dr. Hunter S. Thompson (2008)
Casino Jack and the United States of Money (2010)
Client 9: The Rise and Fall of Eliot Spitzer (2010)
Magic Trip: Ken Kesey's Search for a Kool Place (2011)

WR: Mysteries of the Organism
1971
Directed by Dušan Makavejev
Starring Milena Dravić, Ivica Vidović, Jackie Curtis, and Jagoda Kaloper

How would you describe *WR: Mysteries of the Organism* to someone who has never seen it?

GIBNEY: Oh my God. It's the kind of film that they just don't make anymore. It's a love story between a communist figure skater and a hot, young Yugoslavian woman, mixed in with all sorts of wild documentary stories and performance pieces by artist Tuli Kupferberg. It's a film that's mixed up in a blender.

It's about four separate films, but let's just talk about the "WR" in the title. Can you explain to folks who Wilhelm Reich was?
GIBNEY: I guess you would call him a psychologist. He was deeply interested in how the id [the unconscious, instinctual part of the psyche that drives our pleasure-seeking impulses] was manipulated by the state. He wrote a book called *The Mass Psychology of Fascism*, in which he posited that the master-stroke of fascism was to take the sexual urge, the id, and to manipulate or sublimate it in the service of the state.

And then he became more and more interested in all sorts of other wild theories about a kind of essential spirit that's out there in the land, called "Orgone Energy," and getting in touch with that, and all that kind of thing. But I think for the purposes of this film, the key book is *The Mass Psychology of Fascism*.

The movie is not a wholesale indictment or parody of communism and socialism, which I thought it was. In fact, it's a socialist statement.
GIBNEY: It is a kind of socialist statement. And also, one of the interesting things about it is that it's an indictment of communism, certainly, or Stalinism. But in a peculiar way, it actually equates Stalinism with American imperialism or capitalist imperialism.

In the documentary sequences in Rangeley, Maine, he keeps playing all of these commercial jingles in a way that is playfully reminiscent of the kind of sloganeering propaganda of communism. And indeed, Reich escapes from fascism and communism to come to the United States, only to have his books burned here, which is really, deeply disturbing.

I think that socialism, as a notion that you're somehow actually embracing the dignity of the human being, is something that this film is getting at. There was a resistance to being under the boot of the Soviet Union. It's harder to understand now because we're outside of the Cold War, but Yugoslavia was trying to find a more humane, democratic socialism.

Well, this film was shot from 1968 to 1971 in Yugoslavia and in the United States. After it was released, Makavejev turned down Francis Ford Coppola's offer to direct *Apocalypse Now*. What do *Apocalypse Now* and this film have in common?

GIBNEY: Good question. There was a kind of madness of the state, and certainly *Apocalypse Now* is all about madness, both the madness of the war as it's being prosecuted and the madness of those who are trying to resist it, as embodied by Kurtz. Or maybe they're just embodying it so fulsomely that they become emblematic of it.

So maybe it's that weird zone, because there is a lot of sexuality in *Apocalypse Now*. There's that famous scene where the Playboy Bunnies are helicoptered down among all those horny men, and things get out of hand because their libidos are so supercharged that they have to quickly get the women out. The idea was to come in and give them a little tease, and the tease provoked such a deep well of erotic charge that they had to get the hell out of there before the helicopter was engulfed. So I think there's a little bit of a connection there.

How did you first encounter the film, and what was your reaction to it?

GIBNEY: I think it was another one of those films I saw at a film society in college. That was at a time when I was taking courses in psychology, and so I was certainly familiar with Reich, but I don't claim to be a student of his.

When I first saw it, it was at one of these film festivals, and it just knocked me out. The reason it knocked me out was that it was so formally playful. This guy had something that he wanted to say, and he realized that saying it required an anything-goes approach to filmmaking. Rather than jam all of his ideas into one fictional narrative, he wanted to explode out of it and to have all of these documentary elements that would be both interesting in and of themselves and also inform the fictional narrative in a way that you don't normally get to do.

This was one of the great liberating things about films of the late '60s and early '70s, that they could go anywhere and do anything. Godard had this famous phrase: "In the cinema, however, one isn't supposed, if one is in a room, simply to open the window and film what is going on outside." It was such a simple idea. So *WR: Mysteries of the Organism* is looking out

the window, in addition to seeing what's in the room. It's a great, liberating thing.

When you think about the film, what's the image that comes to your mind? What is the thing that follows you around when you think about the film?

GIBNEY: Tuli Kupferberg. It's not my favorite sequence, but I just think of him roaming around the streets of New York with that gun. I think of that wonderful woman giving that great speech after she just walked outside of the room where her roommate is fucking some guy, so exuberantly and constantly. And she just walks past them as if they're just kids playing in the garden, and walks out to this great hall and gives this fantastic speech.

And then, of course, that moment where Milena Dravić has her head cut off by the Russian skater. In fact, he cuts her head off with his skate, and the head is on a tray in the autopsy room, and she begins to speak. She gives her final words. It was sort of his answer, I think, to Billy Wilder's swimming pool scene in *Sunset Boulevard*.

There's one other scene, which is so great, where Makavejev goes to Rangeley, Maine, and starts interviewing the local people about Wilhelm Reich. It's howlingly funny, because they just remember him as this guy who liked to get his hair cut in a certain way. That's documentary stuff, which doesn't work in a fictional context, but is so rich and fun.

And this is my other curiosity about the film, because unless you read interviews with the director, you don't realize that it's a wholesale indictment. He's a socialist, and at a certain point, Milena Dravić is his mouthpiece.

GIBNEY: That's right. But this was in the age of Coca-Cola, when capitalism was also seen very much as an adjunct of imperialism. It was an economic system that was designed to control and enslave. Things go better with Coke.

So there was that vibe around the world, and the socialism that he was embracing was a utopian vision, which, in its sense of possibility, is a wonderful thing—the idea that you can embrace the individual but also find some kind of greater, collective good without allowing for any corruption on the part of the state. Well, it sounds great, and I'm all for it,

but it turns out to be utopian and may not be possible, given the banality [*laughs*] of humankind.

Sure, but in the way it's read today, the sequences from the dramatic film are so over-the-top that it's hard to take them seriously. The director has said, "It's so nice not to be real all the time," and it has this very novel approach, that you can use a satirical ideal to smuggle in some knowledge, so people can read about it later.

GIBNEY: Well, to me, in talking about some of the films that I've done, my view is that movies should be agent provocateurs. You can't get from a film what you get in a book, which is a kind of grand and detailed, analytical look at something. But what you *can* get are certain searing images, which are so powerful, and so complex, and rich and emotionally strong that they act as agents provocateurs. They get you to go out and want to learn more or want to understand more. And I think that's what this film does. It provokes you. I watched the film recently, and the dramatic sequences are over-the-top. But they're over-the-top in a kind of playful and sort of innocent way—sort of like Milena Dravić is.

How so?

GIBNEY: Sometimes there's the artist's intent and then what they end up doing. And one of the interesting things about that film is the main character, played by Dravić. She's not as wild a libertine as her roommate is. Her roommate is not into talking; she's all into fucking. And she's just constantly fucking and giggling and just naked all the time with her boyfriend, just rolling around on the floor, while Milena talks about it a lot, and she can talk the talk but isn't as comfortable walking the walk.

Then she meets this Russian figure skater who is clearly deeply repressed, and he's the same way—he talks the talk and can't walk the walk. But she's a much more full figure; she's not as deeply repressed as he is. So when they finally have sex, it's too much for him.

I've got to believe this is part of the whole structure of Makavejev's narrative. This is the guy who is the paradigm of Reich's *The Mass Psychology of Fascism*. He's sublimated all of his sexuality in service of the state. So when he actually has an orgasm, it sends him into a rage. He beheads the woman

who has caused him to lose control, which, in its own way, is a powerful metaphor for the relationship of the sexes. And that's very dark but also darkly comic and satirical.

That character is named Vladimir Ilyich, which is also Lenin's actual name. But for a modern audience who doesn't know that, they might not think that he's repressed by the state and then that turns to violence—but just that he's a repressed gay man!

GIBNEY: Right, and that could be. It's hard to understand this film, and maybe that was his intent, I don't know. But it is hard to understand this film unless you immerse yourself somewhat in the history of the time. It's a film that has a lot to say to us today in formal terms—that is to say, the formal freedom that this film embraces. That has a lot to teach us.

But you do really need to put yourself back in that moment, because it is, at the same time, a kind of film of the moment. And also, the whole idea of "free love" is much more difficult for us to understand now, in the era of AIDS, and what we now know—that free love isn't free.

But at the time, that was another aspect of the utopia that we were all seeking. You can see an aspect of the women's liberation movement that's in this, certainly in Milena. You get that in the way she wants to be free and independent as a woman even while she engages her own sexuality. But there's also a kind of macho aspect to this film that viewers today might have difficulty with. Like Rocky and Bullwinkle, you need to set the "Way-Back Machine" to the early '70s to really get what's going on here, because it's much harder to see it unless you do that.

That's why I think it was interesting to me, and I'm not even sure I got it at the time, but hearing the audio montage of the capitalist advertising slogans over the documentary footage of Rangeley, Maine, I realized he was making a very direct comment, that this was commensurate with Soviet propaganda. It was just a different kind of propaganda.

It's very strange that he also chooses to do that over the footage of Jackie Curtis, one of Andy Warhol's muses in *Trash*. It's tough to figure out how to read that.

GIBNEY: I think that in some ways, Makavejev is mocking the freedoms of the West. That is to say, they're false freedoms. But at the same time, he's enjoying them. So I think there's a double-edged satirical quality there, because capitalism is supposed to be pure freedom, right?

But there's something mysteriously enslaving about it. I think that's one of the things he's getting at. And yet he's wholly enjoying all this wild abandon. I think that even in Makavejev, there's a puritanical streak as well, saying, "Purely wild abandon may not get us to where we want to go."

Sure, and that's actually reflected in a very recent interview he did, saying that in the U.S. there seems to be "more sexual freedom than necessary" and, "The times are now vulgar." So it's very interesting that this socialist free spirit now sounds like the state [*laughs*]. There are limits to freedom, to paraphrase him.

GIBNEY: There's a great scene, I think it's in Luis Buñuel's *The Phantom of Liberty*, that's set in the Napoleonic wars. There are a whole bunch of people lined up in a firing squad, and they throw their fists in the air saying, "Down with freedom!"—at which point they're shot. It's just one of those moments.

There is an ambivalence in the film about utter freedom, which is what the capitalist society promises but doesn't really deliver on.

Not long ago British television asked Makavejev to edit the film, to engage in a little bit of self-censorship, to block the explicit bits of sex in the film. He obliged, placing little computerized fish and some pulsating colors over the action.

GIBNEY: I think that's great, actually. I was very dismayed with the way PBS sought to censor the *Enron* film, and I wanted to do exactly what Makavejev did, which is, if there were naked breasts, you would put a black bar over the naked breasts. You would make the censorship explicit. And they wanted me, in as many ways as possible, to make the censorship invisible. I always felt that if you need to censor, then you should make the censorship as visible as possible so that people know what's being censored.

This raises important questions about the act of censoring in other instances, too. I really was pissed off that they made me censor the vulgarity

of the Enron traders. And even when you put bleeps there—[*makes popping bleep sound*]—it somehow sanitizes what they've done. But all of the cuts or changes that they made me make were all designed to hide the censoring force, which, I found, from PBS, really pissed me off. But I'm glad Makavejev embraced the censorship idea and then did so in a playful way, which shines a light on the censorship. That's the way it should be.

When you've been faced with this choice, have you been able to figure out some sort of devious work-around or negotiate your way out of it? Can you talk more about that experience with PBS?
GIBNEY: There were certain language issues, and then there was nudity. A lot of people have raised the question, "Was it necessary for me to put nudity in the *Enron* film? After all, more people could see it if there wasn't nudity in it." And I just felt that at some point—pulling this whole issue earlier of embracing the contradictions—that it's one thing to say that former Enron CEO Lou Pai is addicted to strippers; it's another thing to put you in the strip club. Then you're in Lou Pai's head.

And the way we shot the strip club was also to show—we shot it in mirrors a lot so you could see these multiplying images of female flesh—that Lou Pai was really all about the numbers. Supposedly, in sociobiology, the male procreating instinct and the genetic strategy is to sleep with as many women as possible. So Lou Pai is a perfect paradigm. He goes to these strip clubs. Why? Because there are many women, and they're numbers.

And that's why in that sequence we used the Philip Glass song from *Einstein on the Beach*, about another guy who is all about the numbers. And Enron also was all about the numbers. That's a long way of explaining the kind of thinking that went into that sequence, and therefore it really pissed me off when they wanted me to start eliminating images of nudity, rather than just putting black bars over nipples, which, I think, would have kept the sequences intact and illustrated this prudish aspect of our society, but it nevertheless would have retained the importance of the scene. There's a reason I put it in there; it wasn't just to get some T&A in. It was dismaying.

With the language—that's one thing that really upset me. Having to put bleeps over the offending language of the Enron traders seemed to me a way of actually letting them off the hook. There's a comment that real life makes.

That's one of the great moments in documentary, when you find something that's just unbelievable. It's stranger than fiction. So these guys laughing as the California grid is going down thanks to their efforts—the language was part of that. You can't show or indicate that kind of vile behavior unless you hear it!

Put fucking bleeps in, they sound cute, and then it's really about the swearing. But it's not about the swearing. It's about what you hear in their voices, which is a kind of evil that you need to be able to hear. So that was really disappointing to me, and that I found ultimately even more pernicious than the censorship of the nudity. So I wouldn't say I did as well as Dušan. I kind of gave up, because I felt that people can always see this stuff in other forms—they could get the DVD if they wanted to—but I sure didn't like the way PBS approached it.

It's strange, because they're the network that aired *Tales of the City*, which had nudity and some harsh language. It's strange that they would choose to treat a documentary—

GIBNEY: Yeah, but that was way back when. And the fact is, I was the producer of the *Blues* series that Martin Scorsese did, and in one of the episodes—the one about Chicago blues, directed by Mark Levin, *Godfathers and Sons*—there are quite a few F-bombs. And apparently, one individual complained in the San Mateo area—one individual—and on that basis, the FCC brought a suit against and actually fined that station a considerable amount of money.

PBS, as a result, began to back off. And they apologized: "Oh, you don't understand, we don't want to do this, but we have to." Well, at some point, I just felt that was weak. It's not like you want to be fighting for the word "fuck," that that's *so* important, but there is a kind of freedom of expression that you want to embrace, and when PBS starts caving that way, it just makes even less of an argument for why they should continue to exist.

What was your impression about the different styles of filming in *WR: Mysteries of the Organism*?

GIBNEY: There's the cinema verité stuff, and there's going up to Rangeley, Maine. But then there's this great stuff, this archival footage of Stalin, and

I think also Hitler, conflating communism and Nazism but also seeing the massive displays of the crowds, which have an ecstatic, orgiastic quality to them that then resonates with the personal, individual stories that you're then seeing. It really is something. So there's another style, that kind of archival, montage style, that's in there. He's got it all in the mix.

One of the things I was shocked at, in researching the film, was to find out that the dramatic material was his. It was not stock footage or borrowed from another film. All of the stuff with Milena—he shot that. That's not a mainstream Yugoslavian film that he excerpted.

GIBNEY: Oh, no, I know that. That was directed by him.

I didn't, so because it's such a collage of a film, it made the movie even more mysterious and magnetic to me, because it seemed like we were visiting a film in part, that there were other scenes missing. And the style was so conflicting. This looked almost like a Busby Berkeley production or an early-1960s studio-Hollywood film. So I was really pleasantly shocked to realize, "No, no, no, this is the only place that footage exists— it's only meant for this film."

GIBNEY: I agree, and that's what makes this film so great. He takes this dramatic film and surrounds it with this other material. It's all of a piece, and he decides that for some sequences, it's like an investigation. He's investigating this idea, and part of it is necessary to do as a drama, and part of it is necessary to do as a documentary, because it's important to know the real shit. But in other ways you can do things in drama that you can't explore in nonfiction, in terms of how characters feel and think. So that's what makes it so great.

Relating to my own work, back to *Enron*, people asked, like, "Why would you cheapen up the film by having that re-creation of the guy's suicide up front?" And my view was that it was absolutely critical to have that up front, because psychologically, in a kind of fiction-film moment, you have an emotional identification with that executive—you smell the leather of the seat, you smell the cigarette in the ashtray, you feel the steel of the pistol on his temple—and that helps you to inhabit the rest of the film in a very different way than if you just saw headlines of, ENRON EXECUTIVE COMMITS SUICIDE.

Because that does what a fiction film only can do, which is to get you inside a character for a moment, but then, mixed with the documentary stuff, it makes it sing. You're not saying, "You were there; you're pretending that this is the real thing." You're just saying, "This is how I imagine that this would have happened," which is a thing that only a fiction filmmaker can do. But you put it together with documentary, and then suddenly you're getting a different kind of interpretation of reality, and also a different identification with these executives, so that they're not pure monsters.

Acknowledgments

First, thanks to the filmmakers and their staffs who so generously gave their time and passion to this project. Some directors I pursued for years, waiting for a gap in their schedules. This is really your book, so thanks.

Among the people who introduced me to filmmakers or otherwise helped facilitate an interview, including the directors themselves, plus Nicolette Aizenberg, Brian Andreotti, Terry Armour, Jan Blenkin, Lara Bogenrief, Julian Brooks, Mark Caro, Terence Chang, Charles Coleman, Ian Gibson, Morgan Harris, Larry Jakubecz, Ziggy Kozlowski, David Lee, Sharon Lester, Sally Madgwick, Meghan McElheny, Kirsten McMurray, Will Rowbotham, Richard Ruiz, Brittany Smith, Gail Stanley, Tim Sika, Milos Stehlik, Leo Thompson, Jill Wheeler, and Brenda White.

Second, thanks to my literary agent—rock 'n' roll David Dunton—for believing in me and these last two movie books. I'm forever indebted to Yuval Taylor, my editor, friend, and fellow movie buff. Other superstars at Chicago Review Press/IPG include Amelia Estrich and Mary Kravenas (my resident *Doctor Who* expert).

None of this, of course, would have been possible without the encouragement from people at my (more than) full-time job, so many thanks to Leela de Kretser and Heather Grossmann.

The Best Film You've Never Seen would not have been possible without the eagle eyes and research mojo of Mitchell Armentrout, Shay Bapple, Doni Bloomfield, Gina Brown, Lilian Bürgler, Sheila Burt, Alexis Crawford, Marcella De Laurentiis, Kasia Dworzecka, Michelle Edgar, Jenifer Fischer, Drew Fortune, Megan Frestedt, J. Scott Gordon, Constance Grady, Jessica Galliart, Jay Grooms, Kelin Hall, Esther Han, Jina Hassan, Matthew Hendrickson, Michael Hirtzer, Drew Hunt, Shajiah Jaffri, Laurel Jorgensen, Joey Kahn, Sharon Kim, Alison Knezevich, Rikki Knutti, David Lanzafame, Samantha Leal, Gabriel Mares, Kevin Meil, Nomaan Merchant, Theodore Noble, SunJung Monica Park, Daniel Peake, Caroline Picard, Ryan Ptomey, Nate Radomski, Kristen Radtke, Sofia Resnick Angie Rutkowski, Zack

Seward, Alexandra Sifferlin, Benjamin Summers, Chelsea Trembly, Mia Umanos, Bryan West, Eugenia Williamson, and Emily Wray.

Special gratitude goes out to Anna Borges, Kristina Budgin, Lisa Cisneros, Elysia Liang, Daniel Lewis, Katie MacKendrick, Hatie Parmeter, Rena Schergen, Aaron Vetch, Lisa Weidenfeld, and Qianyi Xu for their detailed research and final edits of the manuscript.

Special thanks to Cherry Dunham Williams, David Frasier, and Zachary Downey at Indiana University's Lilly Library for their help with photos and research materials.

A tip of the hat to David Bradley, Thomas R. Atkins, Dave Kehr, Pauline Kael, the Criterion Collection, and Brian Carmody and Micheal Perzi at Orange Media Relations.

Thanks to my colleagues at the *Chicago Sun-Times* for their support, particularly Jim Kirk and Linda Bergstrom.

Thanks also to the staff and management of the W Hotel in downtown Chicago, who hosted me for two frantic days while I assembled and polished these chapters. Thanks for 1) delivering the sixteen grapefruits I asked for and 2) not asking what they were for.

This book and all my film books owe a debt of gratitude to writers such as Lawrence Grobel, Andrew Sarris, and David Breskin, whose own interview books have provided years of inspiration for me.

Thanks to my friend Rusty Nails, who steered more than one director my way.

To Alec Botnick and EJ Johnson, my agents at William Morris Endeavor— thanks for the encouragement and support.

Without Devon Freeny, my eagle-eyed manuscript editor, I would have been lost. Thanks, Devon, for saving my butt on more than one occasion.

To the fans of these books: Thanks for the love on Facebook, Twitter, Tumblr, and all the avenues of social media. And thanks for coming to the events!

Last: Thanks to my wife Betsy, my best editor and critic, who went as many sleepless nights getting this in as I did. Maybe more. I love you, and you get to pick our movies for a while.

Index